ʒ√

Burt Lancaster

Burt Lancaster

A Filmography and Biography

by

Ed Andreychuk

McFarland & Company, Inc., Publishers
Jefferson, North Carolina, and London

ALSO BY ED ANDREYCHUK

The Golden Corral:
A Roundup of Magnificent Western Films
(McFarland, 1997)

Frontispiece: Burt Lancaster in a publicity still from the 1950s.

Library of Congress Cataloguing-in-Publication Data

Andreychuk, Ed, 1951–
    Burt Lancaster : a filmography and biography / by Ed Andreychuk.
        p.   cm.
    Includes bibliographical references and index.
    ISBN 0-7864-0436-1 (illustrated case binding : 50# alkaline paper) ∞
    1. Lancaster, Burt, 1913–1994.   I. Title.
    PN2287.L246A53   2000
    791.43'028'092—dc21   99-86393
    [B]

British Library Cataloguing-in-Publication data are available

Manufactured in the United States of America

McFarland & Company, Inc., Publishers
    Box 611, Jefferson, North Carolina 28640
    www.mcfarlandpub.com

To all the children in my family—
my daughter, nieces, and nephews—
who I hope will carry Burt Lancaster's
memory into the twenty-first century.

Acknowledgments

Many individuals and groups have assisted me in writing this book. Perhaps there are too many to single out without forgetting someone or some organization, so I offer most humble apologies for any oversights.

My gratitude goes out to the international body of production companies, film studios, television networks, and distribution agencies, for helping to bring forth the Burt Lancaster films, and for sharing stills and information with me.

Special gratitude is extended for press kits from the following groups: Universal Studios (*Ulzana's Raid*), New Line Cinema (*Conversation Piece*), American Cinema (*Zulu Dawn*), Paramount Pictures (*Atlantic City*), Touchstone Pictures (*Tough Guys*), Robert Halmi Inc./ CBS Television (*Barnum*), New Line Television (*The Jeweller's Shop*), Sacis International (*The Betrothed*), and Tribune Entertainment (*Voyage of Terror: The Achille Lauro Affair*).

My thanks to the academies of both Motion Picture and Television Arts and Sciences for the information they provided. For stills, thanks go to the movie trivia shops from coast to coast: Jerry Ohlinger's Movie Material Store in New York, and Cinema Collectors, Collectors Book Store, Eddie Brandt's Saturday Matinee, Kenneth Lawrence's Movie Memorabilia Shop, and Larry Edmund's Bookshop, all in California.

Finally, a nod to my hometown, Baltimore, where invaluable help came from the following: Sharon Williams and 24 Hour Secretary, the Enoch Pratt and Baltimore County library systems, and the now-defunct *News American* newspaper.

Table of Contents

Acknowledgments vi

Introduction 1

Burt Lancaster: A Brief Biography 3

THE FILMS 25
  The 1940s 25
  The 1950s 46
  The 1960s 107
  The 1970s 150
  The 1980s 191
  The 1990s 232

Bibliography 240

Index 241

Introduction

"From Adventuring Giants Like Him—America Drew Its Greatness!" proclaimed ads in 1955 for Burt Lancaster's film *The Kentuckian*. Although those words pertained to the bold frontiersman he portrayed in that movie (which he also directed and produced), they could have also been for the bold filmmaker himself.

A trailblazer in films, Lancaster was once regarded as the biggest of the new post–World War II movie stars. His stardom in Hollywood was indeed swift and unparalleled. He became a star as "The Swede" in his first picture, *The Killers*, in 1946 when he was 32 years old. A stunning physique, undoubtedly beefed up by Lancaster's pre-acting years as an acrobat, showcased a tough yet vulnerable animal magnetism.

Beyond his onscreen presence in films, Lancaster exerted a strong influence in Hollywood through his involvement with the biggest independent production company of the 1950s, Hecht-Hill-Lancaster, starting less than two years after debuting in films. With filmmakers Harold Hecht and James Hill, he helped pioneer a trend of turning television dramas into theatrical films, the foremost of which was the 1955 Academy Award winner for Best Picture, *Marty*.

Burt won an Oscar for Best Actor in 1960 for his enactment of the title role in *Elmer Gantry*. It was the second of four Oscar nominations, which also included 1953's *From Here to Eternity* as Sergeant Warden, 1962's *Birdman of Alcatraz* as Robert Stroud, and 1981's *Atlantic City* as Lou Pasco.

In a film career spanning 45 years, Lancaster was never content to rest on any of his laurels, and he went beyond all boundaries of so-called protocol. Whether bucking the major studios as an independent producer or as a maverick actor, he dared to take risks.

Jeopardizing at times his own popularity, Lancaster honed his craft to go beyond being a star to become an accomplished actor. Though his range was sometimes limited, there was no limit to his passion for earnest film work.

That Lancaster survived as a performer indicated an admirable durability. The transition from star to character actor was done with aplomb, dignity, and graciousness, exemplified by his performance as John W. Davis in his last film, 1991's *Separate But Equal*.

Lancaster's own words from a 1977 interview (to the *Cincinnati Enquirer*) offer a most enlightening reflection on his film persona. He said, "I don't know necessarily that people think of me as a good guy, but I think, from what they've told me ... that some kind of absolute honesty and sincerity, some kind of integrity comes across."

Lancaster remains most famous as an actor. In role after role, his explosive presence gave the impression of being able to open the heavens with the most radiant of smiles and catch lightning bolts with his teeth—or melt those lightning bolts with the steeliest of glances.

Actor, producer, director, even screenwriter and editor, Burt Lancaster did it all in a fabulous film career.

Covered in this book, with extensive credits and cast listings, synopses, commentaries, reviews, and stills, are Burt Lancaster's 72 theatrical films and 13 television films. A brief biography of Lancaster is also included, but the emphasis of the book is on the films.

Burt Lancaster:
A Brief Biography

In 1876, James Lancaster was born in New York, of an English father with the same name and an Irish mother, Susanna née Murray. In 1877, Elizabeth Roberts was born in Connecticut, of an Irish father and mother, James and Jennie (née Smith) Roberts. James Lancaster and Elizabeth Roberts married and lived at 209 East 106th Street in New York City (a predominantly Italian neighborhood in Manhattan known as East Harlem).

Burton Stephen Lancaster was born to them at home on November 2, 1913. He was named for the physician who performed the delivery, Dr. Burton Thom. Little Burt was preceded by a sister, Jane (age four), and brothers James (three) and William (one and a half). His father worked as a clerk at the Madison Square Post Office. Additional income included renting out part of their home to boarders, with the family living on the top floor. When Burt was three years old, his mother gave birth to a fifth child, Florence, who died in 1918 of diphtheria.

At age four, Burt made his acting debut as an angel in a Christmas pageant at the Church of the Son of Man on East 104th Street. Standing before an audience of mostly Irish and German people, he made quite a fuss trying to remove gum stuck on the bottom of his shoe.

Burt was a movie fan as a child. His screen idol then was Douglas Fairbanks Sr.; Burt remembered being dragged home in 1920 by brother William after spending the day at the neighborhood Atlas Theater, watching his hero in the *Mark of Zorro*.

In 1920, Burt also began his education at P.S. 121 (the Galileo) on East 102nd Street; in 1923 he went to P.S. 83 (the Galvani) on 110th Street. Even as a child, he was an avid reader. In 1953 he said, "I read the whole library on 110th Street by the time I was fourteen—everything from Lang's Fairy Tales to Shakespeare. At night, I read with a flashlight, which I hid under my pillow and used after the gas was turned off."

Burt enjoyed classical music and opera as well. His friend Nick Cravat introduced him to opera. Nick, a year older, lived in the same neighborhood, and the two had met when Burt was nine, at a summer camp sponsored by the Union Settlement House on East 104th Street. To go to camp each year, credits had to be earned at the settlement house, and one way to earn them was to appear in plays.

At age eleven, Burt played a dying invalid in *Three Pills in a Bottle* by Booth Tarkington. His performance was so impressive that he was asked to go to drama school. But Burt felt acting was sissy stuff.

Having sung soprano in the choir at the Church of the Son of Man in his youth, Burt had aspirations to become an opera singer—until his voice changed at age 15. In his teenaged years, he outgrew his brothers; previously, he had been a pudgy and short boy.

Although Central Park was not that far away with its play areas, Burt remembered playing stickball and stoopball in the streets and even swimming in the East River. Growing up he found he had a natural aptitude for sports. There were street gangs, and Burt surely had his share of fistfights as a youngster.

Burt gave credit to the Union Settlement House for helping keep him from becoming a juvenile delinquent. Even so, it was at the settlement house that Burt, involved in a fight with another boy as teenagers, was cut with a knife on the thigh. When the wound became infected, Burt had to be hospitalized.

Burt's mother died when he was sixteen years old of intestinal nephritis on November 29, 1929. This happened during his senior year at DeWitt Clinton High School in the Bronx. She was domineering and had a temper, but Burt loved her dearly. He recalled how she often helped their poor neighbors, even strangers, when the Lancasters were financially poor as well.

Elizabeth Lancaster instilled in Burt a sense of being honest and loyal, which he never forgot. Burt seemingly inherited his mother's temper, but he also received a gentleness from his father.

After graduating from DeWitt Clinton in 1930, Burt entered New York University on an athletic scholarship. His specialty was basketball (in his senior year in high school, he helped the varsity team, the Red and Black Courtmen, win the Bronx Championship). In his freshman year at college, Burt met an Australian named Curley Brent at the Union Settlement House. Curley was terrific at performing gymnastic feats on the horizontal bar. Burt became interested learning how to perform on the bar himself, and Nick Cravat got involved as well. They became so involved with it that Burt dropped out of his second year at NYU to form a team with Nick. When it was thought their act was down pat, they bought an old Ford for ninety dollars and headed south, looking for circus work.

The duo became acrobats, calling themselves Lang and Cravat. In the late 1960s (during his jaunt on the television talk-show circuit), Burt recalled initially running into the Kay Brothers Circus. This was in 1932. When asked what they could do, Burt and Nick eagerly put on their homemade tights, but realized they would have to perform on a triple-bar frame instead of the single one they were used to from the settlement house. Burt tried a routine more than once on the three bars, only to fall down each time. His tights were ripped and he was bleeding. He was ready to try again, but someone came over to Burt, put his arms around him, and said, "It's all right kid, you've got the job."

Lang and Cravat worked with an older acrobat and made three dollars a week. They rode in parades, put up

Twenty years old and an acrobat (note the special footwear).

tents, and did other tasks with the circus. Becoming fair bar acrobats, their salary was raised to five dollars a week. They stayed with the Kay Brothers troupe for about thirty weeks. After Nick hurt his nose in a fall and was hospitalized, he wasn't asked to return, so Lancaster quit.

In 1934, Burt met Ora Ernst, a female performer on the horizontal bar. She helped him and Nick get fair bookings in Florida. At age 21, Burt eloped with Ora's 18-year-old daughter, June (also an acrobat). Burt and Nick worked with June and other members of her family in 1935 with the Gorman Brothers Circus, calling themselves the Lancasters. After a few months, Nick, June, and Burt left the circus and performed at Luna Park in New York.

The three signed on in 1937 with the New York–based Federal Theatre Circus, which was part of the Works Project Administration. Nick and Burt did their bar act, and June worked in wardrobe. After being with the WPA for 21 weeks, June and Burt's marriage collapsed. Burt wanted a family, whereas June wanted to become a dancer. He said in 1948, "We never had any fights. We just got tired of each other."

Lancaster and Cravat split temporarily in 1938. Nick joined a bar act with the Ringling Brothers Circus, and Burt worked with the Newton Brothers troupe.

By the late 1930s, the circus business was in a decline. Burt and Nick joined forces again as bar acrobats in vaudeville on the Poli circuit in New England. Owners were not fond of having their floors damaged with holes to support the bar apparatus, so the acrobats worked on a perch act—Cravat, at five feet, three inches, supported a 25-foot pole on his head while Lancaster, at six feet, two inches, did different stunts on the top. Burt sometimes found himself hidden by the proscenium, where audiences could not view his feats. Another acrobat, Jack McCarthy, was also involved with them on the perch act.

With the Barnes-Carruthers Fair Booking Association in 1939, Lancaster, Cravat, and McCarthy joined up as the Three Toppers. They did either the perch act or a horizontal bar act (Burt had put together a movable bar frame that would hold weight and made holes unnecessary).

Plans as big-time acrobats never really came together. Burt finally decided to give up his acrobatics after an injury to his right hand. The injury, which caused a finger infection, happened while performing in St. Louis in 1940. Doctors warned him that amputation might be necessary if he continued, so he left for Chicago with twenty dollars in his pocket.

In Chicago, Burt stayed with a circus family known as the Smiletas. In 1941, he found employment at the Marshall Field Department Store as a floorwalker and then a salesman. To relieve his boredom, he sometimes did handstands in the aisles.

While working at the department store, Lancaster met someone connected to an organization that sold culture events. Burt later looked up this New York City–based business, called the Community Concerts Bureau. He was all set for a job, traveling the country persuading civic leaders to buy concert performances, when he received his draft notice.

Waiting to be inducted, Burt was hired as a singing waiter (but was actually a straight man talking to customers) at a nightclub in New Jersey. He entered the U.S. Army in 1942, training at Fort Riley, Kansas. Burt spent three years with the Special Services, Fifth Army Division. In 1943, he went overseas entertaining troops in North Africa, Italy, and Austria as part of the revue called *Stars and Gripes.* "I had a wonderful time touring Europe as a page turner for a soldier pianist," Lancaster beamed in 1948. Once in his hitch he made sergeant, but was busted back down because he spoke up against an officer who made soldier musicians scrub floors. He was made to jockey trucks through mud.

In Italy, Lancaster met Norma Anderson, a USO entertainer. Back in the United States on a furlough, shortly before his discharge as a private, Burt arranged to see Norma. She was then working for radio producer Ray Knight at the RCA Building in New York City. Going up in an elevator there, Burt noticed he was being stared at by a smaller man. Lancaster didn't like the guy putting his "mince pies" (big, staring eyes) on him. After the elevator door opened, Lancaster went to Knight's office, where he received a phone call from the man on the elevator. His name was Jack Mahlor and, as an associate of stage producer Irving Jacobs, he was looking for a big-framed actor for a new play, *A Sound of Hunting.* Burt was asked to read for the role of the tough-minded sergeant. He did and won the part.

A Sound of Hunting, a three-act play by Harry Brown, opened at the Lyceum Theater on Broadway on November 20, 1945. The basic scenario concerned a group of American soldiers in Italy during World War II, but audiences were understandably weary of the war in 1945. The play ran for only 23 performances. Jacobs's production offered a setting of a war-torn building (by Samuel Leve), which was the focal point for the soldiers, yet this harsh drama seemed too immobile and talky. The performers, nonetheless, were deemed likable under Anthony Brown and Don Richardson's staging.

Of the cast, Sam Levene was credited with the best performance as Private Colucci, the soldier going behind enemy lines in a futile attempt to save a comrade (a sequence not actually seen in the play) while the other men wait in their dreary shelter. But it was Burton Lancaster (as his name was billed in an all-male cast), as Sergeant Joseph Moody, who received the best review. His was a most commanding figure, and he was offered several motion picture proposals.

Lancaster was introduced by Sam Levene to a small-time agent named Harold Hecht. Having acquired a sharp business sense from his years as an acrobat, Burt signed on with Harold because he was impressed with his honesty. Six years older than Burt and knowing many people in the film business, Harold promised that by having fewer clients he would work harder for Burt. Perhaps the real clincher was a goal to produce their own films together in five years.

Producer Hal B. Wallis had seen Burt's performance in *A Sound of Hunting* and was interested in using him at Paramount Pictures. Initially, Wallis made his mark during the 1930s and early 1940s at Warner Bros., but in 1944 he set up an independent production unit with Paramount. Hecht helped negotiate a contract agreement with Wallis based on Lancaster passing a screen test.

Filmed in Hollywood on January 29, 1946, by director Byron Haskin, the test was for a proposed film called *Desert Fury*. Looking younger than his 32 years and with a great physique, Lancaster passed and was signed to a film contract February 7, 1946. It stipulated a $1,250 weekly starting salary. Increased earnings would take place over a seven-year period with not more than two films for Wallis per year. An extra 25 percent of any earnings were allowed for loan-outs to other studios, and Lancaster was also given the option to do one outside picture on his own terms each year.

Desert Fury was to have been Burt Lancaster's debut film, but it was not yet ready for production. So he exercised his one outside picture option by signing a deal (intended to spread over five years with one film a year) with another independent producer named Mark Hellinger. Then with Universal Pictures, Hellinger previously worked with Wallis at Warner Bros. This second contract, signed on April 29, 1946, was also based on passing a screen test, which Burt did, earning him the star-making role of "The Swede" in *The Killers*.

Burt Lancaster's first day actually working on a motion picture began on May 1, 1946, with the scene of the Swede's last prizefight; his first words spoken in the finished picture were: "There's nothin' I can do about it" (to Phil Brown's Nick Adams, a friend warning him that the pair of killers are coming). For his debut, Lancaster was paid a weekly sum of $2,500, which was more than his initial earnings with Wallis.

Four days after *The Killers* was completed, Norma Anderson gave birth to their son, James Steven, on June 30, 1946. With a successful acting career under way and with the divorce of his first marriage recognized, Burt married Norma on December 28, 1946, in Yuma, Arizona. But a tragedy occurred between these wonderful events. Having joined Burt in California to live and assist in his business affairs, brother William died on November 23 from a heart problem known as endocarditis. When Burt and Norma's second son, William Henry, was born almost a year later on November 17, he was named after his late uncle.

Burt Lancaster's movies made in the 1940s were generally summed up as hard-boiled melodramas. Beginning with Hellinger's *The Killers* and ending with Wallis's *Rope of Sand* (1949), Burt seemed bent on a violent jag in a dark, criminal world. *Brute Force* (1947) and *Criss Cross* (1948) were Mark Hellinger conceptions (although the second title was produced after his death, and Lancaster chose to forgo the final two films to be made as part of the Hellinger contract and bought himself free). *Desert Fury* (1947), and *I Walk Alone* and *Sorry, Wrong Number* (in 1948) were Burt's other films of the decade for Hal Wallis. *Kiss the Blood Off My Hands* (1948) was Lancaster and Harold Hecht's first film as independent producers. Paramount's all-star entry, *Variety Girl*, had Burt in a humorous guest bit. This was in 1947 and he was already singled out as a star with more famous Hollywood names. His most dramatic role of this early period came as Chris Keller, the moral son of a corrupt father, in 1948's Universal-International film, *All My Sons*.

Before any of Burt's pictures with Hal Wallis were even released, a new contract was negotiated in 1947 between

A 1940s publicity pose from Hollywood.

caster's name on a theater marquee was said to be worth $1 million in box office earnings. His personal earnings at the time put him on a level with his peers.

During 1948, Burt returned temporarily as an acrobat with Nick Cravat. They appeared on stage at, among other places, Chicago's Oriental Theater in November and New York City's Capitol Theater in December. Their weekly salary was $10,000. Also, in 1949, the duo performed for two weeks with the Cole Brothers Circus and made $11,000 a week.

With Harold Hecht, Burt signed a six-picture deal with Warner Bros. in March 1949. He agreed to appear in three pictures to be produced by the studio and in three with his new production company, with Hecht involved. Prior to filming his first Warner Bros. entry (which was a co-production, *The Flame and the Arrow*), Burt's third child with Norma, Susan Elizabeth, was born on July 5, 1949.

The Flame and the Arrow, in 1950, opened a new facet in Lancaster's motion picture career. His acrobatic jaunts with Cravat in 1948 and 1949 seemed to be a warm-up for displaying their amazing stunts together in this film. Burt's jovial energy in swashbuckling films during the first half of the 1950s was an incredible departure from the stoic demeanor displayed in the previous decade's dark melodramas.

A series of colorful swashbucklers for the production outfit called Hecht-Norma (named for Lancaster's wife),

the actor and producer. It started in January 1948, however, with the filming of *Sorry, Wrong Number*. Lancaster's initial contract revolved around doing *Desert Fury* only, with Wallis able to withdraw, if desired, from the agreed options. But Wallis chose not to withdraw and put Lancaster in *I Walk Alone*.

Now with the new contract, Burt was given a weekly starting salary of $5,000, with five additional option periods for salary increases. Burt also had the option to do eight outside films over a seven-year period, but the producer could still benefit from loan-outs. Although Lancaster actually committed to only six new films (and a television appearance) for Wallis, this aspect of the contract ran longer than seven years because of deferments.

At the end of 1948, Burt Lan-

brought forth, after *The Flame and the Arrow*, *Ten Tall Men* (Columbia, 1951), and *The Crimson Pirate* and *His Majesty O'Keefe* (Warner Bros., 1952 and 1954, respectively). The three pictures for Warner Bros. with Burt simply as an actor (no ties as a producer) were *Jim Thorpe—All American* (1951), and *South Sea Woman* and *Three Sailors and a Girl* (in 1953; with the latter film being a guest bit only).

Burt was loaned out by Hal Wallis to 20th Century–Fox for *Mister 880* (1950) and to Metro-Goldwyn-Mayer (MGM) for *Vengeance Valley* (1951; it was his first western). Wallis's fee for these loan-outs was $150,000 each, with Lancaster getting his 25 percent. A final loan-out by the producer was to Columbia in 1953. Wallis was paid $330,000 (with the actor receiving $73,000) for *From Here to Eternity* (part of the producer's fee was for Columbia and Wallis doing a picture in 1953 without Burt called *Bad for Each Other*).

Come Back, Little Sheba (1952) and *The Rose Tattoo* (1955) were Hal Wallis pictures at Paramount in which Lancaster was considered miscast, although his ambitious earnestness as an actor was very evident. Burt's dramatic stature and masculinity were especially given their due as the tough yet sensitive Sergeant Milton Warden in *From Here to Eternity* (for which he received his first Academy Award nomination). Wallis, fully aware of Lancaster's range as an actor, ended their contract with well-cast roles in *The Rainmaker* (1956) and *Gunfight at the O.K. Corral* (1957).

As part of his commitments to Wallis, Lancaster made his television debut on a segment of NBC's black and white series *The Colgate Comedy Hour*. This particular show was hosted by Dean Martin and Jerry Lewis (who were also under contract to Hal Wallis) and televised in October 1953. Burt appeared with the comedy team as a patient (called Doc Delaney, after his *Come Back, Little Sheba* character) who escapes from an insane asylum. Mildly amusing, the skit was played by all three performers with boyish enthusiasm.

Despite the success with Hecht-Norma Productions, Warner Bros. (initially setting up a $1.1 million budget per film for their three co-productions) was perturbed over the higher costs for *Crimson Pirate* ($1.85 million) and *His Majesty O'Keefe* ($1.55 million). With the completion of the contracted six films, the partnership with Warner Bros. ended; the studio wanted to continue a relationship, but Hecht and Lancaster declined the offer to make new pictures for a lower budget and film only on the Warner Bros. lot.

During the filming of *Crimson Pirate*, Burt and Norma's fourth child, daughter Joanna Mari, was born on July 3, 1951. The couple's third daughter and fifth child, Sighle-Ann (pronounced Sheila), was born July 7, 1954.

After departing ways with Warner Bros., Harold Hecht and Burt Lancaster joined up with United Artists on June 23, 1953 and became Hecht-Lancaster Productions. The initial agreement was for two pictures (westerns, *Apache* and *Vera Cruz*), and included giving them an allowance to develop film properties, the benefit of on-location filming, and a profit margin of 75 percent. On February 8, 1954, a deal was arranged between United Artists and Hecht-Lancaster for seven films costing $12 million. And on April 13, 1956, still another agreement was reached for a total of 18 films worth $40 million.

Burt Lancaster was involved in the production end only (not as an actor) on six of the contracted motion pictures with United Artists. They were in black and white and low budgeted. The titles were *Marty*, *The Bachelor Party*, *The Rabbit Trap*, *Cry Tough*, *Take a Giant Step*, and *Season of Passion*.

Before any involvement with United Artists, the Hecht-Norma company was involved on a film with Columbia Pictures in which Lancaster did not act (it was part of a two-picture deal that included *Ten Tall Men*). Released in February 1952, it was a black and white comedy called *The First Time* and dealt with a married couple awaiting the birth of their first baby. Harold Hecht was the producer, Frank Tashlin the director, and the screenplay was written by Jean Rouveral, Hugo Butler, Dane Lussier, and Tashlin. *The First Time* hardly made an impression at the box office. The couple was engagingly played, however, by Bob Cummings and Barbara Hale with comedic flair.

After its release on April 11, 1955, *Marty* became Hecht and Lancaster's most prestigious motion picture. It won four Academy Awards: for Best Picture (Harold Hecht, producer), Best Actor (Ernest Borgnine), Best Director (Delbert Mann), and Best Screenplay (Paddy Chayefsky). Betsy Blair was nominated for Best Supporting Actress and Joe Mantell for Best Supporting Actor. Joseph LaShelle was nominated for Best Black and White Cinematography; Edward S. Haworth, Walter Simonds, and Robert Priestley shared the nomination for Black and White Art Direction—Set Decoration. More was spent on advertising the picture when it started becoming popular than the initial production costs of a mere $343,000.

A simply told story about a lonely Bronx butcher finding love, *Marty* certainly reached audiences. The contemporary setting made it even more accessible. It was made on location in New York City and based on an original television drama (shown on NBC's *Philco TV Playhouse* on May 24, 1953). Like the movie, the television broadcast was written by Paddy Chayefsky and directed by Delbert Mann. Rod Steiger and Nancy Marchand starred in the telecast as Marty and his new girlfriend, Clara.

Steiger was approached by Hecht-Lancaster to do the film version, but he declined because it meant signing a long-term contract. Ernest Borgnine signed on instead. Previously seen as a heavy hitter (he had small but prominent roles in *From Here to Eternity* and *Vera Cruz*), Borgnine gave a warm and wonderful performance in the title role. Very nice support was given by Betsy Blair as the gentle Clara, Joe Mantell as Marty's feisty pal Angie, and Esther Minciotti as Mrs. Pilletti, Marty's loving mother.

James Hill was a contract writer with MGM who initially worked with Harold Hecht and Burt Lancaster on the script for *His Majesty O'Keefe*. He was first credited as a full partner with them (and the independent production company was then Hecht, Hill, and Lancaster) with the release of *The Bachelor Party* on April 10, 1957. With *Marty*'s success, a trend was started whereby television dramas were made into motion pictures about average people in everyday settings (and scaled as smaller budgeted films).

Unfortunately, the success of *Marty* was never really duplicated, at least not by Hecht, Hill, and Lancaster and their association with United Artists (although

1958's *Separate Tables* came very close, it was derived from a stage play and not a TV drama). For *The Bachelor Party*, Paddy Chayefsky, Delbert Mann, and Harold Hecht collaborated, as with *Marty*, as screenwriter, director, and producer.

Don Murray, E.G. Marshall, Jack Warden, Philip Abbott, and Larry Blyden made up the talented troupe of actors having a bachelor party in the Big Apple. For her performance as the existentialist, Carolyn Jones received an Academy Award nomination for Best Supporting Actress. Though the characters' foibles were interestingly drawn (their loneliness was a common bond), the film lacked the sparks generated by *Marty*; it also cost three times as much to make and so was not a box office hit.

Lancaster's production company was the most successful independent outfit in Hollywood in 1956 with *Trapeze*. In 1955, Burt directed his first film, *The Kentuckian*. The tenure with United Artists certainly brought a respectable group of films to the screen, but the latter part of this association was not as profitable as the first part had been.

Hecht, Hill, and Lancaster films that were not as financially successful as hoped included not only *The Bachelor Party* and *Separate Tables* but all those that followed with or without Burt as a star. These other films were *Sweet Smell of Success* (1957); *Run Silent, Run Deep* (1958); *The Devil's Disciple, The Rabbit Trap, Cry Tough,* and *Take a Giant Step* (1959); *The Unforgiven* (in 1960); and *Season of Passion* (1961).

Starring in *The Rabbit Trap* (released in July 1959) was Ernest Borgnine as a father with his little boy trying to save any rabbits caught in a snare.

The whole plot revolved around the father feeling trapped in his job; although its point was a bit forced, the film was a nice enough diversion.

The characters may have also been rather stereotypical, but Borgnine and Kevin Corcoran (as the son) did okay with their roles. Bethel Leslie was especially good as the wife and mother. J.P. Miller wrote the screenplay from his own earlier television play; Philip Leacock directed and Harry Kleiner produced.

Kleiner produced as well as wrote the screenplay for *Cry Tough* (a September 1959 release). Based on a novel by Irving Shulman, the film, set in New York City's Spanish Harlem, was directed by Paul Stanley. It told the story about a young man who, returning from prison, finds it hard to go straight with his old gangster crowd around. Although it was a look at conditions for Puerto Ricans in a troubled environment, this movie was basically a routine gangster yarn. But strong performances were given by John Saxon as the ex-convict and Linda Cristal as a dance hall girl.

Take a Giant Step (a December 1959 release), like *Cry Tough*, dealt with a minority group—blacks instead of Puerto Ricans. This film focused on a particular teenage boy growing up in a white man's world. Philip Leacock directed; the screenplay by Louis S. Peterson and Julius J. Epstein was derived from a play by Peterson. Epstein also produced. The racial prejudice reflected in the film was noteworthy (and even daring for its day), although not as well as it possibly could have been. As the black youth, Johnny Nash contributed a sensitive performance, as did Ruby Dee as a maid who helps him mature. The thoughtfulness they showed in their roles was a big plus.

Hill, Hecht, and Lancaster were struggling to remain together by the end of the 1950s. Their production company become a larger outfit than what was originally intended. Lavish business offices were kept in both New York and California, with between sixty and seventy employees on an annual payroll of $1 million. Budget overages were incurred with United Artists for $3 million, as well as $2.5 million for unproduced films.

One of the films proposed was called *First Love* and intended for Audrey Hepburn. In December 1956, writer John Van Druten, hired to do the screenplay for $105,000, sued Hecht, Hill, and Lancaster (HHL) because the production company felt his services were not being rendered properly and paid him only $13,333.00. In January 1957, the Screen Writers Branch of the Writers Guild of America (West) asked for a strike against HHL to meet contract agreements, such as in Van Druten's case. The HHL company settled both disputes during March 1957, first by signing a basic agreement contract with the guild and then paying the writer $71,666.67 in an out-of-court agreement.

Also in 1957, Metro-Goldwyn-Mayer was having financial difficulties. The studio offered Burt Lancaster $1 million to play the title role in *Ben-Hur* (this epic film helped save MGM when released to enormous success in 1959, but with Charlton Heston in the lead). Lancaster apparently did not agree with the film's religious theme and turned the project down, opting instead to do another film, also with religion in the story. This other picture was called *Elmer Gantry*.

Heston won the Best Actor Oscar in 1959 for his triumphant performance in *Ben-Hur*, but Lancaster won the award in 1960 for *Elmer Gantry* (his first film with United Artists that neither Harold Hecht nor James Hill was involved in). Burt's own triumph in the title role of the fiery con man is nothing short of magnificent.

While Burt's extroverted energy was never better than in his Oscar-winning role, his introverted power was never better than in his third Oscar-nominated role as Robert Stroud in 1962's *Birdman of Alcatraz*. This final film with Harold Hecht was also in the year that Hecht, Hill, and Lancaster was officially dissolved. After the breakup, Burt replied, "You come to a point where things just don't work anymore. It's like a marriage breaking up and one person saying, 'For the kid's sake, let's get together again.' It never works out."

In December 1961, the last film between HHL and United Artists was released domestically. Filmed in Australia, *Season of Passion* was both directed and produced by Leslie Norman. The screenplay by John Dighton was derived from a play by Ray Lawler. The film was first released in London in 1960 as *Summer of the 17th Doll*.

Ernest Borgnine and John Mills played sugarcane workers who return to their girlfriends each year in the off-season. Anne Baxter portrayed Borgnine's lady, while Angela Lansbury was seen as Mills's prospective new lady after his established one gets married. The original title was in reference to a kewpie doll given to Miss Baxter's character every year.

Although skillfully presented and boasting excellent performances, *Season of Passion*'s modest drama was reflective of the series of films produced in collaboration with United Artists that did not reflect a profit nonetheless. Following the end of HHL, to help reduce the debts owed to United Artists, Harold Hecht produced two films for that company's release (1962's *Taras Bulba* and 1964's *Flight from Ashiya*), and James Hill produced a single picture (*The Happy Thieves*, 1962). To settle his own financial obligations, Burt Lancaster starred in four films released by United Artists between 1961 and 1968. These pictures were *The Young Savages, Birdman of Alcatraz, The Train,* and *The Scalphunters*. Also, in 1964, Burt's interest in the past Hecht-Lancaster films was bought out by United Artists for $920,000 and helped alleviate his share of the debts.

Season of Passion was Ernest Borgnine's last film in the contract that began with *Marty* with Hecht-Lancaster. But in 1956, the actor filed a breach-of-contract suit on September 19 against the producers for $142,000. The grounds of the suit were apparently preempting his services on pictures for other companies and then loaning him back for a large cut (which the producers received and paid Borgnine a small amount). On December 4, Borgnine filed another suit asking for an accounting of his profits for *Marty*. An out-of-court settlement on November 26, 1957, did not dissolve his contract, but prevented preemption of his acting in other films. Reflected in the finances awarded him was an additional 2.5 percent from *Marty*'s earnings.

Despite the unfortunate end of his production company, much worse tragedies occurred at the time in the life of Burt Lancaster. Heart attacks claimed the lives of two of his family members in 1961. A retired New York City policeman, Burt's brother James was working on the set of *Birdman* when he was stricken on January 27. Their father, who had been living with Burt since 1947, died on September 10. That same year, on November 7, Burt's home in Bel Air, California, was one of 300 lost in a massive fire. No one in the Lancaster family was injured, and a new home was rebuilt on the same grounds.

Socially conscious dramas had not proved especially profitable for Lancaster's film company (aside from *Marty*) during the 1950s, but Burt continued his interest as an actor in them in the early 1960s. *Elmer Gantry* and another United Artists release, the star-packed *Judgment at Nuremberg* (1961) proved both artistically and financially sound. But other entries with United Artists did not. *The Young Savages* (1961), *Birdman of Alcatraz* (1962), and *A Child Is Waiting* (1963) fell short of any real box office success.

Lancaster's most extensive film work with a single director was in the 1960s with John Frankenheimer. They did five pictures together, including *Young Savages* and *Birdman of Alcatraz.* Then came *Seven Days in May* (Paramount, 1964), *The Train* (United Artists, 1965), and *The Gypsy Moths* (MGM, 1969).

In 1963, Burt made a guest appearance in the Universal release *The List of Adrian Messenger,* and he also starred in one of his most controversial roles. It was as the Sicilian prince Don Fabrizio in the Italian-made epic *The Leopard* (released domestically by 20th Century–Fox).

United Artists handled the releases of Burt's comedy-flavored westerns, *The Hallelujah Trail* (1965) and *The*

Scalphunters (1968). If nothing else, with their tongue-in-cheek roles, they were a nice change of pace from the highly dramatic films previously done in the 1960s and reminiscent of his swashbuckling roles from the 1950s.

Most appreciatively tongue-in-cheek was Lancaster's performance as adventurer Bill Dolworth in another western, *The Professionals* (Columbia, 1966). Lancaster hit the same outstanding niche here as he had with *Elmer Gantry*; it's not that surprising as Richard Brooks once again directed him, fully realizing the actor's charm and vitality.

Burt's last released motion pictures in the 1960s were a trio of unusual dramas. Along with MGM's *The Gypsy Moths*, there were *The Swimmer* and *Castle Keep* (Columbia, 1968 and 1969, respectively).

As a filmmaker, Lancaster indeed often interested himself in projects that did not prove popular, and he must be commended for his resolve and daring to take risks. The last three films were no exception in this regard. However, he was not entirely unwilling to having his movies make money, and before the 1960s were over he had completed a part in what would be his highest grossing film (in a starring role), *Airport* (1970).

On June 27, 1969, Burt and Norma Lancaster were granted a divorce at the Santa Monica Superior Court in California. They had been married for more than 22 years (although separated since January 1967). Norma, who charged

A Hollywood publicity pose from the 1960s.

Burt with cruelty, was given custody of their three still-minor daughters. The many facets of their relationship are a private matter, except to say that they had drifted apart, and Burt had fallen in love with another woman. Her name was Jackie Bone; he first became involved with her when she was a hairdresser on the set of *The Hallelujah Trail* in 1964.

As mainstream entertainment, Universal's release of *Airport* proved to be one of the top films of 1970. Although Burt's conception of the "ideal" motion picture—"fantastic to look at pictorially, with a tremendous love story, done on a mature level"—was nearly reached here, he was displeased with the film and called it "a piece of junk."

King: A Filmed Record ... Montgomery to Memphis was a three-hour film on Dr. Martin Luther King Jr. and his crusade for civil rights. Filmed in black and white and released by Commonwealth United in March 1970, it received an Academy Award nomination for Best Documentary of the Year. Eli Landau produced *King*; Sidney Lumet and Joseph L. Mankiewicz shared in the direction. Lancaster's personal interest in the civil rights movement brought him to contribute a voice-over with a selected reading on behalf of Dr. King. Many other film-industry notables did likewise, including Harry Belafonte, Charlton Heston, Paul Newman, Sidney Poitier, and Joanne Woodward.

Burt's interest in sports was also reflected through voice-over work. He was heard as a narrator on the CBS television special *Pro Football: Big Game America*, which aired in September 1969. Honoring the fiftieth anniversary of the popular sport, the program, with a documentary profile, compressed its history into a mere hour. The pioneer aspects of football (and early players like Jim Thorpe) were touched on, but the weightier emphasis seemed to be on some of the more current players of the day. The special was not without entertainment value, despite trying to cover perhaps too much ground. Steve Sabol was the director and writer, and Ed Sabol served as executive producer.

On March 8, 1971, Burt was involved as a commentator via closed-circuit television for *Fight of the Champions*, the first heavyweight boxing match between Joe Frazier and Muhammad Ali. He also narrated a prefight documentary short called *The Fighters*, which was developed later into a theatrical film.

With the advent of the 1970s and his own aging, Burt Lancaster expressed a world-weary demeanor with his acting. Still, a highly versatile nature was always exposed. Earlier on he reflected on aging, "I think that getting older means a diminishing of curiosity. As long as you are curious, you defeat age."

A curious attitude certainly led to his participation in the musical play *Knickerbocker Holiday*, during the spring and summer of 1971 (at the Curran Theater in San Francisco and the Dorothy Chandler Pavilion in Los Angeles, respectively). Burt always wanted to do a musical; starring as Pieter Stuyvesant, the militaristic governor (and charming villain) of seventeenth-century New Amsterdam, he danced and sang several songs, including the memorable ballad "September Song." He actually took singing lessons from Frank Sinatra, and displayed on stage was a handsome (if limited) bass vocal range.

However, Lancaster's notable masculinity was deemed quite subdued, and this may have been caused in part by the adjustment of wearing a silver peg leg as befitting his character (a task he rose to rather well). Anita Gillette played the heroine, Tina, and David Holliday the hero, Brom Broeck, whose love was threatened by Stuyvesant.

Knickerbocker Holiday was a revival of a 1938 play with words by Maxwell Anderson and music by Kurt Weill. The Civic Light Opera Company, responsible for the 1971 version, felt that the political satire depicted earlier on was still relevant. Albert Marre directed and Glenn Jordan produced the revival, which was very lavish, yet it proved to be too slow moving to sustain interest beyond its two engagements.

Lancaster's films in the 1970s

seemed to come in threes. After *Airport*, there was the trilogy of westerns: *Valdez Is Coming* and *Lawman* (United Artists, 1971) and *Ulzana's Raid* (Universal, 1972).

Then came three crime films. Two, *Scorpio* (United Artists) and *Executive Action* (National General), were in 1973; one, *The Midnight Man*, was in 1974 (Burt not only starred in this latter entry with Universal but also directed, produced, and wrote the script with filmmaker Roland Kibbee).

Three films during the 1970s had Burt working with very controversial filmmakers. For Luchino Visconti, he was in *Conversation Piece* (New Line Cinema, 1975); for Robert Altman he was in *Buffalo Bill and the Indians* (United Artists, 1976); and for Bernardo Bertolucci he was in *1900* (Paramount, 1977).

In 1977, a trilogy of thrillers was also released with Lancaster starring. They were *The Cassandra Crossing* (Avco Embassy, 1976), *Twilight's Last Gleaming* (Allied Artists, 1977), and *The Island of Dr. Moreau* (American International, 1977).

A wide array of motion pictures with different companies was presented to Burt Lancaster in the 1970s. Yet television films also offered opportunities for the actor. He was in the miniseries *Moses, the Lawgiver* in 1975 and *Victory at Entebbe* in 1976 (both were converted into theatrical films, the first by Avco Embassy and the second overseas by Warner Communications).

Narrating *Pro Football: Big Game America* on CBS television, 1969.

Television input continued with Lancaster's involvement on documentary programming. In October 1977, an apparent interest in the strange and unknown was reflected through his participation as host on an installment of NBC's *Big Event* series. It was called "Psychic Phenomena: Exploring the Unknown," and he introduced several stories (said to have a basis of truth), including one about a surgeon who heals with his mind.

Produced, directed, and written by Alan Neuman, the 90-minute program apparently lacked substantial credence and strong production values. But a 20-hour documentary mini-series, in which Burt was seen and heard as narrator, did have considerable substance despite its initial syndication on only 11 television stations. Starting with a 60-minute telecast on October 7, 1978, *The Unknown War* featured extensive newsreel footage (from German and Russian archives) on a harrowing period in history. For 1,148 days, after Germany invaded Russia during World War II, millions of people died; bombardment, execution, starvation, and freezing were among the causes. Lancaster's three-week stint on the mini-series included actual location filming in Russia.

The strength as well as drawback of *The Unknown War* was the horrors that were vividly depicted. It was presented by New York's Air Time International and the Russian agency Sovinfilm. Roman Karmen was the director and Fred Weiner the producer. Both Weiner and Karmen assisted John Lord and Rod McKuen on the writing from an outline by Harrison Salisbury.

Shortly before this remarkable miniseries was aired, Burt Lancaster gave what may have been his best acting performance of the 1970s as Major Asa Barker in *Go Tell the Spartans* (Avco Embassy, 1978). His blending of world-weary integrity and sarcasm was never better realized during this decade (although his McIntosh in *Ulzana's Raid* came in a close second).

The making of motion pictures had radically changed by 1980 due to escalating costs, and some studios were no longer able to function properly. With millions of dollars needed even for small productions, sometimes films changed hands in distribution and never completely found an audience. Two of these were with Burt Lancaster: *Zulu Dawn*, which went from Orion Pictures in 1979 to American Cinema in 1980 to New World Pictures in 1982, and *Cattle Annie and Little Britches*, which went from Hemdale to Universal in 1981.

Lancaster was extremely fortunate with two other films on which he received his best acclaim of the 1980s: *Atlantic City* (Paramount, 1981) as Lou Pasco, in his fourth and last Oscar-nominated role and *Local Hero* (Warner Bros., 1983) as Felix Happer. So prestigious was *Atlantic City* for Burt that it was regarded as his comeback film. Both of these gems added new luster to his film career, as did a 1983 re-release of *The Leopard*.

Interest in the Luchino Visconti epic was revived through a restoration that featured the original Technicolor prints, 20 minutes of excised footage, and in Italian with English subtitles. Burt's performance as the prince, now seeming to be fully appreciated critically, caused him to comment sarcastically, "When *The Leopard* first came out ... the critics laughed at me. I was a bum. Twenty years later they're saying, 'It's his chef d'oeuvre, his great acting piece.'"

The Osterman Weekend (1983), like *Scorpio* and *Executive Action*, was a film with Lancaster that took a harsh view of the CIA, and he admitted doing it for the money. He performed in *The Life of Verdi* because of his fondness for opera and classical music. As with *The Unknown War*, Burt was heard and seen on the six-part, ten-and-a-half-hour miniseries *The Life of Verdi*, shown on PBS October 24 through November 28, 1983. Made in color by Italy's RAI television and written and directed by Renato

Castellani, it was a lavish treatment on famed opera composer Giuseppe Verdi (who was born in Italy in 1813 and died in 1901). The miniseries used 4,000 costumes, as well as original settings in Leningrad, London, Milan, Paris, and Venice. Despite being a collection of vignettes and requiring some dubbing, the overall grandeur was never dissipated. Exceptionally fine performances were given by Ronald Pickup as Verdi and Carla Fracci as Giuseppina Strepponi, the mistress and second wife of the composer.

During the 1980s, Lancaster acted in a number of television films; the four given accord on the major networks in this period were *Marco Polo* (1982), *Scandal Sheet* (1985), *On Wings of Eagles* (1986), and *Barnum* (1986). Burt appeared in a motion picture called *Little Treasure* (Tri-Star, 1985), for which his daughter Joanna was a producer; and another with his friend Kirk Douglas called *Tough Guys* (Buena Vista, 1986). The two veterans, who first worked together nearly forty years earlier on *I Walk Alone* and made other films as well (*Gunfight at the O.K. Corral* being their most famous) also were in a play in 1981 called *The Boys in Autumn*.

Opening at the Marines' Memorial Theater in San Francisco on September 3 and running to September 20, *The Boys in Autumn* was produced by James McKenzie and George Stevens Jr. (with the John F. Kennedy Center for the Performing Arts). It was written by Bernard Sabath and directed by Tom Moore. The concept, an enchanting one, focused on the whereabouts of those beloved characters from Mark Twain's stories, Tom Sawyer and Huckleberry Finn. World War I has ended when the childhood friends meet again after fifty

years. The place is still Hannibal, Missouri, and the two, now in their twilight years, share the experiences life has dealt them.

Kirk was deemed to be a bit more relaxed on stage as Tom compared to Burt's Huck. Although impressive in their roles, their shared dialogue was considered not up to its fullest potential. Their charisma was felt to be the key to the show's potential, but Lancaster noted, "But both of us knew it wasn't good enough, and it was damned hard work. I was relieved when we agreed that it was too exhausting. I much prefer film."

Fully aware over the years that the art and expense of filmmaking required international collaborations, Burt Lancaster worked overseas on foreign-made films throughout the 1980s. Except for the motion picture *La Pelle* (with Gaumont, 1981), all were television productions. Along with *Marco Polo* and *The Life of Verdi*, there were *Control* (1985), *Sins of the Fathers* (1988), *The Jeweller's Shop* (1989), and *The Betrothed* (1989). *The Phantom of the Opera* and *Voyage of Terror: The Achille Lauro Affair*, made in 1989, were not televised until 1990.

That Lancaster's acting reflected a touching vulnerability in many of his roles went without question. His on-screen persona in this regard seemed to reach the pinnacle of endearment with *Atlantic City*. But the utmost tenderness and graciousness (perhaps due as well for simply surviving into old age) was revealed in his last film (for television in 1991), *Separate But Equal*, and in two others (his last theatrically), *Rocket Gibraltar* (Columbia, 1988) and *Field of Dreams* (Universal, 1989). His glowing final moment in the latter motion picture (with the camera warmly closing in on the peace and serenity of his features) seemed a tribute to his fabulous longevity as an actor.

Field of Dreams (with his small role as Doc Graham), *Rocket Gibraltar*, and *Separate But Equal* (with his starring roles as Levi Rockwell and John W. Davis, respectively) were reflective of how Lancaster's film work had developed since the 1970s. Starring roles in that decade were overlapped with smaller parts (with special billing) in *Buffalo Bill and the Indians*, *The Cassandra Crossing*, and *1900*; he was billed alphabetically in *Victory at Entebbe*.

In the 1980s, smaller roles were also seen in *Marco Polo* (again billed in alphabetical order), *Local Hero*, *The Osterman Weekend*, *Little Treasure*, and *The Betrothed*. Although these films gave Burt special billing, top billing was accorded in smaller roles in both *Sins of the Fathers* and *The Jeweller's Shop* (as it did in the next decade for *Voyage of Terror*).

After the release of *Rocket Gibraltar*, Burt Lancaster had this to say in 1988, "I look for certain special things to come along. Hopefully, a little cameo now and then, or a big picture, like this one—big in a sense of the role it offers." He realized that he was not the box-office star of years ago, and that to endure meant accepting that new, younger stars were stepping into the limelight.

Documentary film work continued for Burt as well. *Legacy of the Hollywood Blacklist* was a 60-minute film shown on PBS in October 1987. Lancaster narrated this documentary produced and directed by Judy Chaikin.

The actor spoke with sympathy of the "Hollywood 10," directors, producers, and writers who were blacklisted by the infamous House Un-American Activities Committee for alleged Communist undertakings in the late 1940s and early 1950s (the McCarthy era). Actors and actresses whose careers had suffered were also given consideration.

Dawn's Early Light: Ralph McGill and the Segregated South was initially a 90-minute documentary film. It was the opening-night presentation at the 1988 Film and Video Festival in Atlanta, Georgia. In August 1989, it was edited to 60 minutes and televised on PBS. Filmmakers Kathleen Dowdy and Jed Dannenbaum reflected on Ralph McGill, editor of the *Atlanta Constitution* from 1942 to 1960, then its publisher until he died in 1969. He was known as "the conscience of the South" for his beliefs on civil rights. Burt Lancaster read excerpts on the program from McGill's Pulitzer Prize–winning column.

Burt shared doing the narration with such personalities as Cecil B. DeMille, Edward G. Robinson, and James Stewart, on the forty-minute documentary short *The Heart of Show Business*. A tribute to Variety Clubs International, it was released theatrically in 1957 by Columbia Pictures.

A 28-minute documentary short, *Race to Oblivion* (1988), also captured Burt's interest. In it, he interviewed Shigeko Sasamoni, a survivor of the 1945 Hiroshima bombing. Produced by Physicians for Social Responsibility, it was distributed on video to schools by Churchill Media and Random House Media.

Besides his documentary and feature work on television, Burt involved himself with a wide assortment of variety and talk shows and Academy Awards programs. After his stint with Martin and Lewis on 1953's *Colgate Comedy Hour*, a mixed bag of variety specials was seen with Burt's participation (along with a parade of other stars). Included were *At This Very Moment* (ABC, April 1962); *Second Annual Super Comedy Bowl: Gridiron Follies* (CBS, January 1972); *Salute to Oscar Hammerstein II* (CBS, July 1972); *I Love Liberty* (ABC, March 1982); *10th Annual Circus of the Stars* (CBS, December 1985); and *Happy Birthday Hollywood* (ABC, May 1987).

Perhaps out of all the variety specials Lancaster did on television, the finest may have been in December 1971 on PBS. Without all the hoopla of the other shows, the public television presentation of *An American Christmas: Words and Music* simply but eloquently expressed the feelings of the holiday season. Burt served as host and storyteller.

Talk show appearances with Burt Lancaster were always engaging. They included with Merv Griffin (summer 1968), Joey Bishop (May 1969), Dick Cavett and David Frost (July 1969), Dinah Shore (June 1972), and Phil Donahue (September 1986). The most controversial talk show he appeared on was Mike Wallace's *PM* in April 1962. When the commentator would not refrain from discussing Burt's arguments with Maximilian Schell (while filming *Judgment at Nuremberg*), Lancaster got up and left.

Academy Awards telecasts involving Burt included the 1961 show to pick up his own Oscar, announcing the Best Actress winner (Sophia Loren) a year later, and acting as one of the hosts on the 1969 and 1971 programs. Among his duties for the 1969 show was announcing the Best Actor (Cliff Robertson); in 1971, among other things, he joined Petula Clark, Sally Kellerman, and Ricardo Montalban in singing the Oscar-nominated song (from *Scrooge*), "Thank You Very Much."

In the Oscar telecast in 1985, Burt joined Kirk Douglas to present the writing awards. Their appearance was highlighted by a clip from their initial jaunt together on the 1958 show, where they sang and did acrobatics for a specialty song, "It's Great Not to Be Nominated."

In January 1980, Lancaster had a life-threatening gallbladder operation and in August 1983 a quadruple heart bypass. While recovering from the heart surgery, he had no choice but to relinquish a starring role in the film *Kiss of the Spider Woman*. William Hurt took over the controversial part of Luis Molina (a homosexual imprisoned in South America) and won the Oscar for Best Actor in 1985. The film acknowledged Burt with a courtesy credit.

The apparent high altitude of its Mexican location was felt by Columbia Pictures to be too risky for Burt's heart in 1988's filming of *Old Gringo*. Originally cast in the title role (the character was Ambrose Bierce, the writer), he was then fired by the studio. A breach-of-contract suit was filed by Burt to collect his salary ($1.5 million), and the matter was resolved out of court. The film, released in 1989, starred Gregory Peck instead.

One of the best and worst years of Burt Lancaster's life was 1990. Five years earlier he had fallen in love with his legal secretary, Susan Scherer, and on September 10, 1990, they were married. The next day they went to South Carolina so Burt could begin work on *Separate But Equal*, not knowing that it would be his final film project.

On November 30, Burt was visiting fellow actor Dana Andrews, who was a patient at a medical center in Los

Angeles being treated for Alzheimer's disease. There, Burt suffered a major stroke, which affected the right side of his body with paralysis and affected his speech.

Variety ran an ad in December 1990 for a proposed sequel to *The Leopard*, with Burt Lancaster and Alain Delon reprising their original roles. Without Lancaster's participation, it remained only a wonderful dream. Although he made a gallant effort to fight the effects of the stroke, Burt decided not to make any public appearances.

However, he was honored for his life's work. On December 15, 1991, the Screen Actors Guild bestowed on Burt their highest honor. Presented to him by Kirk Douglas, the SAG Annual Achievement Award was in recognition of career and humanitarian achievements. His daughter Joanna and his wife, Susie, accepted on his behalf.

New York's American Museum of the Moving Image paid a tribute to Lancaster's films in 1992, calling him "a thinking man's tough guy." Secluded at home, in Century City, California, Burt enjoyed watching his old films. Justifiably, he had every right to be proud of them.

Burt Lancaster died of a heart attack at home on October 20, 1994. He was 80 years old. Susie said he went peacefully: "He was patting my hair and touching my face and he took a sigh and that was it." After his death, he was eulogized on radio, television and in newspapers and magazines. The burial was private.

"It's the passing now of a giant," Kirk Douglas said. "But Burt will never die. We'll always be able to see him swinging from a yardarm in *The Crimson Pirate* ... and shooting with me in *Gunfight at the O.K. Corral*."

A great many of the film performances of Burt Lancaster—an actor for all seasons—will endure. That is truly a wonderful legacy.

The Films

THE 1940S

The Killers
Brute Force
Desert Fury
Variety Girl
I Walk Alone
All My Sons
Sorry, Wrong Number
Kiss the Blood Off My Hands
Criss Cross
Rope of Sand

THE 1950S

The Flame and the Arrow
Mister 880
Vengeance Valley
Jim Thorpe—All American
Ten Tall Men
The Crimson Pirate
Come Back, Little Sheba
South Sea Woman
Three Sailors and a Girl
From Here to Eternity
His Majesty O'Keefe
Apache
Vera Cruz
The Kentuckian
The Rose Tattoo
Trapeze
The Rainmaker
Gunfight at the O.K. Corral
Sweet Smell of Success
Run Silent, Run Deep
Separate Tables
The Devil's Disciple

THE 1960S

The Unforgiven
Elmer Gantry
The Young Savages
Judgment at Nuremberg
Birdman of Alcatraz
A Child Is Waiting
The List of Adrian Messenger
The Leopard
Seven Days in May
The Train
The Hallelujah Trail
The Professionals
The Scalphunters
The Swimmer
Castle Keep
The Gypsy Moths

THE 1970S

Airport
Valdez Is Coming
Lawman
Ulzana's Raid
Scorpio
Executive Action
The Midnight Man
Moses, the Lawgiver
Conversation Piece
Buffalo Bill and the Indians
Victory at Entebbe

The Cassandra Crossing
Twilight's Last Gleaming
The Island of Dr. Moreau
1900
Go Tell the Spartans

THE 1980S

Zulu Dawn
Atlantic City
Cattle Annie and Little Britches
La Pelle
Marco Polo
Local Hero
The Osterman Weekend
Scandal Sheet
Little Treasure
On Wings of Eagles
Tough Guys
Barnum
Control
Sins of the Fathers
Rocket Gibraltar
Field of Dreams
The Jeweller's Shop
The Betrothed

THE 1990S

The Phantom of the Opera
Voyage of Terror: The Achille Lauro Affair
Separate But Equal

The Films

The Killers

A Mark Hellinger Presentation A Universal Release Released August 29, 1946 105 minutes Black and White

CREDITS: Robert Siodmak (Director); Mark Hellinger (Producer); Anthony Veiller (Screenplay); Woody Bredell (Photography); Arthur Hilton (Editor); Jack Otterson and Martin Obzina (Art Directors); Russell A. Gausman and E.R. Robinson (Set Decorators); Vera West (Costumes); Jack P. Pierce (Make-up); D.S. Horsley (Special Effects); Miklos Rozsa (Music Score). Based on the short story by Ernest Hemingway.

CAST: Burt Lancaster (Swede); Ava Gardner (Kitty Collins); Edmond O'Brien (Jim Reardon); Albert Dekker (Jim Colfax); Sam Levene (Lt. Sam Lubinsky); Jack Lambert (Dum-Dum); Jeff Corey (Blinky); John Miljan (Jake); Virginia Christine (Lilly); Vince Barnett (Charleston); Charles D. Brown (Packy Robinson); Donald MacBride (Kenyon); Charles McGraw (Al); William Conrad (Max); Phil Brown (Nick Adams); Queenie Smith (Queenie); Garry Owen (Joe); Harry Hayden (George); Bill Walker (Sam); Wally Scott (Charlie); Gabrielle Windsor (Ginny); Rex Dale (Man); Harry Brown (Paymaster); Beatrice Roberts (Nurse); Howard Freeman (Police Chief); John Berkes (Plinther); John Sheehan (Doctor); Charles Middleton (Farmer Brown); Al Hill (Customer); Noel Cravat (Lou Tringle); Rev. Neal Dodd (Minister); George Anderson (Doctor); Vera Lewis (Mrs. Hirsch); Ann Staunton (Stella); William Ruhl (Mo-torman); Therese Lyon (Housekeeper); Perc Launders, Geoffrey Ingraham, and Howard Negley (Policemen); Ernie Adams (Gimp); Jack Cheatham (Police Driver); Ethan Laidlaw (Conductor); Michael Hale (Pet); Wally Rose (Bartender); Audley Anderson (Assistant Paymaster); Mike Donovan (Timekeeper); Nolan Leary, John Trebach, and Milton Wallace (Waiters).

SYNOPSIS: Two men drive into a New Jersey town one night. They are gangsters coming to kill a man called the Swede. Another man, Nick Adams, warns the Swede of the danger, but the Swede knows they are coming and doesn't care. The killers break into the Swede's room and shoot him dead.

Jim Reardon, an insurance detective, investigates the Swede's murder. He learns that the Swede was depressed several days prior to his demise; it started when a man in an out-of-state car drove through town. The Swede left a beneficiary in Atlantic City—a chambermaid, Queenie, who tells Reardon that she stopped the Swede from attemping suicide six years earlier when a woman ran out on him.

The Swede once was a prizefighter, losing his last bout after suffering a broken hand. He then fell for a woman named Kitty Collins, who was the

25

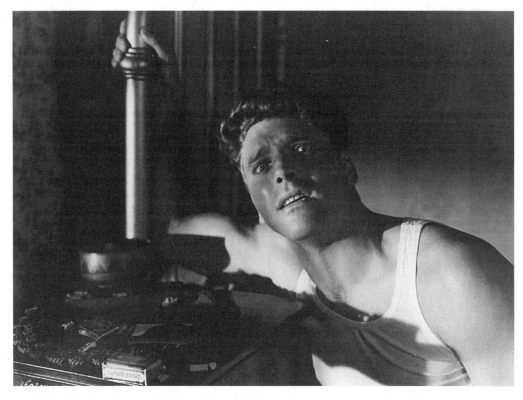

The Killers: **As the Swede, about to be gunned down in his first film.**

mistress of Jim Colfax. The Swede was arrested and sent to prison after taking the rap for a theft Kitty made. Reardon further learns from the Swede's cellmate, Charleston, that after his release the Swede was involved in a caper.

An unusual handkerchief was found on the Swede's body, and Reardon reads in an old newspaper clipping that a similar one was used as a mask in a factory robbery. From the dying words of one of the robbers, Blinky, who is found gunshot, it is discovered that the Swede was in on the crime along with Colfax and a hood called Dum-Dum. After the robbery, the Swede stole the loot from his partners because Kitty told him he was being double-crossed.

Reardon suspects that Kitty was the woman in Atlantic City, and he finds Dum-Dum looking for the stolen money in the Swede's room. Dum-Dum admits to shooting Blinky and then escapes.

Kitty is found in Pittsburgh by Reardon and a police detective named Lubinsky; she reveals running out on the Swede and taking the money with her. As Kitty escapes, Reardon is attacked by the killers, but they are shot by Lubinsky.

Reardon and the police then go to Colfax's house and find him shot by Dum-Dum, who guessed the truth. Dum-Dum is killed by the police. Before he dies, Colfax confesses to planning the whole double-cross and hiring the two killers when he found the Swede while driving through that New Jersey town. Found hiding, Kitty is revealed as Colfax's wife.

The Killers, with Virginia Christine, Burt, and (seated) Ava Gardner.

COMMENTARY: *The Killers* was Mark Hellinger's first independent production and the beginning of a successful trilogy of crime films that hit hard depicting the grime of the underworld (the other two films were *Brute Force* and *The Naked City*). Prior to signing Lancaster, Hellinger wanted Wayne Morris to play the Swede. But Warner Bros., who held the actor's contract, asked for $75,000 for the loan-out, and the producer refused to pay such a high sum then on a low-budget film.

The movie was still well made. Hellinger, director Robert Siodmak, photographer Woody Bredell, and editor Arthur Hilton perfectly visualized the haunting atmosphere and riveting suspense of the underworld. This was certainly reinforced by the source for the film, a 1927 short story by Ernest Hemingway. The screenplay by Anthony Veiller and an uncredited John Huston used Hemingway's conception of a pair of hired gunmen coming after a man and then added the mystery behind the slaying (via flashbacks). Hemingway was very pleased with the results.

The screenplay was nominated for an Academy Award; its sharpness was matched by Siodmak's nomination for Best Director, Hilton's nomination for Film Editing, and Miklos Rozsa's Scoring nomination. Fans of the *Dragnet* television series will recognize the famed four-note opening music. *The Killers'* success as dynamic escapism was also attributable to a remarkable ensemble of performers.

Introduced as "a sensation in his

first screen role," Burt Lancaster easily reinforced this 1946 newspaper advertisement with his sullen yet strong performance as the Swede. He displayed a street smart ruggedness with a handsome demeanor, as well as a naive, even gentle vulnerability. These traits were immensely appealing and helped make him an overnight movie star.

Also helping her own career along very nicely was the beautiful Ava Gardner. She was stunning as the femme fatale who wooed Lancaster's Swede to damnation, thereby helping establish the chilling scenario as a great example of film noir. The film's largest role actually went to Edmond O'Brien as the determined investigator. Strong, standout performances were also given by Albert Dekker, Sam Levene, Jack Lambert, and Charles McGraw and William Conrad as the killers.

REVIEWS: *Life*: "There is not a dull moment in *The Killers*, not a corny line nor a contrived character—nothing but menacing action managed with supreme competence. There is not even a 'name' player in the film, but the standard of performance is worthy of a cast of Academy Award winners."

New Republic: "Lancaster, a hefty actor from the Broadway stage, does an excellent, quiet job that turns Swede into a singularly provocative character."

A tough guy persona and a certain vulnerability helped make Burt a star in the 1940s.

Brute Force

A Mark Hellinger Production A Universal-International Release Released June 30, 1947 98 minutes Black and White

CREDITS: Jules Dassin (Director); Mark Hellinger (Producer); Jules Buck (Associate Producer); Richard Brooks (Screenplay); William Daniels (Photography); Edward Curtiss (Editor); Bernard Herzbrun and John F. DeCuir (Art Directors); Russell A. Gausman and Charles Wyrick (Set Decorators); Rosemary Odell (Costumes); Bud Westmore (Make-up); David S. Horsley (Special Effects); Miklos Rozsa (Music Score). Based on a story by Robert Patterson.

CAST: Burt Lancaster (Joe Collins); Hume Cronyn (Captain Munsey); Charles Bickford (Gallagher); Sam Levene (Louie);

Yvonne DeCarlo (Gina); Ann Blyth (Ruth); Ella Raines (Cora); Anita Colby (Flossie); Howard Duff (Soldier); Art Smith (Dr. Walters); Roman Bohnen (Warden Barnes); John Hoyt (Spencer); Whit Bissell (Tom Lister); Jeff Corey (Freshman); Jack Overman (Kid Coy); Richard Gaines (McCallum); Frank Puglia (Ferrara); Vince Barnett (Muggsy); James Bell (Crenshaw); Sir Lancelot (Calypso); Ray Teal (Jackson); Jay C. Flippen (Hodges); James O'Rear (Wilson); Howland Chamberlin (Gaines); Kenneth Patterson (Bronski); Crane Whitley (Armed Guard in Drainpipe); Charles McGraw (Andy); John Harmon (Roberts); Gene Stutenroth (Hoffman); Wally Rose (Peary); Carl Rhodes (Strella); Guy Beach (Convict Foreman); Edmund Cobb (Bradley); Tom Steele (Machine Gunner); Alex Frazer (Chaplain); Will Lee (Kincaid); Ruth Sanderson (Miss Lawrence); Francis McDonald (Regan); Jack S. Lee (Sergeant); Virginia Farmer (Sadie); William Cozzo, Rex Dale, Frank Marlowe, and Billy Wayne (Prisoners); Paul Bryar (Harry); Glenn Strange (Tompkins); Al Hill (Plonski); Eddy Chandler, Al Ferguson, Kenneth R. MacDonald, Jerry Salvail, and Peter Virgo (Guards); Rex Lease (Hearse Driver); Herbert Haywood (Chef); Blanch Obronska (Young Girl); Hal Malone (Young Inmate); Don McGill (Max); Harry Wilson (Tyrone); Sam Rizhallah (Convict's Son); Kippee Valez (Visitor).

SYNOPSIS: At Westgate Penitentiary, convict Joe Collins returns to his cell after spending ten days in solitary confinement. A setup against him was arranged by head quard Captain Munsey, who had another convict, Wilson, plant a knife on him.

In Cell R17, which he shares with inmates Soldier, Tom Lister, Spencer, Kid Coy, and Freshman, Collins begins planning a prison break. Convict leader Gallagher rebuffs any chance to escape. In the prison machine shop, Wilson is forced by Collins's cellmates into a huge press and is crushed.

A few of the inmates in R17 later reveal why they were sent to prison. Lister was an accountant who embezzled company funds to buy a fur coat for his wife, Cora. Spencer and a woman, Flossie, were con artists, but she ran out on him, letting him get nabbed. Soldier was involved in smuggling food for a woman, Gina, during World War II. When her father tried to tell an MP patrol, Gina shot him and Soldier took the blame. Collins was caught during a gang caper trying to steal money for his invalid girlfriend, Ruth, so she could have an operation.

After Wilson's death, Munsey intimidates Lister into hanging himself. The other inmates of R17 are made to work digging in a massive drainpipe. Warden Barnes and Doctor Walters realize Munsey is actually worse than the prisoners; although key prison personnel, they can do nothing to stop the political machine that sides with the captain for tougher treatment.

Collins's escape plans include moving through the drainpipe, which runs outside the prison walls, and attacking the guard tower from the rear. After his parole falls through, Gallagher agrees to start a riot from inside. Munsey, suspecting something, beats another inmate, Louie, who divulges nothing.

Doctor Walters warns Collins that there is an informer, revealed as Freshman. He is bound to a dump car as his cellmates take positions behind him and ride it out of the drainpipe. Meanwhile, the rioting takes place inside the prison.

Freshman is killed by machine-gun fire set up by Munsey. Spencer and Kid Coy are then shot, but the machine gunners are stopped. From the tower, a guard kills Soldier and wounds Collins. Gallagher crashes a truck into the prison gates, but fails to break through. Collins struggles to the tower and throws Munsey to his death over the railing, before he falls dead from his wounds.

COMMENTARY: Burt Lancaster was chief among the new wave of post-war Hollywood stars, and he was eager to assert his status after his debut in *The*

Killers. On the set of his second released film, *Brute Force*, with Universal (now merged as Universal-International), Burt was undaunted that he offended not only writer Sheilah Graham (by making fun of her when she came to interview him) but director Jules Dassin and producer Mark Hellinger (by feeling

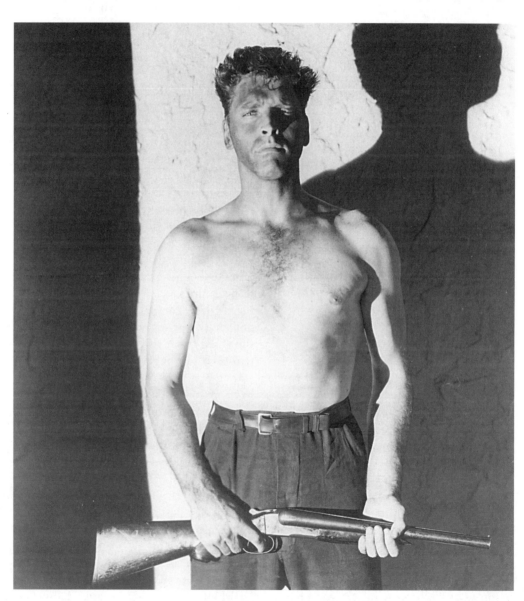

Brute Force: **A publicity pose as Joe Collins.**

it his right to assert, argumentatively if necessary, his creative input into film-making).

Nonetheless, the producer felt he had a passionate ally in Lancaster for his brand of brooding melodrama. Hellinger wanted to show the hardships of men in prison with *Brute Force*, and he presented the prisoners in something of a sympathetic light. With this attitude and the teeming violence, the film made for strong controversy with the then-active Breen Production Code of the Motion Picture Association of America (MPAA)—it was even reputed that some television stations refused to show the more sadistic scenes in later years. Dassin's direction and Richard Brooks's screenplay (from a Robert Patterson story) were with equally passionate acknowledgment for that exciting raw quality that Hellinger was providing.

Even though both were brooding characters, Lancaster realized that Joe Collins was more sophisticated than the Swede in *The Killers*. The Swede gave up after the woman he loved betrayed him, but Collins would not let anything except death deter him from freedom. This steely reserve helped confirm Lancaster as a new energy in film. His vulnerable side was also evident, especially in the tender flashback sequence with the touching heroine, played by Ann Blyth.

A powerhouse cast also included Hume Cronyn (in a striking portrait of how power can induce evil), Charles Bickford, Sam Levene, and Howard Duff (in his film debut). Burt asserted that the actresses—Ann Blyth, Yvonne DeCarlo, Ella Raines, and Anita Colby—were included because of the Hollywood standard that still prevailed in 1947, where romances between men and women were imperative to a film's box office success. *Brute Force* was a tougher film than *The Killers*, but it was not as big a hit. As both an action film and a probe into prison conditions, however, it was stunning.

REVIEWS: *Commonweal:* "Mark Hellinger's production and cast are excellent; and from a cinematic point of view, director Jules Dassin has used his camera exceedingly well to tell an unpleasant but moving story."

New York Times: "Big framed, expressionless Burt Lancaster gives the chief convict a heroic mold."

Desert Fury

A Hal Wallis Production   A Paramount Picture   Released September 24, 1947   96 minutes   Technicolor
CREDITS: Lewis Allen (Director); Hal Wallis (Producer); Robert Rossen (Screenplay); Charles Lang and Edward Cronjager (Photography); Warren Low (Editor); Perry Ferguson (Art Director); Sam Comer and Syd Moore (Set Decorators); Edith Head (Costumes); Gordon Jennings (Special Effects); Miklos Rozsa (Music Score). Based on the novel *Desert Town* by Ramona Stewart.
CAST: John Hodiak (Eddie Bendix); Lizabeth Scott (Paula Haller); Burt Lancaster (Tom Hanson); Wendell Corey (Johnny Ryan); Mary Astor (Fritzi Haller); Kristine Miller (Claire Lindquist); William Harrigan (Judge Berle Lindquist); James Flavin (Sheriff Pat Johnson); Jane Novak (Mrs. Lindquist); Ana Camargo (Rosa); Milton Kibbee (Bartender); Ralph Peters (Cafe Owner); John Farrell (Drunk); Ray Teal (Bus Driver); Harland Tucker (Chuck); Lew Harvey (Doorman); Tom Schamp (Dan); Ed Randolph and Mike Lally (Dealers).

SYNOPSIS: Fritzi Haller is running a gambling casino in Nevada. She does not want her daughter, Paula, to see gangster Eddie Bendix, who is in town with partner Johnny Ryan. Having once had an affair with Bendix, Fritzi knows he is bad; she would rather Paula see Tom Hanson, a deputy sheriff. Tom is in love with Paula, but she seems to favor Bendix.

The gangster is finally revealed as the crook he is by his partner, and so he kills Ryan. Chased by Tom in a car, Bendix drives off a bridge to his own death. By now, Paula realizes just how much Tom means to her.

COMMENTARY: *Desert Fury*, Lancaster's initial film for Hal Wallis, was made before but released (by Paramount in 1947) after *Brute Force*. It was a trite affair—the direction by Lewis Allen was sluggish; the screenplay by Robert Rossen (from the 1945 novel by Ramona Stewart) was weak; most of the fury in the film was felt to be in Miklos Rozsa's music. Producer Wallis made it to showcase his new discoveries, Lizabeth Scott, Wendell Corey, Kristine Miller, and Burt Lancaster.

Lancaster's part of the good-guy deputy required little acting except to fawn over Miss Scott's wayward beauty. A shot of him slugging John Hodiak over a table that seemed a parody of the new star's masculinity. Shot in Sedona, Arizona, *Desert Fury* was Burt's first film in color, and it scored big at the box office, due perhaps to the impact of his previous two released films.

REVIEWS: *Commonweal:* "Expensively made in Technicolor that is

Desert Fury, with (left to right) Burt Lancaster, Mary Astor, and Lizabeth Scott.

used to no particular advantage ... and studded with stars whose talents could have been used better elsewhere, this picture does little more than let its characters talk tough before the camera."

Newsweek: "Outside of a workmanlike stint by Miss Astor, there remain only three impressions worth recording: (1) Lancaster ... makes a much better convict than a cop; (2) Wendell Corey's screen debut as a taciturn thug marks him as a comer; and (3) Miss Scott has wisely left off singing."

Variety Girl

To help fulfill contract obligations to Hal Wallis, Burt Lancaster and Lizabeth Scott appeared briefly together in Paramount's musical comedy *Variety Girl* (1947). Their sequence had Burt as a fellow shooting a cigarette out of Miss Scott's mouth. After the gunsmoke clears, he is seen hanging up a sign for a new assistant. Others in the all-star film included Gary Cooper, Barbara Stanwyck, Bing Crosby, Bob Hope, Dorothy Lamour, and Alan Ladd. Although filmed in black and white, there was an animated Puppetoon sequence in Technicolor.

An entertaining hodgepodge of sketches (revolving around two young ladies played by Mary Hatcher and Olga San Juan as they cavort with the stars on the Paramount lot), *Variety Girl* was produced by Daniel Dare; scripted by Edmund Hartmann, Frank Tashlin, Robert Welch, and Monte Brice; and directed by George Marshall for the benefit of the Variety Clubs of America (founded in 1928) and their work with underprivileged children.

I Walk Alone

A Hal Wallis Production A Paramount Picture Released January 22, 1948 98 minutes Black and White

CREDITS: Byron Haskin (Director); Hal Wallis (Producer); Charles Schnee (Screenplay); Leo Tover (Photography); Arthur Schmidt (Editor); Hans Dreier and Franz Bachelin (Art Directors); Sam Comer and Patrick Delany (Set Decorators); Edith Head (Costumes); Victor Young (Music Score). An adaptation by Robert Smith and John Bright from the Theodore Reeves play *Beggars Are Coming to Town.*

CAST: Burt Lancaster (Frankie Madison); Lizabeth Scott (Kay Lawrence); Wendell Corey (Dave); Kirk Douglas (Noll Turner); Kristine Miller (Mrs. Richardson); Mike Mazurki (Dan); George Rigaud (Maurice); Marc Lawrence (Nick Palestro); Mickey Knox (Skinner); Roger Neury (Felix); John Bishop (Ben); Bruce Lester (Charles); Jean Del Val (Henri); Gino Corrado (George); Freddie Steele (Tiger); Dewey Robinson (Heinz); Fred G. Somers (Butcher); Charles D. Brown (Lt. Hollaran) Walter Anthony Merrill (Schreiber); Bobby Barber (Newsboy); Jack Perrin (Policeman); Bert Moorehouse (Tollgate Policeman); Olin Howlin (Watchman); James Davies (Masseur).

SYNOPSIS: Frankie Madison returns to his old neighborhood after spending 14 years in prison. He goes to see Noll Turner, his former partner in crime who now owns a nightclub. Noll arranges a dinner date between Frankie and a singer named Kay Lawrence. Frankie reveals to Kay that he and Noll were once bootleggers, agreeing to share their spoils regardless of who was imprisoned (Frankie was the one nabbed).

When Noll turns down Frankie's request for his share invested in the nightclub, the ex-convict rounds up some of his cronies and tries to take it. But the situation is different from the old days and involves complicated

I Walk Alone, with (left to right) Wendell Corey, Mike Mazurki, Burt Lancaster, Kirk Douglas, and tough guys.

corporate matters. Frankie even blames Dave, the club's bookkeeper, for the entanglements. Noll has Frankie taken away and beaten.

Dave is appalled by Noll's actions against Frankie and threatens him with financial ruin. Noll then hires a gunman to kill the bookkeeper. Frankie is blamed for the murder. With Kay, he manages to get a confession from Noll, who is then killed by the police when he pulls a gun. Kay and Frankie are left together.

COMMENTARY: Paramount's early 1948 release *I Walk Alone*, despite a smaller budget, was a better film than the previous entry with producer Hal Wallis, *Desert Fury*. But it still was an ordinary crime story, this time directed by Byron Haskin and scripted by Charles

Schnee from Robert Smith and John Bright's adaptation of Theodore Reeves's rather unsuccessful 1945 Broadway play (with Paul Kelly and Luther Adler as the one-time bootleggers).

Wallis, as with *Desert Fury*, used the film as a vehicle for his new stars, including Kirk Douglas, who, like Lancaster, was appearing in his fourth released film in a major role. Burt was typecast in this brooding, tough-guy role all during his filmmaking in the 1940s (with deviations of sort in *All My Sons* and *Sorry, Wrong Number*). The humorous *Harvard Lampoon* included his extremely sullen performance in *I Walk Alone* on their "Worst" list for 1948. The tension between Douglas and Lancaster, fully developed over the next 38 years on the big screen, was engaging. Also effective was the physical attraction between Burt and Lizabeth Scott, which was the case in all three of the films in which they appeared together.

Despite a particularly striking slugfest involving Lancaster's big ex-con and Mike Mazurki's even bigger doorman, the film as a whole lacked the more exciting dynamics of *Brute Force* or *The Killers*. However, Hal Wallis asserted that *I Walk Alone* and *Desert Fury* were bigger at the box office.

REVIEWS: *Commonweal:* "*I Walk Alone* is so much like so many other movies in which these actors have appeared that you'll probably think you've seen it before."

Newsweek: "As Frankie Madison, the confused ex-hooch merchant of *I Walk Alone*, Burt Lancaster is tougher than he is convincing."

All My Sons

A Chester Erskine Production   A Universal-International Release   Released March 27, 1948   94 minutes   Black and White
   CREDITS: Irving Reis (Director); Chester Erskine (Producer and Screenplay); Frank Shaw (Assistant Director); Russell Metty (Photography); Ralph Dawson (Editor); Bernard Herzbrun and Hilyard Brown (Art Directors); Russell A. Gausman and Al Fields (Set Decorators); Leith Stevens (Music Score). Based on Arthur Miller's play.
   CAST: Edward G. Robinson (Joe Keller); Burt Lancaster (Chris Keller); Mady Christians (Kate Keller); Louisa Horton (Ann Deever); Howard Duff (George Deever); Frank Conroy (Herbert Deever); Lloyd Gough (Jim Bayliss); Arlene Francis (Sue Bayliss); Henry Morgan (Frank Lubey); Elizabeth Fraser (Lydia Lubey); Walter Soderling (Charles); Therese Lyon (Minnie); Charles Meredith (Ellsworth); William Johnstone (Attorney); Herbert Vigran (Wertheimer); Harry Harvey (Judge); Pat Flaherty (Bartender); George Sorel (Headwaiter); Helen Brown (Mrs. Hamilton); Herbert Haywood (McGraw); Joseph Kerr (Norton); Jerry Hausner (Halliday); Frank Kreig (Foreman); William Ruhl (Ed); Al Murphy (Tom); Walter Boon (Jorgenson); Richard La Marr (Workman); George Slocum and Victor Zimmerman (Attendants).

SYNOPSIS: Joe Keller is a partner in a factory that makes airplane cylinders. He is accused by his partner's son, George, of selling defective parts to the air force during World War II. Twenty-one young men were killed as a result of the bad cylinders. When Joe stated that he was home ill and had nothing to do with the faulty shipment, partner Herbert Deever was fully blamed and imprisoned.

Having returned from military service, Chris, Joe's oldest son, wants to believe his father's story. Herbert's daughter, Ann, and Chris fall in love, to the resentment not only of her brother but also of Kate Keller, Chris's mother. Ann was engaged to his brother, reportedly killed during his own wartime service; however, Kate refuses to accept his death and feels that Ann should wait for his return.

Visiting Herbert in prison, Chris is told that his father's involvement with the shipment is true. This is further confirmed when Ann reveals a letter from Chris's brother, who knew of their father's wrongdoing and committed suicide by flying a plane with one of the defective cylinders.

Chris attacks his father to make him reveal the truth. Joe admits his guilt, proclaiming that he did it for his family as it would have met financial hardship had the cylinders not been

Top: All My Sons, with (back) Edward G. Robinson, Mady Christians, and (front) Louisa Horton and Burt Lancaster. *Bottom: All My Sons*, Burt Lancaster and Edward G. Robinson.

shipped. Shaken that one of his sons would then kill himself in shame, Joe takes his own life. Chris and Ann leave to start a new life together.

COMMENTARY: Arthur Miller's play *All My Sons* was first produced on the Broadway stage, and it was chosen the Prize Play of the 1946-47 theater season by the New York Drama Critics Circle. The play, directed by Elia Kazan and with Ed Begley and Arthur Kennedy, shared its theme of greedy wartime profiteering with a national capitalistic system made up of many individuals.

Prior to the film's production in the fall of 1947, the House Un-American Activities Committee began a series of hearings on subversive conduct within the film industry. To avoid any repercussions, Chester Erskine, the film's producer and screenwriter, kept the profiteering and its consequences focused on an individual company, and not reflective of the country as a whole. Both the film's stars, Edward G. Robinson and Burt Lancaster (in the Begley-Kennedy roles), were involved with other filmmakers (including Lauren Bacall, Humphrey Bogart, Judy Garland, and Gene Kelly) on the Committee for the First Amendment to protest the HUAC hearings.

Irving Reis directed Erskine's conception of *All My Sons* with a more simplistic perspective, and still it was a noble drama. After its release in 1948 by Universal-International, however, the film was not successful at the box office (although the play had enjoyed a run of nine months). Lancaster said about the film, "Okay, it didn't make money. It was too talky, too preachy. But we took a chance, we tried."

Burt so believed in the film's va-lidity that he took an enormous salary cut after pleading with Hal Wallis (who felt that the actor was miscast) for the loan-out. The long-term contract with the producer (made before *The Killers* and restructured in 1947) stipulated only one outside film a year on his own, and Lancaster already made *Brute Force* in 1947.

Although Robinson's performance as the tragic father was certainly splendid, Lancaster's as the decent son proved to be his most distinguished acting turn of the 1940s. Making her film debut was Louisa Horton as Burt's gentle lady. His sensitive work with his co-stars gave exceptional weight to the touching vulnerability Burt had shown glimpses of in his earlier films. But that pent-up fury, which could explode like a volcano (as it did most remarkably at the climax of *Brute Force*), was also very effective in the final confrontation, which Lancaster shared with Edward G. Robinson.

REVIEWS: *New Republic:* "Irving Reis, who has used the documentary approach in directing large parts of *All My Sons*, has been assigned sound and expert actors, and has been given a valid story to tell. The result is a film so good as to be, these days, astonishing."

Newsweek: "As the affable, misguided villain of the piece, Robinson gives one of his best performances. Lancaster is surprisingly good as the son who comes to know his father for what he is."

Sorry, Wrong Number

A Hal Wallis Production   A Paramount Release   Released September 1, 1948   89 minutes   Black and White

CREDITS: Anatole Litvak (Director); Hal Wallis and Anatole Litvak (Producers); Lucille Fletcher (Screenplay); Sol Polito (Photography); Farciot Edouart (Process Photography); Warren Low (Editor); Hans Dreier and Earl Hedrick (Art Directors); Sam Comer and Bertram Granger (Set Decorators); Edith Head (Costumes); Wally Westmore (Make-up); Gordon Jennings (Special Effects); Franz Waxman (Music Score). Based on Lucille Fletcher's radio play.

CAST: Barbara Stanwyck (Leona Stevenson); Burt Lancaster (Henry Stevenson); Ann Richards (Sally Lord); Wendell Corey (Doctor Alexander); Harold Vermilyea (Waldo Evans); Ed Begley (James Cotterell); Leif Erickson (Fred Lord); William Conrad (Morano); Jimmy Hunt (Peter Lord); Dorothy Neumann (Miss Jennings); Kristine Miller (Dolly); John Bromfield (Joe); Paul Fierro (Harpootlian); Suzanne Dalbert (Cigarette Girl); Joyce Compton (Blonde); Cliff Clark (Sgt. Duffy); Tito Vuolo (Albert).

SYNOPSIS: Leona Stevenson is a bedridden woman, who one night impatiently tries to phone her husband, Henry, at work. She is instead connected to a wrong line and overhears two men planning a murder. Her attempts to interest anyone on this are frustrating because what she heard was vague. However, Leona keeps making calls and learns from a Sally Lord that Henry was being investigated by Sally's husband, Fred, a law attorney.

On the phone, Leona is revealed as a spoiled hypochondriac. Henry actually found out from a Dr. Alexander that she has mental problems. Her father, James Cotterell, has a successful pharmaceutical business, which she will inherit. But Henry resented being supported by her wealth and dominated by her neurotic behavior. With a chemist, Waldo Evans, Henry became involved in stealing drugs with gangsters. Henry's nefarious activities forced him to sign an enormous IOU to a hoodlum named Morano. The only way to pay the debt was by putting a murder contract on Leona to collect her life insurance.

Upon discovering Henry's scheme over the phone, Leona becomes frantic as she now knows that *she* is the intended murder victim. Henry phones her and learns that Morano has been nabbed and that she would have paid off the debt. But the hired killer is in the house. As Henry is about to be apprehended by the law, he implores Leona to go to the window and scream. A passing train muffles her voice, and the killer strikes.

COMMENTARY: *Sorry, Wrong Number* was a famous radio play, starring Agnes Moorehead, when it came to the attention of filmmaker Anatole Litvak.

Sorry, Wrong Number, with (left to right) Burt Lancaster and Paul Fierro.

Lucille Fletcher, the creator of the radio thriller in 1943, was also responsible for the screen treatment (and had to considerably expand on her original 22-minute play). Litvak, who directed (and co-produced) the 1948 Paramount release, kept it as taut and exciting as could be expected. Flashbacks were used as extensively as they were in *The Killers* to unveil the mystery, and this time the result was a longer, complicated scenario that proved less suspenseful. Nonetheless, justification was there for another film noir great (with a manipulative dame, mob, and the rogue in the middle).

Burt Lancaster's role of the weak-willed scamp was certainly another striking departure (like *All My Sons*) from his tough-guy image, offering him his most challenging work for Wallis during the 1940s. *Sorry, Wrong Number* was also the actor's most popular film of this early period in his movie career. The vulnerability of his screen persona was still evident, especially in his last scene, when he feels guilt for his wrongdoing and tries in vain to save his wife's life. But the film truly belonged to Barbara Stanwyck for her tour de force performance (in the Miss Moorehead role) as the irritable, terrified woman. She received an Academy Award nomination (her fourth) for Best Actress, but lost the award to Jane Wyman in *Johnny Belinda*.

REVIEWS: *Newsweek:* "Despite the best efforts of Barbara Stanwyck as the hysterical murderee and Burt Lancaster as her lethal minded husband, the resulting hodgepodge isn't likely to raise many goose pimples."

New York Times: "As the ear bending lady, however, Miss Stanwyck does a quite elaborate job of working herself into a frenzy, as well as playing a nasty dame in the previous self-aggrandizing phases of her life. And a painfully obtuse performance as her stubborn and frustrated spouse who is driven to criminal extremities is given by Burt Lancaster."

Kiss the Blood Off My Hands

A Harold Hecht–Norma Production A Universal-International Presentation Released October 30, 1948   79 minutes Black and White

CREDITS: Norman Foster (Director); Richard Vernon (Producer); Norman Deming (Associate Producer); Leonardo Bercovici (Screenplay); Hugh Gray (Additional Dialogue); Russell Metty (Photography); Milton Carruth (Editor); Bernard Herzbrun and Nathan Juran (Art Directors); Russell A. Gausman and Ruby R. Levitt (Set Decorators); Bud Westmore (Make-up); David S. Horsley (Special Effects); Miklos Rozsa (Music Score). An adaptation by Ben Maddow and Walter Bernstein from the novel by Gerald Butler.

CAST: Joan Fontaine (Jane Wharton); Burt Lancaster (Bill Saunders); Robert Newton (Harry Carter); Lewis L. Russell (Tom Widgery); Jay Novello (Sea Captain); Aminta Dyne (Landlady); Grizelda Hervey (Mrs. Paton); Colin Keith-Johnston (Judge); Reginald Sheffield (Superintendent); Campbell Copelin (Publican); Leland Hodgson (Tipster); Peter Hobbes (Young Father); Thomas P. Dillon (Welshman); Joseph Granby (Theater Manager); Harry Cording, Art Foster, Robin Hughes, and Don MacCracken (Policemen); Harry Allen (Drunk); Valerie Cardew (Change Girl); Ben H. Wright (Cockney Tout); Wally Scott (Hanger-on); Harold Goodwin (Whipper); Keith Hitchcock (Official); Alec Harford (Doctor); Lora Lee Michel (Little Girl); Jimmy Aubrey (Taxi Driver); Leslie Denison (Constable); Arthur Gould-Porter, Kenneth Harvey, Tommy Hughes, and Tom Pilkington (Bookies); Charles McNaughton (Telescope Man); Filippa Rock (Woman); Timothy Bruce, Suzanne Kerr, Patty King, and Anne Whitfield (Children); Colin Kenny (Proprietor); Ola Lorraine (Donald's Mother); Frank Hagney, James Logan, and David McMahon (Seamen); Al Ferguson (Marker); David Dunbar (Large Man); Richard Glynn (Donald); Marilyn Williams (Barmaid); Jack Stoney (Man); Mildred Hale (Woman); Jack Carol, James Fowler, Fred Fox, and Robert Hale (Tipsters); George Bunny (Bookie); Harry Wilson (Man in Pub); Duke Green and Wesley Hopper (Men).

SYNOPSIS: At a London pub following World War II, Bill Saunders (his mind scarred from wartime experiences) slugs the owner in a quarrel and accidentally kills him. Bill flees from the police and hides in an apartment where a woman, Jane Wharton, is sleeping. He frightens her, but leaves her unharmed. The next day, however, he robs a man on the street.

Bill visits Jane at the clinic where she works as a nurse, but at first she doesn't want anything to do with him. Finally able to arrange a date with her, Bill is recognized for his crime at the pub by a hoodlum named Harry Carter. But Bill denies it. He does strike a policeman when taking Jane home and is given six months in jail.

After his release, Bill forms a crooked operation with Harry until he accepts a job as a truck driver at Jane's clinic. To stop Harry from blackmailing him on the pub killing, Bill agrees to help him steal a cargo of penicillin.

On the night of the planned robbery, Jane, believing Bill is delivering the medicine to those in need, decides to ride along with him. The two are now in love. Bill then changes his mind about the robbery, ruining the deal with Harry.

Going to Jane's apartment to force her into rearranging the theft of the medicine, Harry is stabbed with a pair of scissors. Jane runs to Bill and he finds Harry still alive. Harry is taken to his own place and pulls a gun on Bill. The ensuing fight is too much for the crook, and he dies from the stab wound. Although tempted to flee, Bill and Jane decide instead to go to the police and reveal all that has happened.

COMMENTARY: Burt Lancaster secured Harold Hecht's services initially as his agent, following the actor's brief run on Broadway in 1945's *A Sound of Hunting*. Their dream to become independent producers within five years took only a little more than two. As Hecht-Norma Productions (after Harold and Burt's wife), they made a one-picture distribution deal (as part of Burt's loan-out for *All My Sons*) with Universal-International for the 1948 release of *Kiss the Blood Off My Hands*.

Charles K. Feldman Group Productions took those main participants in the film to court in March 1948, just prior to its filming, claiming the rights to Gerald Butler's 1946 novel of the same title. However, another producer, Richard Vernon, had acquired the film rights directly from the author in 1947 and turned them over to Hecht. Thus, Vernon was assigned by Hecht-Norma to produce this first picture. Leonardo Bercovici admittedly never read the novel, but based his screenplay on Walter Bernstein and Ben Maddow's adaptation.

Seemingly a fallen hero pitted against the forces of evil in his films of the 1940s, Lancaster felt with Hecht that it was a safer bet commercially to stay with these tough, brooding, yet sympathetic portrayals. The new production unit further attempted to ensure success by using highly talented craftsmen from

Kiss the Blood Off My Hands: **Publicity pose with Joan Fontaine and Burt Lancaster.**

Burt's previous films—included in this group were photographer Russell Metty, art director Bernard Herzbrun, set decorator Russell A. Gausman, and composer Miklos Rozsa. A former actor, now director, Norman Foster kept things charged up. Though it was not a box office hit, *Kiss the Blood Off My Hands* did generate enough excitement to replenish its production costs of $1.1 million.

Especially realized by Hecht-Norma were the problems associated with a production unit. Although Burt and Joan Fontaine performed diligently, as the woebegone lovers, she was pregnant and caught a bad cold, which confined her to bed for a time, altering the filming schedule. Though set in a postwar London, the film was made in California, for the most part at the Universal Studios in Hollywood, but some exterior shooting in Los Angeles was hampered with weather delays. Robert Newton, singled out as the movie's most flamboyant performance, as the weaseling hood, was considerably hard pressed adjusting to the schedule changes.

REVIEWS: *Rotarian:* "Not so gruesome as the title suggests, yet suspenseful and intensely grim."

New York Times: "Were it not for the restraint and intelligence that Joan Fontaine brings to the role of Jane Wharton the drama no doubt would come apart at the seams…. Mr. Lancaster's performance is good, but he would do well to drop some of his tenseness and get more flexibility into his acting."

Criss Cross

A Universal-International Presentation Released March 12, 1949   87 minutes Black and White

CREDITS: Robert Siodmak (Director); Michel Kraike (Producer); Daniel Fuchs (Screenplay); Franz Planer (Photography); Ted J. Kent (Editor); Bernard Herzbrun and Boris Leven (Art Directors); Russell A. Gausman, Oliver Emert (Set Decorators); Yvonne West (Costumes); Bud Westmore (Make-up); David S. Horsley (Special Effects); Miklos Rozsa (Music Score). Based on the novel by Don Tracy.

CAST: Burt Lancaster (Steve Thompson); Yvonne DeCarlo (Anna); Dan Duryea (Slim Dundee); Stephen McNally (Pete Ramirez); Richard Long (Slade Thompson); Esy Morales (Orchestra Leader); Tom Pedi (Vincent); Percy Helton (Frank); Alan Napier (Finchley); Griff Barnett (Pop); Meg Randall (Helen); Joan Miller (The Lush); Edna M. Holland (Mrs. Thompson); John Doucette (Walt); Marc Krah (Mort); James O'Rear (Waxie); John Miller (Midget); Robert Osterloh (Mr. Nelson); Vincent Renno (Headwaiter); Charles Wagenheim (Waiter); Tony Curtis (Gigolo); Beatrice Roberts and Isabel Randolph (Nurses); Robert Winkler (Clark); Vito Scotti (Track Usher); John Roy (Bartender); Tung Foo (Chinese Cook); Dolores Castle, Jeraldine Jordan, Ann Staunton, and Kippee Valez (Girlfriends); Jean Bane and Diane Stewart (Girls); Stephen Roberts (Doctor); Garry Owen (Johnny); Gene Evans, Kenneth Patterson (Guards); George Lynn (Andy); Michael Cisney (Chester).

SYNOPSIS: Steve Thompson is still in love with his ex-wife, named Anna. He gets into a fight with her new husband, Slim Dundee, but it is a ruse to create a front for the two men. They are planning a robbery on an armored payroll truck of which Steve is a guard.

Driving the truck to the holdup point, Steve reflects on the circumstances leading up to it. Although cop Pete Ramirez suspected something was going on, Steve became entangled with Anna, who then promised to run away with him if he double-crossed Slim with the payroll.

Criss Cross, with Burt Lancaster and Yvonne DeCarlo.

During the robbery, Steve is double-crossed by Slim and his gang. Both men are shot, with Slim escaping and Steve ending up in the hospital.

Steve is kidnapped by one of Slim's henchmen from the hospital, but bribes him to go to a hideout. Having run out on Slim, Anna is there with the stolen payroll. Realizing the henchman will tell Slim where they are, Anna prepares to leave Steve and take the money with her. But Slim arrives and kills them both, as police sirens are heard in the distance.

COMMENTARY: *Criss Cross* was originally planned as Burt Lancaster's third film with producer Mark Hellinger (as part of their five-picture deal starting in 1946 with *The Killers*).

Hellinger's death of a heart attack in 1947, however, left only a partially developed property based on Don Tracy's 1934 novel. Screenwriter Daniel Fuchs and producer Michel Kraike tried to visualize Hellinger's approach, although this type of melodramatic material was clearly becoming a thing of the past.

All things considered, Burt was reluctant to do the film, but was obligated to because Universal-International took over his contract with Hellinger as well as the property. With his earnings from *Kiss the Blood Off My Hands*, Burt was able to buy out the remainder of the five-picture contract.

Upon its release by the studio in 1949, *Criss Cross* seemed to be a rehash of *The Killers*, right down to using some of the same people, including Miklos Rozsa (composing his fifth score for a Lancaster film) and director Robert Siodmak. The director's brooding, dark style and Yvonne DeCarlo's luscious femme fatale were the best things about the film. Lancaster's eternal fall guy, tough yet vulnerable (but also labeled by some critics as "brutish" and "dumb"), was still an assurance that a substantial audience was there (although the film was not a big hit) to catch the star in what newspaper ads of the day called his "most terrific role."

REVIEWS: *Time:* "*Criss Cross* is fairly routine gangster melodrama in which the hero (Burt Lancaster) is led into a whole mess of trouble by his alluring ex-wife (Yvonne DeCarlo). But it is sharply directed by Robert Siodmak and enlivened with some fresh bits of business."

New York Times: "Burt Lancaster eventually gets around to being the same old tough guy of yore. It should not be surprising that his performance is competent, for he has been working at the same type of role for some time."

Rope of Sand

A Hal Wallis Production   A Paramount Picture   Released August 4, 1949   105 minutes   Black and White
    CREDITS: William Dieterle (Director); Hal Wallis (Producer); Walter Doniger (Screenplay); John Paxton (Additional Dialogue); Charles Lang Jr. (Photography); Warren Low (Editor); Hans Dreier and Franz Bachelin (Art Directors); Sam Comer and Grace Gregory (Set Decorators); Edith Head (Costumes); C. Silvera (Make-up); Gordon Jennings (Special Effects); Franz Waxman (Music Score). From a story by Walter Doniger.

CAST: Burt Lancaster (Mike Davis); Paul Henreid (Commandant Paul Vogel); Claude Rains (Arthur Martingale); Peter Lorre (Toady); Corinne Calvet (Suzanne Renaud); Sam Jaffe (Dr. Francis Hunter); John Bromfield (Thompson); Mike Mazurki (Pierson); Kenny Washington (John); Josef Marais and Miranda (South African Veldt Singers); Edmond Breon (Chairman); Hayden Rorke (Ingram); David Hoffman (Waiter); Carl Harbord (Operator of Club); Georges Renavent (Jacques); Ida Moore (Woman); David Thursby (Henry); Trevor Ward (Switchboard Operator); Everett G. Brown, Darby Jones, and Martin Wilkins (Batsuma Chiefs); Byron Ellis (Callboy); James R. Scott (Clerk); Harry Cording, Art Foster, and Blackie Whiteford (Guards); Nestor Paiva (Ship's Captain).

SYNOPSIS: American adventurer Mike Davis returns to the South African mining town of Diamondstad. His intentions are to regain a cache of stolen diamonds and to settle a score with Commandant Vogel, who heads the mine's brutal security. Mine director Arthur Martingale secretly dislikes Vogel and was actually an influence for Mike's return.

Initially, Mike was a guide to a hunter named Ingram, who was the one that took the diamonds from the mine's forbidden area in the desert, but he died before getting them out. Vogel's attempt to force Mike to reveal where the gems were hidden failed.

Now that he is back, Mike is seduced by French beauty Suzanne Renaud, sent by Martingale to make him talk. Instead, she falls in love with Mike.

Vogel's brutality continues toward Mike, although he is able to force the commandant into taking him to the diamonds. After a skirmish in the desert, Mike escapes. The demented Vogel then kills the mine's physician, Dr. Hunter, putting the blame on Suzanne.

Rope of Sand, with (left to right) Claude Rains, Paul Henreid, and Burt Lancaster.

When a barfly named Toady warns Mike of Suzanne's dilemma, he makes a deal with Martingale for her safe return in exchange for the diamonds. With Martingale's sly interference, a gun battle erupts between Vogel and Mike, and the commandant is killed. Mike and Suzanne then leaves Diamondstad together.

COMMENTARY: In 1949, *Rope of Sand* was subject to criticism by the motion picture censors (known as the Johnston Office) for what was deemed an earthy depiction of greed, sex, and violence. Writer Walter Doniger origi-

nally intended for his actually old-fashioned adventure yarn to fuel a reunion between producer Hal Wallis and his *Casablanca* stars, Humphrey Bogart and Ingrid Bergman.

Those two stars did not appear in *Rope of Sand*, but their co-stars from the 1943 classic (also set in Africa), Paul Henreid, Claude Rains, and Peter Lorre, was featured. The intrigue thus was given, under William Dieterle's direction and Charles Lang Jr.'s photography, a substantial grittiness reinforced by the desert scenes filmed in Yuma, Arizona. Although not a Bergman or

Bogart in their romantic paring, French actress Corinne Calvet (in her American film debut) and Lancaster were fetching enough. As the sturdy adventurer, Burt was once more the rough-and-ready man of action caught between good and evil.

Lancaster, often at odds with Doniger over the script during filming, years later regarded the film as his "least favorite." Nonetheless, after its release by Paramount in 1949, *Rope of Sand* proved to be his second most popular movie of the 1940s (right behind Burt's previous Wallis/Paramount picture, *Sorry, Wrong Number*).

The producer's fourth Lancaster film carried the actor's success story to the close of the decade with an assurance that these tough, dark melodramas had scored with audiences and made him a major star with his stolid yet physically powerful presence. For *The Killers, Brute Force, I Walk Alone, Sorry, Wrong Number; Kiss the Blood Off My Hands; Criss Cross;* and *Rope of Sand,* the ingredients of story, acting, direction, music, and black and white photography especially enhanced their somber moods and chilling atmosphere. All except *Rope of Sand* were deemed expressive of the film noir genre with their foreboding sense of doom caught in the web of the underworld.

REVIEWS: *New Republic:* "A picture that features Burt Lancaster, Paul Henreid, Claude Rains, Peter Lorre and Sam Jaffe cannot fail to be a melodrama of corruption and violent passions."

New York Times: "The people you will meet in *Rope of Sand* are not a pleasant bunch but they are all products of good acting and therefore are strangely interesting. The Messrs. Lancaster and Henreid bring forceful authority to their roles."

The 1950s

The Flame and the Arrow

A Norma–F.R. Production Distributed by Warner Bros.   Released July 15, 1950 88 minutes Technicolor

CREDITS: Jacques Tourneur (Director); Frank Ross and Harold Hecht (Producers); Waldo Salt (Screenplay); Ernest Haller (Photography); Alan Crosland Jr. (Editor); Edward Carrere (Art Director); Lyle B. Reifsnider (Set Decorator); Marjorie Best (Wardrobe); Perc Westmore (Make-up); Francis J. Scheid (Sound); Murray Cutter (Orchestrations); Max Steiner (Music Score).

CAST: Burt Lancaster (Dardo); Virginia Mayo (Anne); Robert Douglas (Alessandro); Aline MacMahon (Nonna Bartoli); Frank Allenby (Ulrich); Nick Cravat (Piccolo); Lynne Baggett (Francesca); Gordon Gebert (Rudi); Norman Lloyd (Troubadour); Victor Kilian (Apothecary); Francis Pierlot (Papa Pietro); Robin Hughes (Skinner).

SYNOPSIS: Lombardy in the twelfth century is overrun by Hessian invaders. A daring mountaineer, Dardo, refuses to bow down to the oppression and is branded an outlaw. Ulrich, the Hessian's leader, has Dardo's former wife, Francesca, as his mistress, and seizes Dardo's son by her. Dardo tries to save the boy, Rudi, but Rudi is taken by his mother to Ulrich's castle, and Dardo is wounded with an enemy arrow.

The Flame and the Arrow, with (front) Burt Lancaster and Gordon Gebert, and (back) assorted players.

Upon his recovery, Dardo and a friend, Piccolo, fight for the boy in the castle. Although this attempt to rescue Rudi also fails, Dardo and Piccolo do manage to kidnap Ulrich's niece, Anne.

A nobleman, Alessandro, is taken captive by Ulrich for refusing to pay the high taxes, and Dardo and his outlaw band of followers rescue him. Piccolo is sent to the castle with a message that Dardo will trade Anne for Rudi, but he comes back alone and badly whipped.

Despite saving villager Papa Pietro from Ulrich's wrath and being hanged, Dardo is marched on by other villagers led by Nonna Bartoli. But Papa Pietro convinces the outlaws and villagers to unite and fight Ulrich and his soldiers.

With Ulrich's threat to hang several of the villagers unless he surrenders, Dardo does so and is hanged. But his death is a ruse, as he wore a neck harness, fooling Ulrich until Alessandro betrays the outlaws. Many of them are locked in the castle dungeon.

Now free, Anne reveals Alessandro's deceit and her love for Dardo. Piccolo and Dardo disguise themselves as clowns and join a troupe of acrobats performing in the castle. They rescue their comrades and a battle royal begins. After dueling with swords, Dardo slays Alessandro with his hunting knife. Having killed Rudi's mother and now holding him hostage, Ulrich meets his own end from one of Dardo's arrows. Dardo then embraces Rudi and Anne.

COMMENTARY: Still filming *Rope of Sand* in March 1949, Burt Lancaster's agreement was made to do six films for Warner Bros. (the first was a collaborative effort involving his own production company with Harold Hecht). Though Warner Bros. wanted him to continue his intense tough-guy persona in gangster melodramas, Burt opted for a complete departure as a jovial Robin Hood figure, Dardo the Arrow, in an original screenplay by Waldo Salt called *The Hawk and the Arrow.*

When the story became a film in 1950 (co-produced by Hecht and another independent producer, Frank Ross), it was entitled *The Flame and the Arrow.* Lancaster proved himself to be the most acrobatic swashbuckler since his childhood hero Douglas Fairbanks Sr. had graced the silver screen. He did a backflip from a tree limb, slid down a high tapestry, walked along a long pole, and, for the grand finale, did a fantastic display of gymnastics on six horizontal bars. Audiences accepted with glee this enchanting tale of derring-do. With domestic box office earnings of $3 million, *The Flame and the Arrow* was Burt's most successful film at this stage in his career.

Virginia Mayo was the most beautiful of heroines, and Robert Douglas was the suavest of villains. Lancaster and his friend Nick Cravat were simply wonderful under Jacques Tourneur's spirited direction, as they lightheartedly performed their acrobatics; included was the perch act from their circus days together where the smaller Nick held the bigger Burt aloft on a towering pole. Oscar nominations were given to Max Steiner's lovely, whimsical score and to Ernest Haller's color cinematography. Filming in California included Bronson Canyon, but mostly at Warner's studio in Burbank, where sets were used from two previous swashbucklers, *The Adventures of Robin Hood* and *The Adventures of Don Juan.*

Ironically, *Harvard Lampoon* considered Lancaster's "sturdy Lombard

Burt Lancaster rehearsing his grand finale from *The Flame and the Arrow*.

peasant" the most miscast performance of 1950. His acrobatic background apparently was not known to all, including the humor magazine, and his performance thus met with some criticism. Lancaster, however, went on a publicity tour and performed many of the same acrobatics he accomplished in the film. In October 1950, an extra named Jules Garrison filed a suit against Warner Bros. for refusing to pay a million-dollar offer to anyone who could prove that Burt's stunts were not his own. When the suit eventually came to court in July 1953, it was shown that a Don Turner had doubled for Burt three times, but not on any of the acrobatics. The offer also had not been properly authorized, so the case was dismissed.

REVIEWS: *Time:* "Lancaster is probably the best acrobat now employed as an actor. After a series of gangster films, he obviously relishes his promotion from a hood to a Robin Hood."

Commonweal: "But one really can't take this costume piece seriously. Its social significance doesn't bear close inspection, but its bravado and athletic high jinks are lots of fun."

Mister 880

A 20th Century–Fox Production   Released September 29, 1950   90 minutes   Black and White

CREDITS: Edmund Goulding (Director); Julian Blaustein (Producer); Robert Riskin (Screenplay); Joseph LaShelle (Photography); Robert Fritch (Editor); Lyle Wheeler and George W. Davis (Art Directors); William Travilla (Costumes); Fred Sersen (Special Effects); Lionel Newman (Music Director); Sol Kaplan (Music Score). Based on a series of articles in *The New Yorker* by St. Clair McKelway.

CAST: Burt Lancaster (Steve Buchanan); Dorothy McGuire (Ann Winslow); Edmund Gwenn (Skipper Miller); Millard Mitchell (Mac); Minor Watson (Judge O'Neil); Howard St. John (Chief); Hugh Sanders (Thad Mitchell); James Millican (Olie Johnson); Howland Chamberlin (Duff); Larry Keating (Lee); Kathleen Hughes (Secretary); Geraldine Wall (Miss Gallagher); Mervin Williams (U.S. Attorney); Norman Field (Bailiff); Helen Hatch (Maggie); Robert B. Williams (Sergeant); Ed Max (Mousie); Frank Wilcox (Mr. Beddington); George Adrian (Carlos); Michael Lally (George); Joe McTurk (Gus); Minerva Urecal (Rosie); George Gastine (Waiter); Curt Furberg (German); Joan Valerie (Cashier); Jack Daly (Court Clerk); Dick Ryan (U.S. Marshal); William J. O'Leary (Junkman); Billy Gray (Mickey); Billy Nelson (Driver); Bill McKenzie (Jimmy); Herbert Vigran (Barker); Rico Alaniz (Spanish Interpreter); Victor Desny (Russian Interpreter); Eddie Lee and George Lee (Chinese Interpreters); Sherry Hall (Clerk); John Hiestand (Narrator); Polly Bailey and Bessie Wade (Women); Robert Boon and Dr. D.W. De Roos (Dutchmen).

SYNOPSIS: The U.S. Treasury Department has been trying for ten years to capture a counterfeiter of $1 bills, listed in their files as case #880. Steve Buchanan is the new agent on the case, and what really baffles the department is that Mister 880 uses plain bond paper for printing and even spells Washington's name wrong.

A 73-year-old junk dealer named Skipper Miller, who lives in New York City, is the counterfeiter. He calls his printing press "Cousin Henry." Ann Winslow, a French interpreter at the United Nations building, is also a neighbor of Skipper's, and he cashes a five for her using his phony money. When an unsuspecting Ann uses one of the dollars unknowingly, she is followed by Steve, who feels she isn't the counterfeiter but may be able to lead him to 880. They take a liking to each other, and Steve meets Skipper.

Now friends, the three take a group of children to Coney Island, and some of the phony bills are used. Steve is the one accused, however, of being the crook.

Later, circulars advising merchants on how to spot counterfeit bills are issued to stores that have been part of 880's route over the years. Skipper then buries his printing press. A little boy leads Steve to "Cousin Henry," having seen Skipper's dog digging after it, and even Ann suspects the truth.

At a hearing, Skipper proclaims that he didn't want to become a tax burden—he never collected his government subsidy, and instead printed just enough $1 bills to live on each month (an amount less than the subsidy). Steve ironically defends Skipper in court, and the judge gives him a short jail sentence and a fine of one real dollar bill.

COMMENTARY: *Mister 880* was based on a true story about an elderly counterfeiter, Edward Mueller, who baffled the Treasury Department from 1938 to 1948 (and whose escapades became a three-part *Annals of Crime* story, *Old Eight-Eighty*, in 1949's *The New Yorker* magazine by St. Clair McKelway). Edmund Gwenn, who had enchanted audiences as Kris Kringle in *Miracle on 34th Street* (and won an Academy Award for Best Supporting Actor in 1947), was almost as delightful as Skipper Miller. His lovable playing earned another Oscar nomination for Best Supporting Actor (although he didn't win this time around).

Burt Lancaster and Dorothy McGuire gave, if not quite lovable performances as the romantic couple, at least highly likable ones. Their screen romance seemed to dominate this sentimental tale scripted by Robert Riskin, produced by Julian Blaustein and directed by Edmund Goulding for 20th Century–Fox.

Very wise to undertake another cheerful part after his series of melodramas, Lancaster was initially pegged by Hal Wallis to be reunited with Lizabeth Scott in another melodrama, *Dark City*. But Wallis opted instead for the tremendous loan-out offer for Burt by Fox (with the male lead in the producer's film going to a newcomer named Charlton Heston). *Mister 880* may have been only a mild diversion with audiences in 1950, but it was also quite charming.

Mister 880, with (left to right) Dorothy McGuire, Burt Lancaster, Edmund Gwenn, and players.

REVIEWS: *The New Yorker:* "The role of the young lady is handled by Dorothy McGuire, and that of the operative by Burt Lancaster. Under the direction of Edmund Goulding, they both perform with reasonable competence, but neither of them can stand up to Mr. Gwenn whenever he decides that it's time for an old hand at acting to teach the youngsters a few tricks."

Time: "But the script's neatest trick, unfalteringly pulled off by Edmund Goulding's direction and Edmund Gwenn's superb acting is to give the picture's closing episodes the winning quality of *Miracle on 34th Street.*"

Vengeance Valley

A Metro-Goldwyn-Mayer Picture Released February 16, 1951 82 minutes Technicolor

CREDITS: Richard Thorpe (Director); Nicholas Nayfack (Producer); Irving Ravetch (Screenplay); George J. Folsey (Photography); Conrad A. Nervig (Editor); Cedric Gibbons and Malcolm Brown (Art Directors); Edwin B. Willis and Alfred E. Spencer (Set Decorators); Walter Plunkett (Costumes); William Tuttle (Make-up); Rudolph G. Kopp (Music Score). Based on a novel by Luke Short.

CAST: Burt Lancaster (Owen Daybright); Robert Walker (Lee Strobie); Joanne Dru (Jen Strobie); Sally Forrest (Lily Fasken); John Ireland (Hub Fasken); Carleton Carpenter (Hewie); Ray Collins (Arch Strobie); Ted De Corsia (Herb Backett); Hugh O'Brian (Dick Fasken); Will Wright (Mr. Willoughby); Grace Mills (Mrs. Burke); James Hayward (Con Alvis); James Harrison (Orv Easterly); Stanley Andrews (Mead Calhoun); Glenn Strange (Dave Allard); Paul E. Burns (Dr. Irwin); John R. McKee (Player); Tom Fadden (Obie Rune); Margaret Bert (Mrs. Calhoun); Harvey Dunn (Dealer); Robert E. Griffin (Cal); Roy Butler, Al Ferguson, and Monte Montague (Men); Norman Leavitt, Louis Nicoletti, Dan White, and Robert Wilke (Cowhands).

Vengeance Valley: **riding tall in the saddle.**

SYNOPSIS: A cowhand named Hewie, who works on the Strobie Ranch, tells the story.

Owen Daybright is the foster son of the ranch's owner, Arch Strobie, and also the foreman on the spread. Lee Strobie is Arch's real son and is married to a woman named Jen.

After another woman, Lily Fasken, has his baby, Lee puts the blame on Owen. But Jen suspects the truth when $500 is given to Lily; although staying on the ranch, Jen severs her marital obligations with her husband. In time, it appears that Owen and Jen are attracted to each other.

Meanwhile, Lily's brothers, Hub and Dick Fasken, start trouble with Owen and she comes to his aid. Also helping Owen is Hewie, who it seems is smitten with Lily. Her brothers are then jailed for a week.

Owen, Hewie, and Lee track down some rustled cattle to a nearby ranch owned by Herb Backett. Angry after being caught and beaten up by Owen, Backett makes a deal with Lee to help get the Fasken brothers into the Eastern Division of the big cattle roundup, with the end result being a confrontation with Owen, who is heading the Western Division.

Having been made a partner by Arch, Lee is caught by Owen trying to sell 3,000 head of the cattle and ride off with the money. Lee then sets up Owen in an ambush with the Faskens.

The ambush fails as both brothers are gunned down by Owen aided by cowboys from the roundup. Owen rides after Lee. Forced to draw against Lee, Owen shoots him down.

COMMENTARY: *Vengeance Valley* was Burt Lancaster's first western, and he rode tall in the saddle. As with *Mister 880*, he was loaned out by producer Hal Wallis to another studio, this time Metro-Goldwyn-Mayer. Burt may have been a bit too spry as a cowboy in his fistfights and jumping over a corral, but his performance as a brave and decent western hero was very strong. The supporting cast was equally so. Robert Walker made for a charming bad man forcefully supported in his villainy by John Ireland and Hugh O'Brian. As the epitome of a lanky cowpoke, Carleton Carpenter was reminiscent of a young Gary Cooper. Joanne Dru, with her gentle yet feisty demeanor, was reminiscent of the frontier lady she played earlier in *Red River*.

Irving Ravetch based his screenplay on a Luke Short novel, which initially appeared in seven installments in *The Saturday Evening Post* magazine between December 3, 1949, and January 14, 1950. Produced by Nicholas Nayfack, directed by Richard Thorpe, and released by MGM in 1951, the film, though a bit talky, intelligently presented its adult story with ample action and striking outdoor visuals. Although not a popular western like *Red River*, *Vengeance Valley* nonetheless had a true feeling of that classic's great cowboy spirit.

REVIEWS: *Christian Century:* "Breathtakingly beautiful scenery, photographed in Technicolor in Colorado, provides background for superior Western that gives more than customary attention to character presentation."

New York Times: "*Vengeance Valley* has a considerable amount of excitement, and there is an almost documentary quality about the long sequences which provides a graphic picture of what it is like to be out on the range at roundup time. Richard Thorpe has directed these scenes expertly and he has a fine, sturdy and convincing foreman in Burt Lancaster."

Jim Thorpe— All American

A Warner Bros. Picture   Released August 24, 1951   105 minutes   Black and White

CREDITS: Michael Curtiz (Director); Everett Freeman (Producer); Douglas Morrow and Everett Freeman (Screenplay); Frank Davis (Additional Dialogue); Ernest Haller (Photography); Folmar Blangsted (Editor); Edward Carrere (Art Director);

William Wallace (Set Decorator); Milo Anderson (Costumes); Gordon Bau (Makeup); James Thorpe (Technical Advisor); Max Steiner (Music Score). Based on a story, *Bright Path*, by Douglas Morrow and Vincent X. Flaherty, and the biography by Russell J. Birdwell and James Thorpe.

CAST: Burt Lancaster (Jim Thorpe); Charles Bickford (Pop Warner); Steve Cochran (Peter Allendine); Phyllis Thaxter (Margaret Miller); Dick Wesson (Ed Guyac); Jack Big Head (Little Boy); Suni Warcloud (Wally Denny); Al Mejia (Louis Tewanema); Hubie Kerns (Tom Ashenbrunner); Nestor Paiva (Hiram Thorpe); Jimmy Moss (Jim Thorpe Jr.); Billy Gray (Young Jim Thorpe); Ed Max (Football Manager).

SYNOPSIS: Athletic coach Pop Warner tells the story of Jim Thorpe at a ceremony honoring the famous athlete.

Jim, a Sac and Fox Indian, was born and raised in Oklahoma. As a boy, he hates school, but his father, Hiram Thorpe, convinces him that he needs an education.

In 1907, Jim enters the Indian college in Carlisle, Pennsylvania. He rooms with Ed Guyac and Little Boy. After becoming a track star under Pop's guidance, Jim is attracted to Margaret Miller, also attending the school. Feeling he has to compete for her against an upperclassman on the football team, Peter Allendine, Jim joins the football team.

Jim proposes to Margaret, feeling a bond with her because of their Indian blood. During the summer hiatus, Jim plays semi-professional baseball to keep

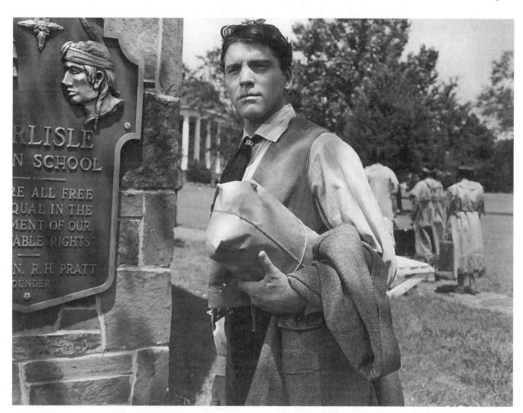

Jim Thorpe—All American: Burt Lancaster in the title role.

in shape. Returning to school for the new term, he discovers that Margaret has dropped out because she actually is not an Indian. Finding her working at the school, he realizes that his love for her has not changed; after he proposes to her again, she readily accepts.

Jim is interested in a coaching job offered by another college when the Carlisle football team (for which he is now an All American player) goes against Penn. His rival for the job is a Penn All American, Tom Ashenbrunner. The two teams battle to a tie. Ashenbrunner is given the coaching job because Jim showed poor leadership, allowing an injured Little Boy to stay in the game. Jim believes he lost because he is an Indian.

Determinedly, Jim goes into the 1912 Olympics in Stockholm, Sweden, and wins the pentathlon and the decathlon. His fame now worldwide, he returns home and marries Margaret. But his Olympic honors are taken away because he unknowingly violated the rules of amateur sports by playing one summer of semi-pro baseball.

Turning professional, Jim becomes a baseball then football player. Margaret gives birth to James Jr., their son. When the boy dies of an illness, Jim blames himself and becomes an alcoholic. Margaret divorces him out of the bitterness and anger that results; Jim becomes a washed-up football player and turns to demeaning work.

Coach Pop Warner returns and helps Jim pick up his life. His own dream of being a coach is fulfilled when he helps a group of boys with their football game.

The ceremony honoring Jim Thorpe ends with Pop announcing that he has been chosen "the greatest male athlete of the first half of the twentieth century."

COMMENTARY: The Associated Press (made up of 393 broadcasters and sports writers) gave 252 votes in February 1950 to Jim Thorpe for the honor of "greatest male athlete." A good many things in the 1951 Warner Bros. release *Jim Thorpe—All American* were indeed based on fact, but a good many things were not or were just left out. Perhaps it would have been too much to list the prodigious number of sports Thorpe was actually involved in, or that he was really married three times and had eight children.

Under director Michael Curtiz and producer Everett Freeman, the film was still a moving and exciting biography of the remarkable sports hero, who was born in May 1888 and died in March 1953 of a heart attack. The screenplay was one Freeman shared with Douglas Morrow, in turn adapted from a story by Morrow and Vincent X. Flaherty called *Bright Path* (Jim Thorpe's tribal name), as well as from a biography by Thorpe and Russell J. Birdwell. Unfortunately, the film was not heralded at the box office.

Burt Lancaster was very proud of the picture, not just for the physical attributes allowed him but also for depicting the racial prejudice reflected against Thorpe being an Indian. The actor was tremendously winning in the title role; combining his own athleticism and vulnerability, Burt's performance was his most effective dramatic one up to this time. Also winning were Phyllis Thaxter as his gentle first wife, Margaret Miller (actually named Iva in real life), and Charles Bickford as the epitome of a firm but understanding coach in Pop Warner.

Thorpe's alma mater Carlisle was then defunct, so part of *Jim Thorpe—All American* was made at Bacone Junior College in Muskogee, Oklahoma. Thorpe was the actual technical advisor on the film, and Lancaster elaborated, "There was even a move by the producers to get his medals back; it would have been a perfect ending for the movie." Yet it took until 1983 for the International Olympic Committee to return Jim Thorpe's Olympic gold medals and recognition in the record books, largely due to the determined efforts of his children.

REVIEWS: *New York Times:* "Warner Bros. could not have assigned a better man ... than Burt Lancaster. He is equipped physically and, what is more important, professionally, for the job of depicting the storied athlete. Mr. Lancaster ... is solidly convincing as the man whose pride would not let him accept handouts and who found joy and sadness in competition."

Newsweek: "And it does follow Thorpe's sports life with more authenticity than is habitual with Hollywood biographies."

Ten Tall Men

A Norma Production   A Columbia Picture   Released October 26, 1951   97 minutes   Technicolor

CREDITS: Willis Goldbeck (Director); Harold Hecht (Producer); Earl Bellamy (Assistant Director); Roland Kibbee and Frank Davis (Screenplay); William Snyder (Photography); William Lyon (Editor); Carl Anderson (Art Director); Jean Louis (Costumes); Morris W. Stoloff (Music Director); David Buttolph (Music Score). Based on a story by James Warner Bellah and Willis Goldbeck.

CAST: Burt Lancaster (Sergeant Mike Kincaid); Jody Lawrence (Mahla); Gilbert Roland (Corporal Luis Delgado); Kieron Moore (Corporal Pierre Molier); George Tobias (Londos); John Dehner (Jardine); Nick Dennis (Mouse); Mike Mazurki (Roshko); Gerald Mohr (Caid Hussin); Ian MacDonald (Lustig); Mari Blanchard (Marie DeLatour); Donald Randolph (Yussif); Robert Clary (Mossul); Henry Rowland (Kurt); Michael Pate (Browning); Stephen Bekassy (Lt. Kruger); Raymond Greenleaf (Sheik Ben Allal); Paul Marion (Eijah); Henri Letondal (Administrator); Philip Van Zandt (Henri); George Khoury (Aide); Nick Cravat and Shimen Ruskin (Disgruntled Riffs); Benny Burt (Beggar); Tom Conroy (Chanter/Hussin's Aide); Charlita and Rita Condi (Belles); Frank Arnold, Alan Ray, and Ralph Volkie (Riffs); JoAnn Arnold, Gwen Caldwell, Diana Dawson, Helen Reichman, Edith Sheets, and Joy Windsor (Ladies in Waiting).

SYNOPSIS: An old merchant and his two daughters are trekking across the desert when they are attacked by Riff bandits. The trio are really disguised foreign legionnaires Mike Kincaid, Luis Delgado, and Pierre Molier. They fight the bandits and capture a chief.

After delivering the prisoner to headquarters in Tarfa, Mike is thrown into the same cell block for kissing his commander's mistress. Mike then learns from the Riffs about a planned attack on the legion. With the main body of legionnaires away, Mike is given seven fellow legionnaire prisoners to stop the Riffs with sabotage. Luis and Pierre join him.

Sneaking into a Riff camp, Mike, Luis, and legionnaire Londos discover that the proposed marriage of chieftain Caid Hussin with another chief's daughter, Mahla, will unite the two tribes and make the attack on Tarfa evident. Mike kidnaps Mahla, and the Riffs chase after the legionnaires.

Ten Tall Men, **with (left to right) Burt Lancaster, Gilbert Roland, Kieron Moore, and comrades.**

Trying to escape on a horse, Mahla injures Londos. He decides to stay behind to hold off the Riffs and in doing so sacrifices his life. Another legionnaire, Browning, is killed in a later Riff strike. Chief Hussin is determined to attack Tarfa even if it means killing Mahla. The legionnaires escape with their captive in a sandstorm.

When they come upon some stolen money, Mike tells them they cannot keep it. But legionnaire Jardine's greed causes him to try to murder Mike. Mahla's screams save him, and Jardine is shot down by a Riff sniper. The legionnaires get the sniper, but Mahla blows up a wrecked truck and they know that the rest of the Riffs will hear the explosion and find them.

Mike uses a diversionary tactic to draw attention away from his comrades, but he is taken by the Riffs with Mahla.

Realizing her affection is for Mike, she stops Caid Hussin from torturing him. The other legionnaires then come to his rescue, and Mike kills Hussin.

Back at Tarfa and with an apparent peace in the wind because of the romantic attraction between Mahla and Mike, the legionnaires are bestowed honors for their gallantry.

COMMENTARY: *Ten Tall Men* was Lancaster's second Technicolor swashbuckling adventure for his own Norma Productions (with partner Harold Hecht as producer). It was released in 1951 by Columbia Pictures. Its tongue-in-cheek escapades (which were partially filmed near Palm Springs, California) included a rascally Burt comically dodging bullets by dashing from boulder to boulder. The action and parody, although not as successful at the box office as what was seen in *The Flame* *and the Arrow*, proved successful enough to warrant that Lancaster and Hecht's next swashbuckler would be their broadest of all. It was called *The Crimson Pirate*.

For *Ten Tall Men*, Burt Lancaster blended his earlier tough-guy persona with his athleticism as the foreign legionnaire, at times ardently regarded as "Sarge" by his comrades. As two of his most trusted pals, Gilbert Roland and Kieron Moore were properly boisterous and heroic as well. Jody Lawrence was a feisty and attractive desert princess. Unfortunately, as a "disgruntled Riff," Nick Cravat had only a minor role; it undoubtedly would have been an added delight seeing him cavort with Burt in feats of acrobatic splendor as they did in *The Flame and the Arrow* and later in *The Crimson Pirate*.

The original story by Willis Goldbeck and James Warner Bellah had the rugged action take place in the Old West between the U.S. Cavalry and the Apache Indians. But the screenplay by Roland Kibbee and Frank Davis also emphasized the lighthearted derring-do and changed the scenario to the Sahara Desert between the French Foreign Legion and Arab tribes. Goldbeck, who also directed a good portion of the picture, was replaced as director by an uncredited Robert Parrish to spruce up the derring-do.

REVIEWS: *Time: "Ten Tall Men*, a tall adventure tale of the French Foreign Legion, treats its old formula so lightheartedly that it becomes the beau jest of the genre."

Newsweek: "Lancaster's persistent ingenuity in topping the natives might bring the film some hard feeling in the Sahara; elsewhere there is fun to be had."

The Crimson Pirate

A Norma Production   Distributed by Warner Bros.   Released August 27, 1952   104 minutes   Technicolor

CREDITS: Robert Siodmak (Director); Harold Hecht (Producer); Guy Agosti (Assistant Director); Norman Deming (Associate Producer); Roland Kibbee (Screenplay); Otto Heller (Photography); H.J. Hodges (Underwater Photography); Jack Harris (Editor); Paul Sheriff (Art Director); Ken Adam (Associate Art Director); Margaret Furse (Costumes); Marjorie Best (Lancaster's and Cravat's Costumes); Tony Sporzini (Make-up); Russell Shearman (Special Effects); Muir Mathieson (Musical Director); William Alwyn (Music Score).

CAST: Burt Lancaster (Vallo); Nick Cravat (Ojo); Eva Bartok (Consuelo); Torin Thatcher (Humble Bellows); James Hayter (Prudence); Leslie Bradley (Baron Gruda); Margot Graham (Bianca); Noel Purcell (Pablo Murphy); Frederick Leicester (El Libre); Eliot Makeham (Governor); Frank Pettingill (Colonel); Dagmar Wynter (La Signorita); Christopher Lee (Attache).

SYNOPSIS: During the eighteenth century, on their pirate brig in the Caribbean, Captain Vallo and his crew pretend they have died of scurvy. The ruse allows the pirates to capture Baron Gruda, the king of Spain's agent, and the 30-gun galleon he is on. But Vallo sets Gruda free after making a deal to lure the rebel leader called El Libre from a nearby island.

Vallo and a shipmate, Ojo, are chased on the island by the governor's soldiers in the effort to find the rebel leader. Rebel Pablo Murphy captures the two pirates, planning to trade them for the 30 guns aboard the galleon. But another rebel, Consuelo, helps Vallo and Ojo return to the ship. Her father is El Libre, being held prisoner on another island, and Vallo feigns interest to help in his rescue.

On this other island, Vallo, masquerading as Baron Gruda, is accompanied by Consuelo and Ojo. The colonel there releases El Libre and a scientist named Prudence. Although soon recognized as the Crimson Pirate, Vallo escapes with his party.

Back on the galleon, Consuelo learns of Vallo's initial plan with Gruda. But the pirate captain has fallen in love with her and changes his mind. Another pirate, Humble Bellows, learns of this and plans with Gruda against Vallo.

Consuelo and her father are released by Vallo; however, soldiers are nearby and capture her and kill El Libre. Vallo, Ojo and Prudence are cast adrift in a dinghy, but the scientist saves them from a watery grave. Bellows and the other pirates are double-crossed by Gruda and tied up in a net aboard their brig. On his island, Pablo Murphy is tortured by the king's agent to persuade Consuelo to marry the governor.

Vallo unites the island rebels, although Pablo strikes out on his own and is killed by Gruda's aide, Attache. With Prudence's skills, a large balloon and explosives are among the wonders created, and Vallo and Ojo use them to rescue their comrades.

Baron Gruda is now aboard the galleon with Consuelo as his hostage, and the pirates secretly swim underwater to it from their brig. Choosing to sacrifice his life for his shipmates, Humble Bellows stays behind to deceive Gruda into believing that the pirate ship is manned. The ploy works, and the brig is blown to pieces.

Sneaking aboard the galleon, the rest of the pirates engage in a rousing

The Crimson Pirate: **Burt Lancaster (center) with Nick Cravat (wearing vest) and a band of cutthroat pirates.**

free-for-all with the king's men. Gruda is killed. After being rescued, Consuelo is embraced by Vallo.

COMMENTARY: *The Crimson Pirate* was the swashbuckler to end all swashbucklers with its riotous good charm. Burt Lancaster and Harold Hecht had a field day making it for Norma Productions in partnership with Warner Bros. during 1951; its subsequent release by Warner Bros. was in 1952. Taking advantage of Warners' frozen European assets, colorful Mediterranean locations on the island of Ischia and in the Bay of Naples were utilized. Two seaworthy vessels from a previous Warner Bros. adventure, *Captain Horatio Hornblower*, were also used.

Robert Siodmak was the accredited director, and his flair for scenarios with elaborate double-crosses (*The Killers, Criss Cross*) was evident. But Lancaster and writer Roland Kibbee were at the helm for the 18-minute climactic battle royal (with its prominent mixture of action and broad humor), while the director was filming interiors at Teddington Studios in England.

Lancaster's tendency for arguing with directors drew even more attention on *The Crimson Pirate* when he called Siodmak a "silly old has-been." The high level of energy that Burt invested in filmmaking in general seemed to be his reasons for being frustrated at times.

The spirited energy Burt brought to the role of the jolly pirate captain was even more flamboyant than his Dardo in *The Flame and Arrow* and Kincaid in *Ten Tall Men*. Indeed, he was never more

Nick Cravat and Burt Lancaster in *The Crimson Pirate*.

handsome or dashing than as Vallo. Nick Cravat, as he had on *The Flame and the Arrow*, added tremendous support as his sidekick and again remained mute to compensate for the lack of acting ability with dialogue, although it was often easy to compare his amusing antics with the great Harpo Marx. In *The Crimson Pirate*, the pair was once more incredibly fearless with their acrobatics as they swung from poles, did backflips, climbed ropes and swung from them, and trampolined through open windows.

Although the film was a bit farcical with its abundance of derring-do and hijinks, it was another rousing success at the box office (although not as big as *The Flame and the Arrow*). William Alwyn's music score was as lively as the action, and the Technicolor photography by Otto Heller was magnificently vivid. Hungarian actress Eva Bartok, in her American film debut, was a very captivating heroine, and Torin Thatcher made an excellent pirate of the old school.

Burt Lancaster surely relived his boyhood memories of the Douglas Fairbanks Sr. swashbucklers he loved while making this film and *The Flame and the Arrow*. *The Crimson Pirate* was compared favorably with Fairbanks's own 1926 silent swashbuckler, *The Black Pirate*, and the sequence with the pirates swimming underwater was even duplicated.

REVIEWS: *Commonweal:* "The backgrounds are beautiful to behold and the pirate stuff with Burt Lancaster swinging a mean cutlass is exciting from beginning to end."

Saturday Review: "Lancaster may come nowhere near the senior Fairbanks in ease and grace, but he displays here the same boundless energy and enthusiasm for mischief that made Fairbanks such fun to watch."

Come Back, Little Sheba

A Hal Wallis Production   A Paramount Picture   Released December 24, 1952   Black and White

CREDITS: Daniel Mann (Director); Hal Wallis (Producer); Ketti Frings (Screenplay); James Wong Howe (Photography); Warren Low (Editor); Hal Pereira and Henry Bumstead (Art Directors); Sam Comer and Ross Dowd (Set Decorators); Edith Head (Costumes); Wally Westmore (Make-up); Gordon Jennings (Special Effects); Don McKay and Walter Oberst (Sound); Franz Waxman (Music Score). Based on the play by William Inge. Produced on the stage by The Theatre Guild.

CAST: Burt Lancaster (Doc Delaney); Shirley Booth (Lola Delaney); Terry Moore (Marie Buckholder); Richard Jaeckel (Turk Fisher); Philip Ober (Ed Anderson); Edwin Max (Elmo Chester); Lisa Golm (Mrs. Coffman); Walter Kelley (Bruce); Paul McVey (Postman); Peter Leeds (Milkman); Anthony Jochim (Mr. Cruthers); Kitty McHugh (Pearl Stinson); Virginia Mullen (Henrietta); William Haade (Intern); Virginia Hall (Blonde); Beverly Mook (Judy Coffman).

SYNOPSIS: Marie Buckholder answers an ad for a room to rent at the Delaney home so she can be closer to her college. She meets Lola and later Doc Delaney, a middle-aged couple. Initially not interested in having a boarder, Doc is taken with Marie's youthful charm and rents out Lola's sewing room to her.

Doc is a member of Alcoholics Anonymous. He is accompanied by Lola to his first AA birthday, having not had a drink for over a year. The Delaneys learn that Marie has her sights on a young man back home named Bruce. Thus Doc disapproves when Marie begins a friendship with the brash track star at the college, Turk Fisher.

While Doc keeps busy with his chiropractic work as well as helping other alcoholics, Lola lounges around at home during the day and eavesdrops on Marie and Turk in the evening.

Seeing Turk take Marie out one particular evening causes Lola to reflect with Doc on their daughter. Lola lost the child during her pregnancy twenty years earlier and was unable to have more children. Lola reminds Doc that he might have become a full M.D. if he didn't have to drop out of school and support a wife. Doc reminds her that he also might have continued his medical studies if he hadn't used all the money his family left him by spending it on alcohol. Doc wants to put the disappointments of his past behind him, but Lola longs for her youth, when she was pretty instead of frumpy. Lola's sorrow is made even worse by calling out to her little lost dog, Sheba, hoping she will come back.

During another night out with Turk, Marie forgets her key, so Turk slips in through the window to unlock the door. Seeing them go into her room, Doc assumes that it is for sex. But Marie rebuffs Turk's advances, and he leaves.

Doc is upset and takes a bottle of whiskey with him the next day. Lola

Come Back, Little Sheba, with Shirley Booth and Burt Lancaster.

Come Back, Little Sheba, with Shirley Booth and Burt Lancaster.

becomes worried when he fails to show up for a dinner party with Bruce and Marie. When Doc does come home, he is drunk. Verbally and physically, he attacks Lola. Doc is soon taken to the hospital by two AA friends, Ed Anderson and Elmo Chester.

Returning home after a few days, Doc learns that Marie and Bruce have married. Lola and Doc reveal that there is still love in their own marriage.

COMMENTARY: Burt Lancaster's participation in the film version of *Come Back, Little Sheba* assuredly boosted his stature as an actor of com-

mendable merit. However, being too young (at 38) and too physically imposing (even with the boost from Wally Westmore's make-up and Edith Head's costumes), he was rightly judged as somewhat miscast as the more mature Doc. Burt never saw the original stage version of William Inge's 1949 play of the same title (which played on Broadway in 1950 for 191 performances); in actuality, he didn't want to be influenced by Sidney Blackmer's interpretation of the stage role. For his own interpretation, Burt (who was 12 years younger than Blackmer) was basically very quiet, even gentle, with his drunk scene being considerably forceful.

Earlier in his film career, Lancaster played a man beaten down by the pressures of a marriage in *Sorry, Wrong Number*. Once more, he had to persuade producer Hal Wallis to let him play a part he truly wanted but that Wallis knew he was not right for. Still under contract to the producer, Burt had managed to get out of any direct film commitments to him since 1949's *Rope of Sand* (although Wallis benefited financially from the loan-outs to 20th Century–Fox and Metro-Goldwyn-Mayer).

Upon securing the film rights to Inge's play, Wallis and Paramount Pictures had Ketti Frings develop the screenplay. Both the play's Lola, Shirley Booth, and its director, Daniel Mann, made successful transitions to the film production. Everyone involved helped to make it a drama of overwhelming poignancy. Franz Waxman's score was a lovely accompaniment, conveying the tender melancholy of the all-too-human story with almost mystic refrain. Warren Low was nominated for an Academy Award for Film Editing. Terry Moore's radiant energy as Marie earned her an Oscar nomination for Best Supporting Actress.

Yet the film's true heart belongs to Shirley Booth for her wonderfully natural performance as the forlorn wife. Having won a Tony Award earlier on for her stage performance, she went on to win the Academy Award for Best Actress in 1952. Lancaster later confessed, "Shirley Booth is the finest actress I have ever worked with."

Initially, one of the reasons Hal Wallis let Burt do the film was his formidable box office strength. That Shirley was chosen for the film met with some controversy over her box office potential (although she was a popular stage actress of many years). Following its 1952 release by Paramount, *Come Back, Little Sheba* proved even more successful once film audiences became aware of the brilliant leading actress. With reported box office earnings of $3.5 million, the movie was actually Burt Lancaster's most profitable yet.

REVIEWS: *Newsweek:* "*Come Back, Little Sheba* is one of Hollywood's few outstanding movies of the year."

New York Times: "Enough cannot be said for the excellence of the performance Miss Booth gives in this, her first screen appearance—which, in itself, is something of a surprise. Her skillful and knowing creation of a depressingly common type—the immature, mawkish, lazy housewife—is visualization at its best. And the excellence of Mr. Lancaster as the frustrated, inarticulate spouse, weak-willed and sweetly passive, should not be overlooked."

South Sea Woman

A Warner Bros. Picture Released June 3, 1953 99 minutes Black and White

CREDITS: Arthur Lubin (Director); Sam Bischoff (Producer); Edwin Blum (Screenplay); Ted McCord (Photography); Clarence Kolster (Editor); Edward Carrere (Art Director); William L. Keuhl (Set Decorator); Moss Mabry (Costumes); Gordon Bau (Make-up); H.F. Koenekamp (Special Effects); Lester Horton (Choreography); David Buttolph (Music Score). An adaptation by Earl Baldwin and Stanley Shapiro from the play *General Court Martial* by William M. Rankin.

CAST: Burt Lancaster (Sgt. James O'Hearn); Virginia Mayo (Ginger Martin);

Chuck Connors (Davey White); Arthur Shields (Donovan, U.S.N.R.); Barry Kelley (Col. Hickman); Leon Askin (Marchand); Veola Vonn (Madame Duval); Robert Sweeney (Lt. Miller); Hayden Rorke (Lt. Fears); Raymond Greenleaf (Admiral Peabody); Paul Burke (Ensign Hoyt); Henri Letondal (Alphonse); William O'Leary (Smith); John Alderson (Fitzroy); Georges Saurel (Jacques); Viola Daniels (Suzette); Alena Awes (Mimi); Rudolph Andres (Van Dorck); Noel Cravat (Fatso); Peter Chong (Woo Ching); Cliff Clark (Parker); John Damler (Kellogg); Jacqueline Duval (Julie); Paul Bryar (Captain of the Gendarmes); Robert Kino, Frank Kumagai, Keye Luke, Edo Mito, and Rollin Moriyama (Japanese Officers); Tony Garsen (Orderly); Guy de Vestal and Gregory Gay (Free French); Strother Martin (Young Marine); Jim Hayward (Masterson); Grace Lem (Mama Ching); Danny Chang (Wong); Paul Liu (Ho); Gisele Verlaine (Olga); Al Hill and Jack Kenney (Bartenders).

SYNOPSIS: Marine sergeant Jim O'Hearn is on trial at an American military court in 1942. Charged with desertion, Jim refuses to defend himself. It is revealed that he and a woman named Ginger Martin were found on a raft in the Pacific. Ginger is called to the stand; she informs the court that, while working in a Shanghai saloon, marine private Davey White proposed to her. The bar's owner tried to keep her from leaving, and Jim helped them get away. They stole a boat and drifted out to sea after Davey and Jim got into a fight. Picked up by a Chinese junk, the three were then made to swim ashore because of the marines' brawling.

South Sea Woman: **Burt Lancaster with Chuck Connors and Virginia Mayo.**

They swam onto the island of Namoo. Marchand, its governor, tells the court the marines claimed to be deserters. But they said that only because of the governor's hatred of Americans and because they didn't want to be jailed. On the witness stand, Ginger tells how Jim tried to get passage on a Dutch captain's ship for himself and Davey.

Jim finally speaks out, revealing that the "Dutch" captain was a German unloading radar equipment. He further informs the court that he mustered up a crew, did away with the captain and his men, and took over the ship. Davey was forced to go aboard by Jim. Their destination was Pearl Harbor, recently bombed by the Japanese.

En route, Ginger was found stowing away, and the ship was attacked by the Japanese. With a handful of grenades, Davey sacrificed his life to blow up an enemy destroyer. In the chaos, Jim and Ginger ended up on the raft, where they were picked up by an American ship. The court then drops the charge of desertion against Jim and recommends Davey for the Medal of Honor. Jim reveals his own love to Ginger.

COMMENTARY: After its 1953 release by Warner Bros., *South Sea Woman* proved to be a muddled war comedy/drama. Burt Lancaster was forced to make it to help fulfill his contract with the studio. The film may have been the poorest production of his career since *Desert Fury*, not even having the value of Technicolor that the earlier film had.

Any attempt to take advantage of exotic location filming was forsaken (to save money, Warner Bros. and producer Sam Bischoff instead built a cyclorama on their Burbank sound stages to convey a South Sea island) because Harold Hecht and Lancaster had gone beyond the production costs by the studio for *The Crimson Pirate* and the forthcoming release *His Majesty O'Keefe* (with the latter actually made before *South Sea Woman* and Burt's last entry in the six-picture deal for Warner Bros., *Three Sailors and a Girl*).

Director Arthur Lubin's previous experience with the comedy antics of Abbott and Costello undoubtedly helped to make the South Sea romp, with its pair of gung-ho, rollicking marines, as much fun as possible. Burt and newcomer Chuck Connors seemed to be enjoying themselves amid the frenetic action and silliness. Even lovely Virginia Mayo, seemingly bewildered by it all, ably joined in. But their hijinks were not as briskly shared by the ticket-buying public.

REVIEWS: *Christian Science Monitor:* "With a little free-handed borrowing from the Flagg-and-Quirt routine of *What Price Glory?* the authors of *South Sea Woman* manage to piece out their 99 minutes of noise, romance, sentimentality and violence."

New York Times: "Assisted by a roughneck named Chuck Connors, who is the picture of a raw-boned Marine, Mr. Lancaster makes a noble effort to keep the show going on sheer gall."

Still in uniform as a marine, Lancaster made a cameo appearance in the musical *Three Sailors and a Girl*. Roland Kibbee (who wrote the screenplay with Devery Freeman, based on George S. Kaufman's play *The Butter and Egg Man*) as an uncredited favor to Burt helped with the writing on *South Sea Woman* (in which its credited writers, Edwin Blum, Earl Baldwin, and Stanley Shapiro, labored on a William M. Rankin play). As a return favor to

Kibbee, Lancaster agreed to an unbilled bit in the musical. But fans had to wait until the end of this November 23, 1953, release to glimpse the actor looking for a break in show business from a wily producer played by Sam Levene.

Produced in Technicolor by Sammy Cahn and directed by Roy Del Ruth, *Three Sailors and a Girl* was not received as one of the great Hollywood musicals. The story was an ordinary one about a group of show business aspiring types trying to concoct a Broadway musical. But the talented cast included Jane Powell as the girl, and Gordon MacRae, Gene Nelson, and Jack E. Leonard as the sailors.

From Here to Eternity

A Columbia Picture   Released August 5, 1953   118 minutes   Black and White
CREDITS: Fred Zinnemann (Director); Buddy Adler (Producer); Earl Bellamy (Assistant Director); Daniel Taradash (Screenplay); Burnett Guffey (Photography); William Lyon (Editor); Cary Odell (Art Director); Frank Tuttle (Set Decorator); Jean Louis (Gowns); Clay Campbell (Make-up); Mushy Callahan (Boxing Advisor); Brig. Gen. Kendall J. Fielder (Technical Advisor); Morris Stoloff (Musical Director); George Duning (Background Music). Based on the novel by James Jones.
CAST: Burt Lancaster (1st Sgt. Milton Warden); Montgomery Clift (Pvt. Robert E. Lee Prewitt); Deborah Kerr (Karen Holmes); Donna Reed (Lorene); Frank Sinatra (Pvt. Angelo Maggio); Philip Ober (Capt. Dana Holmes); Mickey Shaughnessy (Sgt. Leva); Harry Bellaver (Mazzioli); Ernest Borgnine (Sgt. Fatso Judson); Jack Warden (Cpl. Buckley); John Dennis (Sgt. Ike Galovitch); Merle Travis (Sal Anderson); Tim Ryan (Sgt. Pete Karelsen); Arthur Keegan (Treadwell); Barbara Morrison (Mrs. Kipfer); George Reeves (Sgt. Maylon Stark); Jean Willes (Annette); Claude Akins (Sgt. Baldy Dhom); Robert Wilke (Sgt. Henderson); Douglas Henderson (Cpl. Champ Wilson); Robert Karnes (Sgt. Turp Thornhill); Don Dubbins (Friday Clark); John Cason (Cpl. Paluso); Kristine Miller (Georgette); John Bryant (Capt. Ross); Joan Shawlee (Sandra); Angela Stevens (Jean); Mary Carver (Nancy); Vicki Bakken (Suzanne); Margaret Barstow (Roxanne); Delia Salvi (Billie); Willis Bouchey (Lt. Colonel); Al Sargent (Nair); William Lundmark (Bill); Weaver Levy (Bartender); Tyler McVey (Maj. Stern); Robert Healy (Soldier); Brick Sullivan (Military Guard); Freeman Lusk (Col. Wood); Robert Pike (Maj. Bonds); Carleton Young (Col. Ayres); Fay Roope (Gen. Slater); Manny Klein and his trumpet.

SYNOPSIS: Private Robert E. Lee Prewitt is transferred to Hawaii's Schofield Army Barracks in 1941. He is greeted by a fellow private, Angelo Maggio, and Sergeant Milton Warden before being placed under the command of Captain Dana Holmes. Knowing Prewitt was once an army boxer, Holmes urges him to fight again for the company. Prewitt refuses, however, and Holmes has the men on the boxing team give him a hard time.

Karen Holmes, the captain's wife, searches for him at his office and meets Warden. It is revealed that her marriage is shaky, and she has a loose reputation. Warden, looking for a casual affair, visits her at home. Warden and Karen begin seeing each other secretly. One evening they go to a secluded beach and make love. Learning about Karen's past, which included a miscarriage and an unloving husband, Warden is sympathetic.

Prewitt and Maggio visit a local club while on leave. When a hostess named Lorene is attracted to Prewitt, he reveals that he doesn't box anymore because he accidentally blinded a man in

From Here to Eternity, **with Philip Ober, Burt Lancaster, and Montgomery Clift.**

a sparring match. At the club, Maggio gets into an argument with Fatso Judson, the stockade sergeant.

Although Warden breaks up a bar fight on the base later between the two, Judson threatens to get Maggio if he ends up in the stockade. When Maggio walks out on guard duty and gets drunk, he is thrown into it to Judson's satisfaction.

So he and Karen can openly share their newfound love and return to the United States after her impending divorce, Warden reluctantly agrees to become an officer. Prewitt is still harassed by the boxing team and is forced into a fistfight with one of them.

When Prewitt and Warden are later drunk together sitting in the road, Maggio stumbles by. Having escaped from the stockade, after being badly beaten by Judson, he dies in Prewitt's arms.

At Schofield, Prewitt plays "Taps" on the bugle for Maggio. He gets into a knife fight in town with Judson and kills him. Cut badly, Prewitt stays with Lorene and goes AWOL.

Capt. Holmes is ordered to resign from the army because of his treatment of Prewitt. When Warden, who hates officers, cannot sign the papers that will make him one, Karen then decides to return to the United States with her husband.

The Japanese bomb Pearl Harbor, including Schofield Barracks, on December 7, 1941. In the thick of the danger, Warden shows that his true love is to the army as an enlisted man. Prewitt is another such man and leaves Lorene to try to return to his company. He is mistaken for a saboteur and gunned down by American soldiers. After the bombing, Karen and Lorene stand together aboard a ship bound for the United States.

COMMENTARY: James Jones's novel *From Here to Eternity* reflected on the bitter truths of army life at a barracks in Hawaii of 1941—a time that led to America's entry into World War II. Jones had been in the U.S. Army and began writing his book after he left in 1944. Ultimately, it sold over three million copies and earned him the National Book Award for 1952. Harry Cohn, then head of Columbia Pictures, visualized it as a great movie and bought the rights. Daniel Taradash spent almost a year writing the screenplay. The book's profanity, brutal stockade description, and pages involving the soldiers with homosexuals were left out due to the strict movie censorship codes in 1953. Nonetheless, the film version was a harsh enough depiction of military life; the stirring honesty was its best feature.

The vivid characterizations were excellent. Burt Lancaster's Sergeant Warden was a solid man, tough but fair and compassionate. The role was Lancaster's most important individual work

From Here to Eternity: **Burt Lancaster and Deborah Kerr in one of the most famous love scenes in film history.**

in the 1950s. Montgomery Clift and Frank Sinatra gave perhaps their best performances as Privates Prewitt and Maggio. Sinatra, having career problems prior to the film, had the foresight to know that this part would make him a star again. Often seen as refined ladies, Donna Reed and Deborah Kerr were surprising in their respective roles as Lorene (a club hostess, underlined as a prostitute in the book) and Karen (the promiscuous wife involved with Lancaster's sergeant). The famous love scene between Burt and Deborah was filmed in three days on Blowhole Beach in Oahu, Hawaii. The Motion Picture Association originally forbade publicity stills to be used of the two kissing only in swimsuits and lying on the beach with the sea rushing over them. Apparently, it was the water that was objectionable.

It was clear following its Columbia release in 1953 that *From Here to Eternity* would reach classic status. The stunning realism was in its story and characterization and masterfully enhanced by Fred Zinnemann's direction, Burnett Guffey's photography and William Lyon's editing. The film received 13 Academy Award nominations and won eight of them: Best Picture (producer, Buddy Adler), Best Supporting Actor (Frank Sinatra), Best Supporting Actress (Donna Reed), Director (Zinnemann), Screenplay (Daniel Taradash), Black and White Cinematography (Guffey), Film Editing (Lyon), and Sound Recording (Columbia Sound Dept.; sound director, John P. Livadary). The other five nominations were for Best Actors (Burt Lancaster, Montgomery Clift), Best Actress (Deborah Kerr), Costume Design (Jean Louis), and Scoring of a Dramatic or Comedy Picture (Morris Stoloff and George Duning).

Clift and Lancaster both lost the Oscar to William Holden in *Stalag 17*, and Miss Kerr lost to Audrey Hepburn in *Roman Holiday*. *Julius Caesar*, *The Robe*, *Roman Holiday*, and *Shane* were the nominees that ran against *From Here to Eternity* for Best Picture. It was also named Best Picture by the New York Film Critics, and Fred Zinnemann was chosen Best Director and Burt Lancaster, Best Actor. Made for $2 million, *From Here to Eternity* earned $12.2 million. It was not only one of the biggest hits of the year but also Lancaster's top box office film until 1970's *Airport*.

REVIEWS: *Commonweal:* "Buddy Adler's production with its barracks background and Honolulu locale are beautifully photographed; and his good cast respond to Zinnemann's direction with performances so praiseworthy that it is difficult to name any one as the picture's best."

Time: "Burt Lancaster as Sergeant Warden is the model of a man among men, absolutely convincing in an instinctive awareness of the subtle, elaborate structure of force and honor on which a male society is based."

His Majesty O'Keefe

A Norma Production   A Warner Bros. Presentation   Released January 27, 1954 91 minutes   Technicolor
CREDITS: Byron Haskin (Director); Harold Hecht (Producer); Norman Deming (Associate Producer); Borden Chase and James Hill (Screenplay); Otto Heller (Photography); Manuel del Campo (Editor); Arthur Ridout (Dubbing Editor); Edward S. Haworth and W. Simpson Robinson (Art Directors); Liz Hennings and Marjorie Best (Costumes); Stuart Freeborn (Make-up); Daniel Nagrin (Choreography); Louis Levy (Music Director); Robert Farnon (Music

Score). Suggested from the novel by Lawrence Klingman and Gerald Green.

CAST: Burt Lancaster (Capt. David O'Keefe); Joan Rice (Dalabo); Andre Morell (Alfred Tetens); Abraham Sofaer (Fatumak); Archie Savage (Boogulroo); Benson Fong (Mr. Chou); Philip Ahn (Sien Tang); Tessa Prendergast (Kakofel); Lloyd Berrell (Inifels); Charles Horvath (Bully Hayes); Guy Doleman (Weber); Grant Taylor (Lt. Brenner); Alexander Archdale (Harris); Harvey Adams (Friedlander); Jim Crawford (Rhee); Warwick Ray (Garcia); Paddy Mulelly (Beldon); Niranjan Singh (Singh).

SYNOPSIS: Captain David O'-Keefe tells this tale, which begins in 1870 in the South Pacific. After holding a mutinous crew back at gunpoint for four days aboard his ship, he is finally subdued and flung over the side.

Swept ashore exhausted on the island of Yap, O'Keefe is revived by Fatumak, a native. O'Keefe then meets Alfred Tetens, a white man representing a German trading company that deals in the valuable market of copra (the oil extracted from the dry meat of the island's abundant supply of coconuts).

When another native, Boogulroo, challenges Alfred to a fight as is the annual custom, O'Keefe accepts the challenge instead. Deemed a great warrior, O'Keefe fails, however, to convince the natives to help him amass a fortune in copra.

Taken to Hong Kong by the Germans, O'Keefe first fails in his quest for a ship and crew to return to Yap (so determined is he for the copra). Infamous pirate Bully Hayes, representing a Spanish trading company, offers him a ship to carry slaves, but O'Keefe refuses the offer. Meeting two Chinamen—Chou and Sien Tang—O'Keefe accepts their offer of a ship, a crew, and an equal share in any copra profits.

Sailing to Yap, O'Keefe stumbles on an island of fierce natives. He is injured, but manages to escape. On a friendly island, O'Keefe recovers and falls in love with a half-caste girl, Dalabo, who accepts his marriage proposal. Before leaving this isle, O'Keefe finds the men of Yap struggling to remove sacred stones called *fei* from a mountain. Using gunpowder, he makes the task much easier.

O'Keefe insists that the natives on Yap supply him with copra for helping them. All reluctantly agree except for Boogulroo and his followers, who are especially angry that the traditional way of obtaining *fei* has been violated. Now wealthy with his copra, O'Keefe marries Dalabo in Hong Kong.

Greedy for even more copra, O'-Keefe finds the natives on Yap being terrorized and enslaved by Bully Hayes and his pirates. With his own crew and the native men, O'Keefe defeats them. The grateful islanders then honor him as their king. O'Keefe banishes Boogulroo and his men to the hills after being threatened with a spear.

Members of the German trading company trick O'Keefe and Alfred in an attempt to start a civil war between the natives. Alfred is killed by a native spear. Realizing he was wrong for his greed and disturbing the native traditions, O'Keefe is humbled when Boogulroo and all the islanders unite around their king.

COMMENTARY: With its release in 1954, *His Majesty O'Keefe* was Burt Lancaster's last film distributed by Warner Bros. (as part of the six films contracted initially in 1949). It proved to be not as popular as the previous two swashbucklers with the studio (which Burt's film partner, Harold Hecht,

His Majesty O'Keefe: Burt Lancaster (center) with cast members.

helped to produce), *The Crimson Pirate* and *The Flame and the Arrow.* Derived from Lawrence Klingman and Gerald Green's best-seller of the same title about a real-life figure, an initial script by Frank Nugent and Laurence Stallings was deemed unacceptable shortly before production commenced in 1952. Borden Chase and James Hill actually worked on the screenplay during the filming; the results, though entertaining, were a bit uneven, perhaps due to the haste in writing it. Director Byron Haskin, aware of the script problems, did the best job possible.

Although the acrobatic prowess of Lancaster's Vallo or Dardo in the earlier swashbucklers was now not as evident, his robust O'Keefe was still physically imposing. In fact, only his Vallo cut a more dashing and handsome figure. Burt's natural athleticism was particularly striking, when sliding at breakneck speed down a rope from a mountainside and in the island brawl with Charles Horvath's Bully Hayes (also a real-life figure).

On the Warner Home Video, Robert Farnon and Louis Levy are accredited, respectively, as composer and music director of the film. Yet Dimitri Tiomkin reportedly was also involved in the scoring and musical direction. With lyricist Paul Francis Webster, Tiomkin also wrote the film's enchanting love song, "Emerald Isle," which exemplifed the touching romance between O'Keefe and Joan Rice's delightful island maiden.

His Majesty O'Keefe's finest attribute, however, was the colorful location filming in the Fiji Islands. As with *The Crimson Pirate*, the sumptuous surroundings were photographed by Otto Heller. On the isle of Viti Levu, a sound stage, cutting room, and native village were among the accessories constructed. During an interim in filming, Lancaster spoke about filmmaking to the people at Suva, the capital of the tropical paradise.

REVIEWS: *America:* "Casts the redoubtable Burt Lancaster in the role, based loosely on fact, of an American adventurer who made himself king (literally) of the Pacific island of Yap some eighty years ago."

Library Journal: "History has been selected and romanticized much more than in the 1950 novel, but the picture has a pleasing authentic tone and is full of color and excitement."

Apache

A Hecht-Lancaster Presentation   Released through United Artists   Released July 9, 1954   91 minutes   Technicolor

CREDITS: Robert Aldrich (Director); Harold Hecht (Producer); Sid Sidman (Assistant Director); James R. Webb (Screenplay); Ernest Laszlo (Photography); Alan Crosland Jr. (Editor); Nicolai Remisoff (Production Designer); Joseph Kish (Set Decorator); Norma (Costumes); Robert Schiffer and Harry Maret (Make-up); Lee Zavitz (Special Effects); Jack Solomon (Sound); W. Lloyd Young (Music Editor); David Raksin (Music Score). Based on the novel *Broncho Apache* by Paul I. Wellman.

CAST: Burt Lancaster (Massai); Jean Peters (Nalinle); John McIntire (Al Sieber); Charles Buchinsky (Hondo); John Dehner (Weddle); Ian MacDonald (Glagg); Paul Guilfoyle (Santos); Walter Sande (Lt. Colonel Beck); Morris Ankrum (Dawson); Monte Blue (Geronimo).

SYNOPSIS: Massai is the last Apache Indian to surrender to the U.S. Army in 1886. Shipped by train to a Florida exile with old Geronimo and other Apaches, Massai escapes before reaching this destination. He begins the long journey back to his homeland in New Mexico on foot.

On the trek, Massai confronts the brutal elements of nature. Passing through the bustling community of St. Louis, he is forced to flee from the suspicions of a mob of white citizens. Temporary refuge is found at a farm owned by a Cherokee Indian, Dawson, who has adapted to the white man's life. Dawson gives Massai a bag of seed corn.

The weary Apache reaches his homeland. He tells Santos, the chief, and Santos's daughter, Nalinle, about the Cherokee. But Santos betrays Massai, and he is taken prisoner by the army once more. Indian agent Weddle, who despises his burden, plans on killing Massai.

After escaping, Massai kills Weddle and starts a one-man war against the army. Forced to go with Massai as a hostage, Nalinle suspects that he might kill her for her father's betrayal. When Massai abandons her instead, Nalinle follows, declaring her love for him. Realizing his own love for her, Massai marries Nalinle in an Indian ceremony. Together they journey into the mountains to live, planting a field of corn.

Army scouts Al Sieber and Hondo, tracking Massai, find him when Nalinle is giving birth. Accompanying soldiers surround Massai in his cornfield as he wages a last-ditch battle. Sieber and the Apache are fighting when a baby's cry is heard. Massai stops fighting. Realizing the war is over, Sieber lets him return to his family.

Apache: **Burt Lancaster's energy in films was incredible.**

COMMENTARY: Although originally under development at Warner Bros. by Harold Hecht and Burt Lancaster, Paul I. Wellman's 1950 novel *Broncho Apache* was the basis for the producing team's initial film with United Artists (as part of their two-picture deal made in June 1953). James R. Webb's screenplay was a sympathetic treatment of Native Americans, following on the path blazed by 1950's *Broken Arrow*, and was derived somewhat from historical events. Unlike *Broken Arrow*, whose Indian heroine is killed by white men, *Apache's* heroine and hero survive.

Despite the death of the warrior called Massai in Wellman's novel, United Artists was insistent on a more upbeat ending. Both Lancaster and director Robert Aldrich actually favored the ending where the Apache is killed. On UA's demand that he survive, Burt later said, "I must say that though I hated the idea, I went along with them and the picture was very successful, so I will never know how the other ending would have done."

That the film was a box office success was proven after its 1954 release by the studio, with earnings of $3 million. Lancaster's portrayal of a blue-eyed Indian met with some skepticism, but he was effective in capturing both the rugged stolidity and vulnerability of his Massai. The vulnerability was most noteworthy when he wanders through the strange surroundings of St. Louis. His ruggedness was the key to the film's true success because of the robust action on display.

Whether galloping on horseback, running and jumping over hills, or fighting tooth and nail, Burt's physical daring was always incredible. At one point, he actually injured himself in a horse fall

and was sidelined for a month with torn right hip and leg muscles. Jean Peters showed an amazing fortitude in her own right as Nalinle, Massai's wife (although, like Lancaster, she faced scrutiny over not seeming like a true Indian). John McIntire lent his usual crusty bearing to the role of Al Sieber, the famous scout. The Indian scout named Hondo was played by Charles Buchinsky (later known as Charles Bronson) with his trademark stoicism, but without the opportunity to do his own robust muscle flexing (that came later).

Hecht produced and Aldrich directed *Apache* with a remarkable hardiness. Photographer Ernest Laszlo's western landscapes (locations near Sedona, Arizona, and Sonora, California) were stunningly showcased. However, the film did not achieve the classic status it sought by comparing itself in 1954 advertisements to *High Noon* and *Shane*. Although it cast an optimistic view on Native American portrayals in Hollywood films, *Apache* is known more as a surefire Lancaster action film.

REVIEWS: *Variety:* "Lancaster and Miss Peters play their Indian roles understandingly without usual screen stereotyping."

Time: "Ernest Laszlo's photography and Robert Aldrich's direction help make the film appear a little grander that it really is. There are some fine shots of a realistic Indian village and of hazy plains and sawtooth mountains."

Vera Cruz

A Hecht-Lancaster Production   Released through United Artists   Released December 25, 1954   94 minutes   Technicolor SuperScope

CREDITS: Robert Aldrich (Director); James Hill (Producer); Jack R. Berne (Assistant Director); Roland Kibbee and James R. Webb (Screenplay); Ernest Laszlo (Photography); Alan Crosland Jr. (Editor); Alfred Ybarra (Production Designer); Norma (Costumes); Robert Schiffer (Makeup); Russell Shearman (Special Effects); Manuel Topete and Galdino Samperio (Sound); Robert Carlisle (Music and Effects Editor); Raul Lavista (Orchestrations and Conducting); Hugo Friedhofer (Music Score). From a story by Borden Chase.

CAST: Gary Cooper (Ben Trane); Burt Lancaster (Joe Erin); Denise Darcel (Countess Marie Duvarre); Cesar Romero (Marquis de Labordere); Sarita Montiel (Nina); George Macready (Emperor Maximilian); Ernest Borgnine (Donnegan); Henry Brandon (Danette); Charles Buchinsky (Pittsburgh); Jack Elam (Tex); Morris Ankrum (General Ramirez); James McCallion (Little Bit); Jack Lambert (Charlie); James Seay (Abilene); Archie Savage (Ballard); Charles Horvath (Reno); Juan Garcia (Pedro).

SYNOPSIS: In 1866, Ben Trane, a former Confederate officer in the Civil War, rides into Mexico during a revolution and inadvertently joins forces with American outlaw Joe Erin and his gang.

This group of mercenaries is eager to fight for the highest price, and the Marquis de Labordere, an officer in the service of Emperor Maximilian, offers them the lucrative opportunity to fight against the Juarista rebels. Taking over another gang, Joe kills the leader, Charlie, and an underling. Ben has his wallet stolen by a señorita named Nina, whom he rescued from one of the gang's members, Little Bit. Rebel leader General Ramirez orders the mercenary

Vera Cruz, **with Gary Cooper and Burt Lancaster.**

gunmen to fight without pay against the emperor. But Joe forces the general and his rebels to leave after threatening to have two gunmen, Donnegan and Pittsburgh, kill several peasant children.

The marquis takes the mercenaries to the emperor's palace, where Maximilian plots to reward their services with death. Another of the emperor's officers, Danette, takes an instant dislike to Joe's crudity. Joe and Ben show their proficiency with firearms before agreeing to escort, with the marquis and Danette, the Countess Marie Duvarre to the port city of Vera Cruz so she can sail to Europe.

On the road, Ben and Joe discover a hidden fortune in gold in Marie's coach that is to enlarge the emperor's military strength. The two plan to steal it with her, although the marquis overhears their scheme. The band of gunmen and accompanying soldiers escape an ambush by the rebels, but there are casualties on both sides.

Finding out that Marie is plotting to keep all the gold, Joe then schemes with her to keep it from Ben. Meanwhile, Nina tries to convince Ben that the gold belongs to the rebels. After the marquis escapes with the gold, Ben, Joe, and his gang chase after it.

Again confronted by the Juaristas, with Little Bit getting killed, the mercenaries agree to fight with them for a partial payment of gold. Together they storm Vera Cruz against Maximilian's soldiers. Pittsburgh and Donnegan are among those killed, as are Danette and the marquis. When one of the gunmen, Ballard, retrieves the gold, he is shot down by Joe, who wants all of it for himself. Ben now believes Nina is right about the gold. Forced into a showdown, Ben shoots Joe dead.

COMMENTARY: Even though *Apache* scored well with audiences, the next film, *Vera Cruz* (in the two-picture deal between Hecht-Lancaster Productions and United Artists), was even bigger at the box office. Yet before either of these westerns was released, H-L and UA signed a new seven-picture deal together.

Domestic earnings for *Vera Cruz* (Harold Hecht and Burt Lancaster's most profitable film together at this time) reached over $4.5 million. Undoubtedly, the star teaming of Gary Cooper and Lancaster helped provide the box office magic after a Christmas 1954 release. Ads for the film heralded it as "The Battle of the Giants!"

Vera Cruz had Cooper against Lancaster, fist against fist, gun against gun, and was loaded with wild action. The bullets almost flew around corners. As broad as could be, the film had a dash of swashbuckler in it. As exciting entertainment, it was highly enjoyable, although criticism may have been justified for its outrageousness. Liberties were undoubtedly taken with history in regard to the actual Mexican revolution in 1866 as depicted in the film.

Burt was clearly having fun as the dirty, grinning outlaw, and he was wickedly amusing. Apparently United Artists had no qualms about the death of such a devil-may-care character (as they had on the possible demise of Burt's noble Indian in *Apache*). The original intention was for Cary Grant to play the outlaw (with Lancaster playing the other straightforward lead), but he declined because of a dislike of working with horses. Fortunately, Cooper was interested in the lead; his portrayal of a soft-spoken and strong western figure had by then become an endearing and enduring trademark in his own film career. The supporting cast was big— Ernest Borgnine and Charles Bronson (still using his real name of Buchinsky at the time) were among the tough gunmen who rode with Burt and Coop. Denise Darcel and Sarita Montiel were breathtaking in their beauty.

James Hill, who had worked on the screenplay of *His Majesty O'Keefe*, now produced his first film for Hecht-Lancaster (in time he would become a full partner in the company). Having differences on *Apache* with Lancaster did not deter Robert Aldrich from directing again. The director's penchant for violence in his films was still in sharp contrast with the theatrics of *Vera Cruz*. Others who had worked on *Apache* and returned were editor Alan Crosland Jr., photographer Ernest Laszlo, and screenwriter James R. Webb.

Webb worked on the script with Roland Kibbee (this assuredly accounts for the lively blend of action and humor) from a story by Borden Chase. Filmed in Mexico (exteriors were done in Cuernavaca; interior shooting took place at Churubusco Studio in Mexico City), a new big screen concept was introduced called SuperScope, which really caught some bizarre camera angles. This process fit well with a rollicking picture like *Vera Cruz*, but proved to be a passing fad in Hollywood filmmaking.

REVIEWS: *Newsweek:* "The long Cooper walk and the saturnine Lancaster smile are features of an enormous landscape sunnily rendered in SuperScope and Technicolor, with stunning views of baroque churches and the great brooding ruins of the Aztecs. The story is adventurous piffle."

Saturday Review: "Burt Lancaster, with a derisive smile which alone could make the movie worth a visit if you like smiles, throws a great deal of energy into making himself dangerously likable."

The Kentuckian

A Hecht-Lancaster Production   Released through United Artists   Released September 1, 1955   104 minutes   Technicolor CinemaScope

CREDITS: Burt Lancaster (Director); Harold Hecht (Producer); Richard Maybery (Assistant Director); A.B. Guthrie Jr. (Screenplay); Ernest Laszlo (Photography); William B. Murphy and George E. Luckenbacher (Editors); Edward S. Haworth (Production Designer); Robert Priestley (Set Decorator); Norma (Costumes); Robert Schiffer (Make-up); Russell Shearman (Special Effects); John Kean and Paul Schmutz Sr. (Sound); Irving Gordon (Songs); Bernard Herrmann (Music Score). Based on the novel *The Gabriel Horn* by Felix Holt.

CAST: Burt Lancaster (Big Eli Wakefield); Dianne Foster (Hannah Bolen); Diana Lynn (Susie Span); John McIntire (Zack Wakefield); Una Merkel (Sophie Wakefield); Walter Matthau (Stan Bodine); Donald MacDonald (Little Eli Wakefield); John Carradine (Fletcher); John Litel (Babson); Rhys Williams (Constable); Edward Norris (Gambler); Clem Bevans (Pilot); Lee Erickson (Luke); Lisa Ferraday (Woman Gambler); Douglas Spencer and Paul Wexler (Fromes Brothers).

SYNOPSIS: Eli Wakefield and his boy, Little Eli, have a dream to go to Texas in the year 1820. With their hunting dog, Faro, they are traveling through the Kentucky wilderness. Hot on their trail are two Fromes brothers, who are keeping a feud going against the Wakefields.

In the village of Prideville, Big Eli is wrongfully accused by the constable of killing another Fromes, and he is thrown in jail. A bound servant woman, Hannah Bolen, looks after Little Eli and

Burt Lancaster in the title role of *The Kentuckian*.

soon helps his father escape. The two help Hannah by buying her freedom with their saved Texas money.

To continue their journey to Texas, more money must be raised, so Eli works in Humility for his brother, Zack. Hannah goes to work for the town's tavern owner, Stan Bodine, who is handy with a bullwhip.

Fishing for mussels for his brother, Eli finds a freshwater pearl and wonders if it is valuable. Although such pearls are worthless, a snake oil salesman, Fletcher, fools Eli into writing about it to the president of the United States.

While writing the letter, Eli is introduced by Zack and his wife, Sophie, to schoolteacher Susie Span. The townsmen ridicule Eli over the pearl, as do the schoolchildren to Little Eli. Father and son's problems are temporarily forgotten when the riverboat run by Captain Babson arrives destined for Texas.

Eli and his boy return on the riverboat from a short business trip to another town for Zack, under the pretense that the pearl had some value. Turning a gambling scam to their favor, the two are forced to jump overboard with their earnings.

Disliking Eli, especially for taking Susie away from him, Bodine agitates a fight between Little Eli and another boy. When Big Eli intervenes, Bodine viciously attacks him with a bullwhip. Only when Hannah drives a wagon over the whip does Eli beat him.

When Eli tells his son of plans to marry Susie—who is delicate and has an invalid mother—the boy runs off because it means forgetting about Texas. When he learns it was Hannah who stopped the whip, Eli reflects on his true feelings.

Babson offers Eli a chance to travel free to Texas as his lieutenant. But the Fromes brothers are holding Little Eli and Hannah hostage in Bodine's cabin. When he refuses to load his rifle, Bodine is killed by the brothers. Babson is also killed. Hannah shoots one of the brothers, and the other fires at her but misses. Eli, with Babson when he fell, runs across a creek and slays the second brother. Showing his love now to Hannah, Eli implores her to go with him and his son to Texas.

COMMENTARY: During filming of *Vera Cruz*, director Robert Aldrich did not welcome Burt Lancaster's forceful energy as he tried to be everywhere and caused some interference. Burt defended his reputation for being difficult, however, when he stated, "I had always felt that I had a kind of director's attitude towards my work. I was constantly worrying about the writing of the scripts I acted in, always wanting to change the staging of the scenes, always feeling it could be done a different way."

So in 1954, Lancaster put in an application to join the Screen Directors Guild, but he was rejected because he publicly expressed harsh views of the guild. He was instead given a waiver to direct one picture, *The Kentuckian*. Produced by Harold Hecht, it was the third film in the collaboration between Hecht-Lancaster Productions and United Artists. As director, Burt may have let it run too long and wide, but the action scenes were quite exciting. He even managed to convey some of the spiritual feeling for the American frontier, which gave the film a poetic touch.

The Kentuckian was given colorful support from those on both sides of the camera. Ernest Laszlo's beautiful photography included locations in Kentucky

The Kentuckian, with Dianne Foster, Burt Lancaster, and Donald MacDonald in a publicity pose.

and Indiana's Lincoln Pioneer Village. Bernard Herrmann's score was unforgettable. Any charm that the film had began with A.B. Guthrie's script from Felix Holt's 1951 novel, *The Gabriel Horn* (used for calling in the story's hunting dog, the horn was a symbol of the pioneer boy's growing up when he mastered it).

Donald MacDonald portrayed Lancaster's son very endearingly; he was spunky without losing that precious bewilderment of childhood. For his own performance as the bold frontiersman, Lancaster was the image of the stouthearted American folk hero. He conveyed a good-hearted boyishness as well as a great manly fortitude. A painting was even done of him in the title role by Thomas Hart Benton. A striking counterpart to Lancaster was seen in Dianne Foster's female pioneer. Attractive performances were also given by Diana Lynn, John McIntire, Una Merkel, John Carradine, and John Litel as frontier folks trying to carve out a civilized path in the wilderness.

Sharing a fine film debut with young MacDonald was Walter Matthau. Not yet appreciated for his beguiling comic flair, his cantankerous film persona, however, was accented in his role as town bully. During the elaborate bullwhip fight between him and Lancaster, Matthau was doubled by an expert whip handler named Whip Wilson. Burt was slightly cut by Wilson across the shoulders when he urged him to "hit me and make it look real."

That *The Kentuckian* might have benefited from a more skilled director cannot be ignored, despite all good intentions. The box office success of Burt's two previous western adventures was not continued after the film's 1955 release. He reflected afterward on his direction: "I actually found it the hardest job of my life. I had no time for anything. It's no life really. Nobody works harder than the director if he's at all serious."

REVIEWS: *America:* "Some of the picture has the charm of a folk tale and some of it the charmless but authentic feeling for frontier crudity, narrow prejudice and, in one prolonged bullwhip fight, brutality. But as a whole the direction has neither the style nor the pace to sustain interest over the long pull."

Catholic World: "However, there is a convincing handling of human relationships in *The Kentuckian* which lifts it above other outdoor dramas. Mr. Lancaster is obviously a sincere craftsman, and in this case, both as actor and director, he imparts intelligence and dignity to his dual chores."

The Rose Tattoo

A Hal Wallis Production   A Paramount Picture   Released December 12, 1955   116 minutes   Black and White   VistaVision

CREDITS: Daniel Mann (Director); Hal Wallis (Producer); Richard McWhorter (Assistant Director); Tennessee Williams (Screenplay); Hal Kanter (Adaptation); James Wong Howe (Photography); Farciot Edouart (Process Photography); Warren Low (Editor); Hal Pereira and Tambi Larsen (Art Directors); Sam Comer and Arthur Krams (Set Decorators); Edith Head (Costumes); Wally Westmore (Make-up); John P. Fulton (Special Effects); Harold Lewis and Gene Garvin (Sound); Alex North (Music Score). From the play by Tennessee Williams. Produced on the New York stage by Cheryl Crawford.

CAST: Burt Lancaster (Alvaro Mangiacavallo); Anna Magnani (Serafina Delle Rose); Marisa Pavan (Rosa Delle Rose); Ben

0 207- 50

The Rose Tattoo, as **Alvaro.**

Cooper (Jack Hunter); Virginia Grey (Estelle Hohengarten); Jo Van Fleet (Bessie); Sandro Giglio (Father De Leo); Mimi Aguglia (Assunta); Florence Sundstrom (Flora); Dorrit Kelton (Schoolteacher); Rossana San Marco (Peppina); Augusta Merighi (Guiseppina); Rosa Rey (Mariella); Georgia Simmons (The Strega); Zolya Talma (Miss Mangiacavallo); George Humbert (Pop Mangiacavallo); May Lee (Mamma Shigura); Lewis Charles and Virgil Osborne (Taxi Drivers); Larry Chance (Rosario Delle Rose); Jean Hart (Violetta); Roger Gunderson (Doctor); Roland Vildo (Salvatore); Fred Taylor (Cashier); Albert Atkins (Mario).

The Rose Tattoo, with Burt Lancaster and Anna Magnani.

SYNOPSIS: In a Sicilian American community in Florida, Estelle Hohengarten asks seamstress Serafina Delle Rose to make a silk shirt for the man she loves. Serafina does her sewing from her home, where she lives with her husband, Rosario, and their teenage daughter, Rosa. Overhearing Serafina's conversation with Estelle, Rosario abruptly leaves in his truck. That night, he is chased in the truck by police because it contains contraband. When the vehicle overturns, Rosario is killed. He is cremated by his wife, who miscarries another pregnancy. When Estelle comes to the house to see his ashes, she is driven away by the neighboring women.

Three years later, Rosa meets a nice sailor, Jack Hunter, at a high school dance and falls in love. Serafina, who stills mourns her late husband, is unkempt now and doesn't leave the house, much to her daughter's embarrassment. Thinking Jack has a girl in every port, Serafina makes him take a vow to respect Rosa's innocence.

Trying to learn the truth about her late husband's suspected infidelity, Serafina visits her priest, Father De Leo. Upset, she is taken home by a truck driver named Alvaro Mangiacavallo. Although she is attracted to Alvaro's fine physique and happy-go-lucky attitude, Serafina is torn by her memories of Rosario.

That evening, Alvaro has a rose tattooed on his chest (just like Rosario had) hoping to please Serafina. However, her reaction is of surprise, and it flames her obsession to learn of her deceased husband's rumored lover. Reluctantly, Alvaro takes her to confront Estelle, who admits to the affair with Rosario.

Returning home, Serafina destroys the urn containing Rosario's ashes. Alvaro tries to comfort her. Soon he gets drunk and passes out on her floor. Rosa returns from an outing with Jack, wanting to marry him.

The next morning, Rosa is startled by a bare-chested Alvaro. Serafina pushes him out of the house while he proclaims his love to her. When Jack and Rosa express their wish to marry, Serafina surprisingly gives her blessing. Alvaro returns to find Serafina waiting openly for him.

COMMENTARY: In 1947, Burt Lancaster was up for the Broadway role of Stanley Kowalski in Tennessee Williams's play *A Streetcar Named Desire*. Burt was involved with filming *All My Sons*, so the part went to and made a star out of Marlon Brando.

Hal Wallis was interested in producing a film of Williams's play *The Rose Tattoo* (which came to Broadway in February 1951 and ran over eight months). But Wallis wanted two specific things when he purchased the movie rights—that Tennessee Williams write the screenplay (which he did, with Hal Kanter helping with the adaptation) and that Italian actress Anna Magnani play Serafina.

The play was originally written with Magnani in mind, but she turned it down, apparently because she felt her English speaking skills were not good enough. Maureen Stapleton instead performed triumphantly in the stage version. When Wallis and Paramount Pictures were ready for filming in 1954, Magnani felt her English would suffice for the transition. Her English may have been a bit broken at times, but her performance was nonetheless the finest thing about the film. She was stunningly moving and passionate as the widow who comes out of her remorse to find a new love.

Although the film, like the play, accented Williams's sometimes tragic outlook on life, an especially captivating humor radiated from the budding relationship between the widow and the good-hearted, silly truck driver she meets. A second, perhaps even more tender romance is revealed in the love between her daughter and a sailor (played endearingly by Marisa Pavan and Ben Cooper).

Though Lancaster displayed enormous energy and amusement as Alvaro (Eli Wallach played the part on Broadway), he was overshadowed by Magnani. It may have been only a supporting role, yet he was first billed to help ensure that *The Rose Tattoo* was a box office hit after a 1955 release. It helped solidify his 1947 contract renewal with Hal Wallis.

Since 1952's *Come Back, Little Sheba*, Burt managed to continue to get deferments on the Wallis contract, although the producer capitalized from the loan-out for *From Here to Eternity*. As with *Mister 880* and *Vengeance Valley*, Wallis was given $150,000 for the actor's services for the Columbia classic.

Daniel Mann directed both the stage and film versions of *The Rose Tattoo* (as he had with *Come Back, Little Sheba*), and again he was passed over for an Academy Award nomination. The even more distinguished *Rose Tattoo*, however, was nominated for eight of the awards: Best Picture, Best Actress (Anna Magnani), Best Supporting Actress (Marisa Pavan), Black and White Cinematography (James Wong Howe), Editing (Warren Low), Costume Design (Edith Head), Music Score (Alex North), and Art Direction and Set Decoration (Hal Pereira, Tambi Larsen and Sam Comer, Arthur Krams).

The film won three of the Oscars: Best Actress, Art Direction and Set Decoration, and for Howe's photography (which included location filming in Key West, Florida). *Marty*, Harold Hecht and Burt Lancaster's own distinguished film with United Artists (which earned an Oscar for Best Actor Ernest Borgnine), beat out *Rose Tattoo* for Best Picture of 1955.

REVIEWS: *Commonweal:* "Hal Wallis has given *The Rose Tattoo* a good production photographed handsomely in black and white in VistaVision, and Daniel Mann has directed well his large cast, including those playing the neighbors of the volatile widow in this largely-Italian village in southern United States."

Library Journal: "Anna Magnani, playing her first English speaking part, gives an electrifying performance as the unglamourous, love-starved Serafina. In each speech and every gesture, she is Sicilian to the core. As her loutish lover, Mangiacavallo, Burt Lancaster tries valiantly, but, in spite of a great deal of physical activity, the Sicilian spirit does not come through."

Trapeze

A Hecht-Lancaster Presentation   A Susan Productions' Picture   Released through United Artists   Released May 30, 1956   106 minutes   DeLuxe Color CinemaScope
   CREDITS: Carol Reed (Director); James Hill (Producer); Michel Romanoff and Robert Gendre (Assistant Directors); James R. Webb (Screenplay); Liam O'Brien (Adaptation); Robert Krasker (Photography); Bert Bates (Editor); Rino Mondellini (Production Designer); Colasanti (Costumes); Louis Bunnemaison (Make-up); Walter Castle (Photographic Effects); R.L. Lannan (Special Effects); Fay Alexander and J. Bouglione (Technical Advisors); Muir Mathieson (Conductor); Malcolm Arnold (Music Score). Based on the novel *The Killing Frost* by Max Catto.
   CAST: Burt Lancaster (Mike Ribble); Tony Curtis (Tino Orsini); Gina Lollobrigida (Lola); Katy Jurado (Rosa); Thomas Gomez (Bouglione); John Puleo (Max); Minor Watson (John Ringling North); Gerard Landry (Chikki); Jean-Pierre Kerien (Otto); Sidney James (Snake Charmer); Gabrielle Fontan (Old Woman); Gamil Ratib (Stefan); Pierre Tabard (Paul); Michel

Thomas (Ringmaster); Gimma Boys; Los Arriolas; Edward Hagopian.

SYNOPSIS: Trapeze artist Mike Ribble is performing before a circus audience. Failing at a triple somersault, he falls to the net and onto the floor.

Acrobat Tino Orsini seeks out Mike in the Paris circus, where he now works as a rigger because of a busted ankle from the earlier fall. Mike tries to discourage the younger man when he asks to be taught how to do the triple somersault. Circus performer Rosa helps Mike realize the strength of a new trapeze act with him catching Tino. But she is against the dangerous triple.

Believing that Tino has the skills to master the triple, Mike works with him vigorously. Another acrobat, Lola, whose tumbling act has been let go in favor of the trapeze act, tries to seduce Mike into letting her join.

After her ploy with Mike fails, Lola romances Tino and convinces circus owner Bouglione of the glamorous attraction of putting a woman into the act. Learning from Rosa that Lola is really in love with him, Mike thinks that by romancing her himself this will help get him the triple with Tino, who seems more interested in Lola than his work.

When a lion breaks loose, Mike is clawed on his wrist. Seeing Lola's genuine concern for his injury makes Mike reflect that he does really love her. Tino, who loves her as well, learns that they

Trapeze, **with Tony Curtis and Burt Lancaster.**

are having an affair and hits Mike. A catcher named Otto replaces Mike because Tino will have nothing to do with him or the triple.

On the night circus impresario John Ringling North is in the audience and expects to see the triple somersault, Mike takes Otto's place. Bouglione finds out and has the protective netting taken down, feeling the acrobats will not perform the triple. He doesn't want to lose Tino to a contract with North.

Angry at first seeing Mike as catcher, Tino is reminded by his mentor that he swung without a net the first time they met. Performing the triple somersault, Tino goes on with John Ringling North to Madison Square Garden. Tino wants to keep the act together, but Mike knows there is too much between them and leaves. Mike is soon joined by Lola, and they walk off into the night.

COMMENTARY: In the spring of 1956, Hecht and Lancaster became the biggest independent production company in Hollywood. This was fortified with the new $40 million contract with United Artists and the release of their biggest box office success together, *Trapeze*. Produced by James Hill for $4 million, the film grossed over $7.2 million domestically. It was Lancaster's dream to make a definitive film about the circus.

Carol Reed's direction caught the thrills of the trapeze and the color and awe surrounding the world of the circus. There was even a raw feel for the behind the scenes goings-on. Robert Krasker's photography, especially of the acrobatics, was nothing short of fascinating. *Trapeze*'s filming included the Cirque d'Hiver (the actual circus in Paris, France, where the flying trapeze was introduced by Leotard in 1859).

The film was held up to some scrutiny when author Daniel Fuchs sued Hecht and Lancaster, claiming the story was taken from his work *The Daring Young Man*. This was not true, as James R. Webb wrote the screenplay from Liam O'Brien's adaptation of the 1950 Max Catto novel *The Killing Frost* (James Jones of *From Here to Eternity* fame initially worked, although uncredited, on the adaptation as well).

The novel focused on three acrobats, but there was no obsession with a triple somersault; instead, Tino Orsini is condemned for the death of one Sarah Linden, actually killed by Mike Ribble. This bizarre twist gave way to the film's only real drawback—the clichéd (if still romantic) love triangle provided by the writers.

The novel's Sarah became Lola in the film to accent the charms of Italian actress Gina Lollobrigida in her English film debut. As stunning as she was in the role of the beautiful seductress, it was the interaction on the trapeze between Tony Curtis's flyer and Burt Lancaster's catcher that supplied *Trapeze*'s dynamics.

Lancaster seemed the ideal choice for the fallen acrobat. Both a worldly demeanor and his great athleticism helped win him the Best Actor award at the 1956 Berlin International Film Festival. Many of the actual acrobatic feats were his own, but Burt was doubled at times by Eddie Ward, an aerialist with Ringling Brothers.

An acrobat named Fay Alexander doubled for Curtis and also served as the film's technical advisor for the flying sequences. Curtis and Lollobrigida even went into training to give off the real aura of acrobats and were as equally believable as Burt. The performances of all three stars are among their very finest.

Trapeze, with Tony Curtis, Gina Lollobrigida, and Burt Lancaster.

REVIEWS: *Commonweal:* "Certainly there is plenty of excitement from beginning to end. James Hill's production in DeLuxe Color is excellent, and, for a change, CinemaScope is employed to add to the effectiveness of the movement, and not just to show off some scenery."

Newsweek: "Lancaster, as a quite literally broken veteran whose life's passion is to hand on to posterity his precious 'triple'—three aerial somersaults before the catch—is unusually touching."

The Rainmaker

A Hal Wallis Production   A Paramount Picture   Released December 13, 1956   122 minutes   Technicolor VistaVision

CREDITS: Joseph Anthony (Director); Hal Wallis (Producer); C.C. Coleman Jr. (Assistant Director); Paul Nathan (Associate Producer); N. Richard Nash (Screenplay); Charles Lang Jr. (Photography); Warren Low (Editor); Hal Pereira and Walter Tyler (Art Directors); Sam Comer and Arthur Krams (Set Decorators); Edith Head (Costumes); Wally Westmore (Make-up); John P. Fulton (Special Effects); Harold

Lewis and Winston Leverett (Sound); Alex North (Music Score). Based on N. Richard Nash's play.

CAST: Burt Lancaster (Starbuck); Katharine Hepburn (Lizzie Curry); Wendell Corey (File); Lloyd Bridges (Noah Curry); Earl Holliman (Jim Curry); Cameron Prud'homme (H.C. Curry); Wallace Ford (Sheriff Thomas); Yvonne Lime (Snookie); Dottie Bee Baker (Belinda); Dan White (Deputy); Ken Becker (Phil Mackey); Michael Bachus (Sheriff); Stan Jones, John Benson, James Stone, Tony Merrill, and Joe Brown (Townsmen).

SYNOPSIS: In a small Kansas town, confidence man Starbuck is bamboozling the folks to buy his tornado rods. When they catch onto his scheme, he is forced to flee in his horse-drawn wagon.

Lizzie Curry returns to her family's farm from a trip to see kinfolk. Believing she is an old maid, Lizzie feels that her father, H.C., and brothers, Noah and Jim, hoped she would find a man to marry while she was away. The Curry men do try to fix her up with Deputy Sheriff File from their own town. Although he likes Lizzie, File is in no hurry to marry a second time (his ex-wife left him for another man).

The entire region is in the midst of a terrible drought. Starbuck appears at the Curry home; knowing they are desperate for rainfall for their crops, for $100 in advance he promises to make it rain within 24 hours. The Currys reluctantly gamble on the con man.

The Rainmaker, with (left to right) Katharine Hepburn, Lloyd Bridges, Burt Lancaster, Cameron Prud'homme, and Earl Holliman.

Although Noah is especially a pessimist against Starbuck actually making it rain, Jim plays along exuberantly. He follows Starbuck's instructions, however silly they seem, including beating a big drum incessantly.

In the interim, Starbuck helps Jim stand up to his domineering older brother. Perhaps more important, Starbuck romances Lizzie and makes her believe in herself as a beautiful woman.

When File arrives to arrest the con man, the Currys urge him to let Starbuck go. The deputy is understanding; however, seeing Starbuck make a play for Lizzie's hand in marriage forces File to realize that he loves her and doesn't want to lose her to another.

Lizzie chooses the security of File over the dream-peddling of Starbuck. As it hasn't rained in the designated time, Starbuck returns the $100 and leaves. No sooner is he gone than it begins to rain, to his surprise. He returns gleefully for the money. As Starbuck rides away, he leaves the Currys and File dancing for joy over the rain.

COMMENTARY: Burt Lancaster's performance as Starbuck in *The Rainmaker* was filled with the kind of flamboyant energy that his admirers find truly exhilarating. Yet also evident was the vulnerability that makes many of his performances so deeply touching. Hal Wallis produced this 1956 Paramount release fully realizing Lancaster's charismatic personality as an actor. Ironically, the film concluded Burt's contract with Wallis (*The Rainmaker* was actually made after the filming in 1956 of the producer's *Gunfight at the O.K. Corral*).

Initially, Wallis had purchased the film rights with Burt in mind, but then opted for William Holden to play Starbuck. Holden didn't feel quite right for the part, thus dropping out and opening the door for Lancaster (who was given the opportunity when he agreed to do *Gunfight*).

For *The Rainmaker*, N. Richard Nash based his screenplay from his own play first seen as a television drama (on NBC's *Philco Playhouse*, August 16, 1953). The play then came to the New York stage (in October 1954, running for 125 performances). Darren McGavin played Starbuck in both of these versions. The movie version contained a stagey look at times (it was shot mainly at the Paramount Studios in Hollywood under the stage play's director, Joseph Anthony). The story's blending of comedy with drama was particularly enriched by the delightful ensemble of players.

Katharine Hepburn radiated her own special charm, although she may have been a bit too mature and sophisticated as the country lass Lizzie (Joan Potter originated the role on television and Geraldine Page on stage). Nonetheless, Hepburn conveyed both the character's vulnerability and spiritedness so well that she was nominated for her seventh Academy Award as Best Actress (although she lost to Ingrid Bergman in *Anastasia*).

At this stage in his career, Burt may have met his toughest female co-star with Hepburn. When he was late for the first day of filming, she chewed him out; thereafter he was right on time. There may have been an edge in their respective acting styles, but their romance in the film was handled with a fine sensitivity and awareness for each other's talent.

Excellent support for the two stars came from Lloyd Bridges and Earl Holliman as Lizzie's brothers, from Wendell Corey as the fellow who wins her, and from Cameron Prud'homme as her pa (he also played the father in the original television and stage versions). *The Rainmaker*, which also benefited from an Oscar-nominated music score by Alex North, was hardly the big box office hit that *Trapeze* was, yet both films (along with the late 1955 release of *The Rose Tattoo*) helped make 1956 one of Lancaster's most popular years in motion pictures.

REVIEWS: *Commonweal:* "Although *The Rainmaker* is too long and not very convincing as a movie, it has its exciting moments, thanks to its actors who know how to put over life's escapist and realistic moods, and who conclude that a path between the two is best."

New York Times: "Lancaster is superb as the necromancer, and Katharine Hepburn seems to have been created for the role of the frightened yet dauntless woman facing middle age and loneliness."

Gunfight at the O.K. Corral

A Hal Wallis Production   A Paramount Picture   Released May 30, 1957   122 minutes   Technicolor VistaVision
CREDITS: John Sturges (Director); Hal Wallis (Producer); Michael D. Moore (Assistant Director); Paul Nathan (Associate Producer); Leon Uris (Screenplay); Charles Lang Jr. (Photography); Warren Low (Editor); Hal Pereira and Walter Tyler (Art Directors); Sam Comer and Arthur Krams (Set Decorators); Edith Head (Costumes); Wally Westmore (Make-up); John P. Fulton (Special Effects); Dimitri Tiomkin (Music Score). Title song by Dimitri Tiomkin and Ned Washington; sung by Frankie Laine. Suggested by the magazine article "The Killer" by George Scullin.

CAST: Burt Lancaster (Wyatt Earp); Kirk Douglas (Doc Holliday); Rhonda Fleming (Laura Denbow); Jo Van Fleet (Kate Fisher); John Ireland (Johnny Ringo); Lyle Bettger (Ike Clanton); Frank Faylen (Cotton Wilson); Earl Holliman (Charlie Bassett); Ted De Corsia (Shanghai Pierce); Dennis Hopper (Billy Clanton); Whit Bissell (John P. Clum); George Mathews (John Shanssey); John Hudson (Virgil Earp); DeForest Kelley (Morgan Earp); Martin Milner (James Earp); Kenneth Tobey (Bat Masterson); Lee Van Cleef (Ed Bailey); Joan Camden (Betty Earp); Olive Carey (Mrs. Clanton); Brian Hutton (Rick); Nelson Leigh (Mayor Kelley); Jack Elam (Tom McLowery); Don Castle (Drunken Cowboy); Mickey Simpson (Frank McLowery); Charles Herbert (Tommy Earp); Tony Merrill (Barber); Lee Roberts (Finn Clanton); Frank Carter (Hotel Clerk); Edward Ingram (Deputy); Bing Russell (Bartender); Henry Wills (Alby); Dorothy Abbott (Girl); William S. Meigs (Wayne); John Benson (Rig Driver); Richard J. Reeves (Foreman); John Maxwell (Merchant); Harry B. Mendoza (Cockeyed Frank Loving); Tony Joachim (Old Timer); Trude Wyler (Social Hall Guest); Robert C. Swan (Shaugnessy Man); Roger Creed (Deputy/Killer/Townsman); Bill Williams (Stuntman); Frank Hagney and Ethan Laidlaw (Bartenders); Paul Gary and Morgan Lane (Killers); Len Hendry, Gregg Martell, and Dennis Moore (Cowboys); James Davies, Joe Forte, Max Power, and Courtland Shepard (Card Players).

SYNOPSIS: Three men on horseback ride into Fort Griffin, Texas, and one, Ed Bailey, is killed in a saloon fight with gambler Doc Holliday. Sheriff Cotton Wilson arrests Doc and places him in a guarded hotel room, even though the killing was in self-defense. Lawman Wyatt Earp, of Dodge City, Kansas, is trailing outlaw Ike Clanton. Despite disliking Doc, Wyatt dislikes lynch mobs even more and helps the gambler escape from one with his mistress, Kate Fisher.

Doc and Kate go to Dodge City. Knowing the gambler needs to make some money, Wyatt allows him to stay, but only after he promises no more killings. Wyatt runs into a problem with a female gambler, Laura Denbow, but reaches a compromise by setting up a special gaming table for her.

With all but one of his deputies out of town, Wyatt deputizes Doc to help catch some outlaws. Doc is determined to help the lawman and does so when the outlaws try to ambush their camp along the trail.

When regular deputy Charlie Bassett informs Doc that Kate has taken up with gunman Johnny Ringo, the gambler seeks them out. Remembering his promise to Wyatt, Doc allows Ringo to humiliate him in front of Kate. Wyatt in the meantime has fallen in love with Laura.

Cattleman Shanghai Pierce comes to town with his cowboys and Ringo on a drunken shooting spree. Wyatt confronts them alone after Charlie is wounded. Doc stands at the lawman's side and wounds Ringo.

Wyatt plans on giving up being a lawman to marry Laura and settle down in California. But their love is threatened when Wyatt receives word that his brothers, Virgil and Morgan (both lawmen), need his help in Tombstone, Arizona.

Doc accompanies Wyatt to Tombstone, although his brothers dislike the gambler. The Earps unite to try to stop Ike Clanton from running a rustled herd of cattle through their area. Kate arrives in town and takes up again with Ringo, who is now part of Clanton's gang; Cotton Wilson is part of the gang as well.

Billy Clanton, Ike's younger brother, is befriended by Wyatt. After Wyatt's appointment as U.S. Marshal, Ike and his men try to assassinate him, but kill Wyatt's own younger brother, James, instead. Suffering from alcoholism and tuberculosis, Doc collapses confronting Kate on the murder. The Earps want vengeance, and Billy is sent to tell Wyatt that the showdown will be at the O.K. Corral.

Doc is able to join the Earps in their fight. Ike kills Cotton when he runs off. While Morgan and Virgil are wounded, so is Billy. His brothers, Finn and Ike, are killed by Doc and Wyatt as are brothers, Tom and Frank McLowery. Ringo is shot down by Doc, who is forced to kill Billy to save Wyatt. Disturbed that Billy had to die, Wyatt throws down his badge.

In the aftermath, Doc is urged by Wyatt to seek medical help. As Doc joins a card game, Wyatt rides out of Tombstone to join Laura in California.

COMMENTARY: *Gunfight at the O.K. Corral* was Burt Lancaster's last released film for Hal Wallis. Both Kirk Douglas and Lancaster had started their film careers contracted to the producer. After *I Walk Alone* (Burt and Kirk's initial teaming together for Wallis), Douglas was able to get out of his contract. Burt's took longer, of course, because of the various loan-outs and deferments. During production on *Gunfight* the famous friendship between Douglas and Lancaster really took off.

In the story of the friendship between peace officer Wyatt Earp and gambler Doc Holliday, liberties with history were assuredly taken by screenwriter Leon Uris from George Scullin's 1954 *Holiday Magazine* article (entitled "The Killer," it told of the life and times of Doc Holliday). The actual gunfight (on October 26, 1881) lasted 30 seconds.

Gunfight at the O.K. Corral, with Kirk Douglas, Burt Lancaster, John Hudson, and DeForest Kelley.

Neither Ike and Finn (Phineas) Clanton nor Johnny Ringo were part of the gunplay; Ike was there but ran away (and James Earp, Wyatt's older not younger brother, was not killed prior to it).

Despite historical inaccuracies, *Gunfight*'s value for exciting, spectacular entertainment could not be faulted. The gun battle in the film lasted 11 minutes and took a few days to shoot (in Old Tucson, Arizona). Charles Lang Jr.'s photography of the Arizona landscape was stunning. Frankie Laine sang a haunting ballad written by Dimitri Tiomkin and Ned Washington (the same duo who brought the even more famous *High Noon* ballad to the screen). *Gunfight at the O.K. Corral* was nominated for Academy Awards for Film Editing (Warren Low) and Sound (George Dutton, Sound Director; Paramount Sound Department).

John Sturges was virtually a master in utilizing the wide-screen effect (this film was Lancaster's best in the VistaVision process), and the director was fully able to capture the mythic quality around the legend of Doc Holliday and Wyatt Earp. Burt portrayed Wyatt as the stoic, fearless lawman he was alleged to be in the Old West. The performance is one of his strongest and most memorable. Kirk Douglas perhaps was even better as the more flamboyant Doc; caught especially well were the character's sicknesses and anger. John Ireland and Lyle Bettger were first-rate as the main villains, Ringo and Ike, as were Rhonda Fleming and Jo Van Fleet as Wild West ladies Laura Denbow (a fictitious character) and Kate Fisher (actually Doc's mistress). After its 1957 release by Paramount Pictures, *Gunfight at the O.K. Corral* proved to be Burt Lancaster's most popular western of the 1950s.

REVIEWS: *America:* "The Technicolor scenery is distractingly beautiful, but otherwise the mood of John Sturges' direction is realistic, even sordid."

Saturday Review: "As played by Burt Lancaster, directed by John Sturges, and written by Leon Uris, Wyatt Earp is a good sturdy, quiet fellow who dresses neatly and speaks good English, and who is more likely to quiet a fellow down by hitting him over the head with a gun than by shooting him."

Sweet Smell of Success

A Hecht, Hill and Lancaster Presentation   A Norma-Curtleigh Production   Released through United Artists   Released June 27, 1957   96 minutes   Black and White

CREDITS: Alexander Mackendrick (Director); James Hill (Producer); Harold Hecht (Executive Producer); Clifford Odets and Ernest Lehman (Screenplay); James Wong Howe (Photography); Alan Crosland Jr. (Editor); Edward Carrere (Art Director); Mary Grant (Costumes); Robert Schiffer (Make-up); Jack Solomon (Sound); Chico Hamilton and Fred Katz (Songs); Elmer Bernstein (Music Score). From the novelette *Tell Me About It Tomorrow* by Ernest Lehman.

CAST: Burt Lancaster (J.J. Hunsecker); Tony Curtis (Sidney Falco); Susan Harrison (Susan Hunsecker); Martin Milner (Steve Dallas); Sam Levene (Frank D'Angelo); Barbara Nichols (Rita); Jeff Donnell (Sally); Joseph Leon (Robard); Edith Atwater (Mary); Emile Meyer (Harry Kello); Joe Frisco (Herbie Temple); David White (Otis Elwell); Lawrence Dobkin (Leo Bartha); Lurene Tuttle (Mrs. Bartha); Queenie Smith (Mildred Tam); Autumn Russell (Linda); Jay Adler (Manny Davis); Lewis Charles (Al Evans); The Chico Hamilton Quintet.

SYNOPSIS: J.J. Hunsecker is a New York–based syndicated newspaper columnist whose readership is 60 million. Sidney Falco is a press agent. Both men are ruthless—Sidney will do anything to sell the columnist an item, for J.J. has the power to destroy or help anyone he chooses.

Not wanting his younger sister, Susan, to see jazz musician Steve Dallas, J.J. conspires with Sidney to end the romance. Since it could mean writing J.J.'s column while he is on vacation, Sidney arranges for another columnist, Otis Elwell, to print a smear accusing Steve of being a Communist and smoking marijuana. To her disdain, Rita, Sidney's girlfriend, is used sexually to lure Otis into the scheme.

So overbearing is J.J., feeling Steve is not good enough for her, that Susan does agree to stop seeing him. Steve's angry retort bruises J.J.'s ego. He has Sidney plant some marijuana on the musician. Harry Kello, a cop who owes J.J. some favors, then arrests Steve.

Susan tries to commit suicide, but Sidney stops her. To try to undermine his previous actions, J.J. has Harry go after Sidney for planting the dope. Sidney is beaten and dragged away to jail. But the damage has already been done. Susan walks out of her brother's life to go to Steve.

COMMENTARY: By the end of 1956, James Hill was a full partner with Harold Hecht and Burt Lancaster. Their first films together (released in 1957 by United Artists) were two New York–based stories: *The Bachelor Party* (without Burt as an actor) and *Sweet Smell of Success* (with Burt openly boasting of it as one of his favorite roles). Neither picture, however, was a box office success (Hecht produced the first and Hill the latter).

Despite his British roots, director Alexander Mackendrick perfectly conveyed the seedy turmoil of New York City life in *Sweet Smell of Success* (his meticulous craftsmanship also helped extend production costs). Interiors were done in Hollywood (at the Goldwyn Studios), and actual exteriors were shot in Manhattan. The story was initially

Sweet Smell of Success: **Burt Lancaster as J.J. Hunsecker.**

Sweet Smell of Success, with Burt Lancaster and Tony Curtis.

based on one that appeared in 1950 in *Cosmopolitan Magazine* written by Ernest Lehman (who also worked on the screenplay, as did Clifford Odets).

Lancaster was indeed pleased with the film (Hecht was not), and his interpretation of a manipulative and powerful figure (allegedly based on columnist Walter Winchell). The smoldering tension generated by Burt was also a reflection of part of his own personality.

Both Burt and Tony Curtis as the press hound were terrific in this dis-

turbing yet engrossing film. It was co-financed by Tony's own production company, Curtleigh. Curtis's more energetic performance is considered to be his very best; Lancaster agreed that his younger co-star deserved an Oscar (he wasn't even nominated). Susan Harrison and Martin Milner were a welcome relief as the decent couple caught in the web of immorality. Regarded as Burt's first big failure for his own company, *Sweet Smell of Success*, over the years, nonetheless has achieved a cult status.

REVIEWS: *Library Journal:* "It is not much of a story, but it serves to show the depths of human perfidy among those who are drugged by the sweet smell of success.... It is moodily photographed by the expert James Wong Howe, and strikingly worded in the supercharged dialogue of Clifford Odets."

Commonweal: "Excellent in the repellent lead roles are Burt Lancaster, as the sinister columnist who thinks he is a god who can make or break people, and Tony Curtis, as the press agent who's willing to do any kind of dirty work in his dog-eat-dog publicity business."

Run Silent, Run Deep

A Hecht, Hill and Lancaster Presentation   A Jeffrey Productions Inc. Picture   Released through United Artists   Released March 27, 1958   94 minutes   Black and White

CREDITS: Robert Wise (Director); Harold Hecht (Producer); Emmett Emerson (Assistant Director); William Schorr (Associate Producer); John Gay (Screenplay); Russell Harlan (Photography); George Boemler (Editor); Edward Carrere (Art Director); Ross Dowd (Set Director); Frank Prehoda (Make-up); Howard Lydecker, Clifford Stine, and Arnold Gillespie (Special Effects); Fred Lau (Sound); Rear Admiral Rob Roy McGregor (Technical Consultant); Franz Waxman (Music Score). Based on the novel by Commander Edward L. Beach.

CAST: Clark Gable (Commander Richardson); Burt Lancaster (Lt. Jim Bledsoe); Jack Warden (Mueller); Brad Dexter (Cartwright); Don Rickles (Ruby); Nick Cravat (Russo); Joe Maross (Kohler); Mary LaRoche (Laura); Eddie Foy III (Larto); Rudy Bond (Cullen); H.M. Wynant (Hendrix); John Bryant (Beckman); Ken Lynch (Frank); Joel Fluellen (Bragg); Jimmie Bates (Jessie); John Gibson (Capt. Blunt).

SYNOPSIS: During World War II, Commander Richardson loses his American submarine to the Japanese. It is sunk, apparently by an enemy destroyer called *Bongo Pete*, off the Japan coast in the Bongo Straits.

A year later, another American sub, the *Nerka*, docks at Pearl Harbor under its executive officer, Lt. Jim Bledsoe. Richardson, now on administrative duty, sees an opportunity to return to combat and face the Bongo Pete. Bledsoe and his crew are upset that Richardson is given command.

Aboard the *Nerka*, Richardson has the men constantly drill in actual crash diving and torpedo firing simulation. The men are annoyed and confused by this until the *Nerka* sinks an enemy destroyer with a much-practiced "down the throat shot."

When it is realized that Richardson is defying orders by returning to the Bungo Straits, there is talk of mutiny, but Bledsoe stops it. There is further antagonism between Cartwright, an officer who opposes Richardson, and Mueller, a crewman who supports the commander.

In the Straits, the *Nerka* is attacked by Japanese planes and by the Bongo Pete with depth charges. There are a few men killed on the sub, and Richardson suffers a life-threatening concussion. The *Nerka* tries to fool the enemy into thinking it is destroyed by sending its dead to the surface through the torpedo tubes.

Feeling there is only more death if the *Nerka* stays in the Straits, Bledsoe takes command and is prepared to return to Pearl Harbor. He changes his mind when a radio message indeed

On the set of *Run Silent, Run Deep*, with (left to right) Harold Hecht, Burt Lancaster, Clark Gable, and James Hill.

declares the submarine lost (and it is discerned that the Japanese initially detected them through the garbage dumped over the side). Using this knowledge to advantage, the *Nerka*, under Bledsoe, gets close enough and sinks the *Bongo Pete*.

A greater danger appears in a Japanese submarine—it was this ship, Richardson now realizes, that brought down the first sub. Richardson goes to Bledsoe's side to help sink the enemy submarine. Dying from his concussion, Richardson is then honored with a military burial at sea.

COMMENTARY: United Artists bought the movie rights to Commander Edward L. Beach's 1955 best-selling novel, *Run Silent, Run Deep*, and asked Hecht, Hill, and Lancaster to turn it into a film. After the box office failure of *Sweet Smell of Success*, HHL was eager to make what was believed to be a purely commercial drama. John Gay's screenplay actually enhanced the book's tension between the two main officers.

The HHL group was fortunate to secure veteran Hollywood legend Clark Gable to star alongside Burt Lancaster (as was Hecht and Lancaster with Gary

Cooper for *Vera Cruz*). At age 57, Gable may have been a bit too old for the submarine commander, but his obsession for revenge made the character the film's most intriguing. However, Lancaster's executive officer was a more likable part; his tough but fair demeanor was reflective, if not as substantive, of his sergeant in *From Here to Eternity*. Jack Warden, Brad Dexter, Don Rickles, and Nick Cravat (in a nice speaking role as a crewman who gets stuck outside the sub as it submerges) were among those offering solid support.

Run Silent, Run Deep's submarine warfare was certainly its strongest feature, conveyed suspensefully and with almost a documentary presentation by producer Harold Hecht and director Robert Wise, and through Russell Harlan's black and white cinematography. Commander Beach (an uncredited technical advisor) and Rear Admiral Rob Roy McGregor (technical consultant) were undoubtedly very influential in the authenticity displayed. The Flotilla 1 sub also received credit for its cooperation during filming (but also used was the sub *USS Redfish* in San Diego). The underwater photography used miniatures. For all the painstaking care that went into it, *Run Silent, Run Deep* seemed just a bit routine and was not the box office hit envisioned after its 1958 release.

REVIEWS: *New York Times:* "A better film about war beneath the ocean and about guys in the 'silent service' has not been made."

Variety: "Both Gable and Lancaster give strong, convincing performances."

Run Silent, Run Deep, **with Burt Lancaster and Clark Gable.**

Separate Tables

A Hecht, Hill and Lancaster Presentation   A Clifton Productions Inc.   Picture Released through United Artists   Released December 18, 1958   98 minutes   Black and White

CREDITS: Delbert Mann (Director); Harold Hecht (Producer); Thomas P. Shaw (Assistant Director); Harry Horner (Associate Producer, Production Designer); Terence Rattigan and John Gay (Screenplay); Charles Lang Jr. (Photography); Marjorie Fowler and Charles Ennis (Editors); Edward Carrere (Art Director); Edward G. Boyle (Set Decorator); Edith Head (Miss Hayworth's Gowns); Mary Grant (Costumes); Harry Maret and Frank Prehoda (Make-up); Fred Lau Sound); David Raksin (Music Score). Title song by Harry Warren and Harold Adamson; sung by Vic Damone. Based on Terence Rattigan's play.

CAST: Rita Hayworth (Ann Shankland); Deborah Kerr (Sybil Railton-Bell); David Niven (Major Pollock); Burt Lancaster (John Malcolm); Wendy Hiller (Pat Cooper); Gladys Cooper (Mrs. Railton-Bell); Cathleen Nesbitt (Lady Matheson); Felix Aylmer (Mr. Fowler); Rod Taylor (Charles); Audrey Dalton (Jean); Priscilla Morgan (Doreen); May Hallatt (Miss Meacham); Hilda Plowright (Mabel).

SYNOPSIS: The English Beauregard Hotel is the home for a group of lonely people. Sybil Railton-Bell seems interested in one Major Pollock, and they walk together. She is dominated by her mother, Mrs. Railton-Bell, who does not approve of Sybil's attraction to the major. He seems disturbed by a newspaper article.

A visitor to the hotel, Ann Shankland, arrives and is greeted by its proprietress, Pat Cooper. Ann is looking for resident John Malcolm, who is in love with Pat. When he first appears, it is obvious that he has been drinking; seeing Ann brings a reminder that they once shared a stormy marriage.

Mrs. Railton-Bell finds the article that concerns the major—it reveals his arrest for indecent behavior to several women at a local theater and that his military stories and ranking are fraudulent. She is intent on having him leave the hotel and involves the other residents. When John tries to get Sybil to disagree with her mother, the younger woman becomes hysterical.

A spark of passion remains between John and Ann, but they soon quarrel bitterly over Pat. Upset, Ann is comforted by Pat, who is also aware of the trouble with the major.

Both Ann and Major Pollock prepare to leave in the morning. Sybil is actually sorry that he will be going and offers him money. He refuses, telling her they are so much alike because they are afraid of people. Pat tries to persuade John that he and Ann are still in love. The major is told by Pat that he doesn't have to leave.

In the dining room, breakfast is being served at the separate tables. John sits down at Ann's table. When the major sits at his own table, John is the first to bid him "Good morning." Mrs. Railton-Bell wants Sybil to then leave with her from their table. Refusing, Sybil stays and talks with the major, who has decided to remain at the hotel. Pat moves about with her morning duties.

COMMENTARY: Terence Rattigan's play *Separate Tables* originated on the London stage in 1954 as a pair of one-act stories that concerned four desperately lonely people residing at the same seaside hotel in Bournemouth, England. Margaret Leighton and Eric Portman shared the four roles, each playing two characters magnificently. The first story—"Table by the Window"—told of the relationship between Mrs.

Separate Tables, with (left to right) Deborah Kerr, Gladys Cooper, Cathleen Nesbitt, and Burt Lancaster.

Shankland and Mr. Malcolm. The second, "Table Number Seven," related the story between Miss Railton-Bell and Major Pollock. In 1956, the Producers Theatre in association with Hecht and Lancaster brought the successful play to Broadway with the same leads (although Geraldine Page eventually took over for Leighton). Again, the play was a success, with a New York run of 332 performances (its London engagement lasted 726 performances).

In late 1957, Hecht, Hill, and Lancaster began film production of *Separate Tables* (with the understanding that writer Rattigan would be involved with the screenplay, which he

was with John Gay). HHL hired Laurence Olivier to direct the film and play the major, with his wife, Vivien Leigh, and Spencer Tracy to co-star. Burt Lancaster then opted to do the Tracy role, but Olivier did not think he was up to it. In short order, after arguing with Burt on how the character of John Malcolm, a writer with a drinking problem should be played, Olivier withdrew from the project, as did Miss Leigh.

Delbert Mann was asked to direct, but he had misgivings about being able to helm the English setting properly. Producer Harold Hecht helped convince him otherwise. The esteemed director of *Marty* brought forth *Separate Tables'* warmest and most vulnerable qualities, particularly with the British leads, Deborah Kerr and David Niven. The pair totally absorbed themselves in their unglamorous and heartwarming performances. Both Rita Hayworth and Lancaster were Americanized for the film; although quite good in their intensity, they seemed a bit too glamorous and vibrant compared to their co-stars. Another English performer, Wendy Hiller, radiated kindness and understanding as the caretaker of these troubled souls.

The film was successful with audiences after its 1958 release by United Artists (yet the earnings of $3.7 million were not nearly what HHL had wanted). Six Academy Award nominations were received: Best Picture, Best Actor (David Niven), Best Supporting Actress (Wendy Hiller), Screenplay Based on Material from Another Medium (Terence Rattigan, John Gay), Black and White Cinematography (Charles Lang Jr.), and Music Scoring of a Dramatic or Comedy Picture (David Raksin).

Niven and Hiller were Oscar winners. Kerr's nomination was her fifth since 1949, but she lost to Susan Hayward in *I Want to Live!* The musical romance of *Gigi* took the Best Picture honor over the more stringent (yet equally delicate) romantic strains of *Separate Tables*.

REVIEWS: *Commonweal:* "Harold

Separate Tables, with **Burt Lancaster and Rita Hayworth.**

Hecht has given the film an outstanding production; and Delbert Mann has handled his brilliant cast expertly."

America: "In the film Deborah Kerr and David Niven play very effectively a pair of almost psychopathically lonely and inhibited misfits while, somewhat less effectively, Rita Hayworth and Burt Lancaster are the estranged husband and wife who destroy one another apart as surely as they did together."

The Devil's Disciple

A Hecht-Hill-Lancaster Films, Limited and Brynaprod, S.A., Presentation Released through United Artists   Released August 20, 1959   82 minutes   Black and White

CREDITS: Guy Hamilton (Director); Harold Hecht (Producer); Adrian Pryce-Jones (Assistant Director); John Dighton and Roland Kibbee (Screenplay); Jack Hildyard (Photography); Alan Osbiston (Editor); Terrence Verity and Edward Carrere (Art Directors); Scott Slimon (Set Decorator); Mary Grant (Costumes); Alan Binns (Technical Advisor); John Hollingsworth (Music Director); Richard Rodney Bennett (Music Score). From the play by George Bernard Shaw.

CAST: Burt Lancaster (Anthony Anderson); Kirk Douglas (Richard Dudgeon); Laurence Olivier (General Burgoyne); Janette Scott (Judith Anderson); Eva LeGallienne (Widow Dudgeon); Harry Andrews (Major Swindon); Basil Sydney (Lawyer Hawkins); George Rose (British Sergeant); Neil McCallum (Christopher Dudgeon); Mervyn Johns (Reverend Maindeck Parshotter); David Horne (William Dudgeon); Jenny Jones (Essie); Erik Chitty (Titus Dudgeon); Betty Henderson (Storekeeper's Wife).

SYNOPSIS: In 1777, the American Revolution is taking place in the New England colonies. Rebel Timothy Dudgeon has been sentenced to be hanged in Springtown by the British military under the command of General Burgoyne. Reverend Anthony Anderson of Websterbridge is asked for help by Timothy's youngest son, Christopher.

Arriving too late to intercede, Anderson tries to remove the hanged man but is stopped by the British. Dudgeon is to remain as an example to any other rebels against King George of England. Later, however, Richard Dudgeon removes his father's body and buries him at Anderson's church.

At the reading of the will, Richard inherits his father's property. The widow Dudgeon despises Richard, her eldest son, and puts a curse on him.

General Burgoyne is soon aware of where Timothy is buried and dispatches soldiers to arrest Anthony. While the reverend is away comforting the widow Dudgeon, Richard bravely masquerades as Anderson and is arrested. Only with reluctance does Judith, Anthony's wife, go along with the deception. When Anderson learns of this and rides off, Judith thinks he is a coward.

Anderson in vain tries to secure help from patriot Lawyer Hawkins for Richard. At Dudgeon's hearing, presided over by Burgoyne in Websterbridge, he is sentenced to be hanged even after Judith reveals the masquerade. Judith believes she loves Richard for his heroism. Richard would prefer to be shot, but Burgoyne points out that the British soldier is not a very good marksman.

In Springtown, Anthony singlehandedly defeats a group of British soldiers and intercepts an important message for Burgoyne. Anderson goes to the general, informing him Springtown has been captured by the rebels and that the message relates the additional British troops are not coming. Burgoyne then releases Dudgeon and invites him to tea. Judith is perplexed at having to choose between Richard and her seemingly new husband. She runs off, Anthony chases after her on horseback, and the couple ride away together.

COMMENTARY: Irish playwright George Bernard Shaw wrote *The Devil's Disciple* in 1897, regarding it as not one of his best plays. Nonetheless, its satire revolving around the ineptitude of the British war machine (during the

American Revolution) was reflective of his esteemed wit and romance. The play saw a multitude of stage productions over the years, and the most highly regarded seemed to be in New York City in 1950 (with a run of 125 performances). Several folks involved in this particular staging collaborated on the *Hallmark Hall of Fame* presentation seen on NBC November 20, 1955 (including Maurice Evans as Dick Dudgeon and Dennis Price as General Burgoyne).

Burt Lancaster referred to Shaw as his "favorite author" and involved his film company in the big-screen transition. The idea initially was for Gary Cooper to play clergyman Anthony Anderson (Ralph Bellamy had played the part on the television showing) and Montgomery Clift as Dudgeon. But this didn't pan out. Instead Kirk Douglas's own Bryna Productions joined Hecht, Hill, and Lancaster for the motion picture. Douglas then played Dudgeon and Lancaster the clergyman.

After Shaw died, the rights to several of his properties went to Gabriel Pascal, who died before an agreement was reached for the movie rights. However, permission was obtained from those controlling Pascal's estate, and the rights were purchased for $600,000. The story's New England setting was then produced in England by Harold Hecht.

Anthony Asquith was originally meant to direct the film, but he was replaced by Alexander Mackendrick, who was in turn replaced by Guy Hamilton. Setting aside any differences he had with Lancaster over *Separate Tables*,

Laurence Olivier agreed to co-star as the jaunty British general (actually based on a historic figure known as "Gentleman Johnny" Burgoyne). Olivier's performance, especially showcasing the witticisms, was the film's true saving grace.

Screenwriters John Dighton and Roland Kibbee were wise to make use of the author's humor, but they were perhaps unwise to place the emphasis on the muscular heroics between Burt and Kirk. While amusing, their antics were not exactly what was expected from a treatment of Shaw. For the first part of *The Devil's Disciple*, Burt's reverend was stoic to the extreme; like a breath of fresh air, he turns into a bold yet whimsical fighting man. Kirk's rogue of the title (who has given his soul to the devil) was more vivid during the first part rather than the last.

"Burt, Kirk and Larry are coming— by George!" proclaimed the ads in newspapers for the film's 1959 release by United Artists. This alone may account for why audiences, even admirers of Shaw, did not make it as lucrative at the box office as desired.

REVIEWS: *Commonweal:* "Except for occasional Shaw flashes amidst the rewritten lines and added scenes, the movie is confused and dull and hardly accounts for all the talent that went into its making."

Time: "In a climactic scene of comic derring-do, ex-acrobat Lancaster makes heroic hash of a colonial courthouse and all the Redcoats in it. Otherwise he is as stiff and starchy as the clerical collar he eventually gives up."

The Devil's Disciple: **Burt Lancaster and Kirk Douglas hamming it up in a publicity pose.**

The 1960s

The Unforgiven

A Hecht-Hill-Lancaster Presentation A James Productions Inc. Picture Released through United Artists Released April 6, 1960 125 minutes Technicolor Panavision

CREDITS: John Huston (Director); James Hill (Producer); Ben Maddow (Screenplay); Franz Planer Lloyd (Editor); Stephen Grimes (Art Director); Dorothy Jeakins (Costumes); Frank McCoy and Frank Larue (Make-up); Dave Koehler (Special Effects); Basil Fenton Smith (Sound); Dimitri Tiomkin (Music Score). Based on the novel by Alan LeMay.

CAST: Burt Lancaster (Ben Zachary); Audrey Hepburn (Rachel Zachary); Audie Murphy (Cash Zachary); John Saxon (Johnny Portugal); Charles Bickford (Zeb Rawlins); Lillian Gish (Mattilda Zachary); Albert Salmi (Charlie Rawlins); Joseph Wiseman (Abe Kelsey); June Walker (Hagar Rawlins); Kipp Hamilton (Georgia Rawlins); Arnold Merritt (Jude Rawlins); Carlos Rivas (Lost Bird); Doug McClure (Andy Zachary).

SYNOPSIS: Cattleman Ben Zachary returns to his home in the Texas Panhandle of the 1870s, having hired men in Wichita. One of the men is a half-breed named Johnny Portugal. Ben is greeted along the trail by his brothers, Cash and Andy, and sister, Rachel. Their mother, Mattilda, is surprised with a piano all the way from the Kansas cow town.

Ben and neighbor Zeb Rawlins are partners in the cattle business and learn that a crazed range rider has been scaring the women. Cash and Ben try to catch the rider, Abe Kelsey, but he escapes in a sandstorm.

Three Kiowa Indians come to the Zachary ranch and want to trade horses for Rachel. They tell Ben that Kelsey claims she is a Kiowa. When Ben refuses to trade, a war lance is thrown into the door.

Zeb's son, Charlie, wishes to marry Rachel. But he is ambushed and killed by the Indians. At Charlie's funeral, Rachel is scorned by his mother, Hagar. Kelsey must be found and the truth be known about Rachel before Zeb will continue the partnership.

The Zachary brothers and others follow Kelsey's trail. When the rider is seen on a distant ridge, on a horse stolen from the Zacharys,. Johnny Portugal chases after and captures him.

Back at the Rawlins' place, a noose is put around Kelsey's neck. He swears that Rachel is an Indian who was taken by Mattilda's late husband as a baby and could have been traded back for his own son kidnapped by the Indians. Ben counteracts that his father found Rachel in a white settler's wagon after an Indian attack in which Kelsey's boy was killed. Mattilda rushes at Kelsey causing him to hang. Zeb will have nothing more to do with the Zacharys until Rachel is sent away.

Returning home, the Zacharys find an old Indian scroll there that does substantiate Kelsey's story. Mattilda then admits that it's true. Cash is embittered and leaves his family.

When the Indians return for Rachel, she tries to go with them to prevent an attack. However, Ben orders Andy to shoot one, and the Indians attack in full force. Many are killed. Now that Rachel is known not to really be his

The Unforgiven, **with Burt Lancaster and Audrey Hepburn.**

sister, Ben realizes they are free to marry. Just as the Indians are breaking into the Zachary home, Cash, who had heard gunfire from the distance, rushes back to help defeat them. Rachel is forced to shoot her actual Indian brother, Lost Bird. Mattilda lies dead from the struggle.

COMMENTARY: Hecht, Hill, and Lancaster accomplished a vast amount of film work during 1959, yet it was a very unfortunate time. The release of *The Devil's Disciple* was the company's fourth motion picture in a row starring Burt that did not exactly light up the box office as intended. There was also the release of three financially unsuccessful films made by HHL without Burt as an actor (*The Rabbit Trap*, *Cry*

Tough, and *Take a Giant Step*). Thus, HHL mentioned in 1959 that it would soon disband, although some hope remained that, like *Trapeze*, a western epic called *The Unforgiven* (filmed that winter and produced by James Hill) would be a big hit.

Even before Alan LeMay's novel of frontier racism was published in 1957, HHL had already purchased the screen rights (knowing that another LeMay story, *The Searchers*, was made into a great western by John Ford). *The Rabbit Trap*'s screenwriter, J.P. Miller, initially was involved on this HHL project as was *Separate Tables*' director, Delbert Mann. Both Miller and Mann left the project when they concurred that Hill and his partners were more interested in the story as a commercial property rather than an authentic depiction of the West. Ben Maddow and John Huston then came aboard as screenwriter and director, respectively.

Huston remarked in his 1980 autobiography, *An Open Book*, that *The Unforgiven* was the one film he disliked making in his long career. Instead of just the harsh racial theme in an equally harsh land that was the initial main concern envisioned by all, the picture was loaded with incredible action and bigger-than-life heroics. It was apparently heavily edited as well, most noticeably in the way the horseman played by the star of *Cry Tough*, John Saxon, seemed to just disappear.

Burt Lancaster's rugged yet vulnerable screen persona made him a splendid choice for the gritty westerner he played, unbending and nearly invincible in his strength for the family he loves. Audrey Hepburn was deemed too delicate and thus miscast as his equally vulnerable female counterpart. (The always radiant actress was perhaps not given enough credit for her fortitude, especially in coming back to work after only three weeks off for falling from a horse and breaking several bones in her back during filming.)

A stalwart western figure in many films, Audie Murphy may have given his best performance as Lancaster's brother facing his own bigotry. The timeworn pioneers played by Charles Bickford and Lillian Gish were so convincing that

The Unforgiven, with Burt Lancaster and Audie Murphy.

they seemed part of the raw terrain in which they lived.

Perhaps the most memorable performance was given by Joseph Wiseman, whose ghostly range rider was especially reflective of *The Unforgiven*'s many haunting and tragic elements. That the film was exciting yet touching cannot be denied. Yet on its 1960 release by United Artists, the film failed at the box office. The production costs surely did not help—*The Unforgiven* was Hecht, Hill, and Lancaster's costliest film of all at $5.5 million. The sod house used by the Zachary family (built on location in Durango, Mexico) cost $300,000 alone, as did the individual services of Hepburn, Lancaster, and Huston.

REVIEWS: *Newsweek:* "The large cast could hardly have been better chosen, while Huston's direction is fast and lusty, and Dimitri Tiomkin has supplied music to match."

New York Times: "As the girl, Audrey Hepburn is a bit too polished, too fragile and civilized among such tough and stubborn types as Burt Lancaster as the man of the family, Lillian Gish as the thin-lipped frontier mother, and Audie Murphy as a redskin-hating son."

Elmer Gantry

From Elmer Gantry Productions   Released through United Artists   Released July 7, 1960   147 minutes   Eastman Color   CREDITS: Richard Brooks (Director and Screenplay); Bernard Smith (Producer); Thomas P. Shaw (Assistant Director); John Alton (Photography); Marjorie Fowler (Editor); Edward Carrere (Art Director); Bill Calvert and Frank Tuttle (Set Decorators); Dorothy Jeakins (Costumes); Robert Schiffer and Harry Maret (Make-up); Harry Mills (Sound); Andre Previn (Music Score). Based on the novel by Sinclair Lewis.

CAST: Burt Lancaster (Elmer Gantry); Jean Simmons (Sister Sharon Falconer); Dean Jagger (William L. Morgan); Arthur Kennedy (Jim Lefferts); Shirley Jones (Lulu Bains); Patti Page (Sister Rachel); Edward Andrews (George Babbitt); John McIntire (Rev. Pengilly); Joe Maross (Pete); Hugh Marlowe (Rev. Garrison); Philip Ober (Rev. Planck); Everett Glass (Rev. Brown); Michael Whalen (Rev. Phillips); Wendell Holmes (Rev. Ulrich); Barry Kelley (Captain Holt); Rex Ingram (Preacher); Dayton Lummis (Eddington); Ray Walker, Ralph Dumke, George Cisar, and Norman Leavitt (Friends); Larry J. Blake (Bartender); John Qualen (Sam);

George Selk (Valet); Guy Wilkerson (Cleanup Man); Milton Parsons (Revivalist); Dan Riss (Speaker); Jean Willes and Sally Fraser (Prostitutes); Peter Brocco (Benny); Casey Adams (Deaf Man); George Flower (Cheerleader).

SYNOPSIS: Elmer Gantry is a hard-drinking, womanizing fellow with a penchant for preaching. Down on his luck as a traveling salesman in the Midwest, Elmer sees a more lucrative opportunity in the revival troupe of Sister Sharon Falconer. He charms his way into her organization initially using her leading choir singer, Sister Rachel.

Sharon has a sweet way of sermonizing, but her manager, Bill Morgan, is against Gantry's loud and crude style. Bill informs Sharon that Elmer was expelled from a theological seminary for seducing the deacon's daughter, named Lulu Bains. Behind Sharon's sweet exterior there is a shrewd businesswoman, and her main concern is Elmer's evangelistic skill in converting sinners.

Gantry encourages Sharon to accept an invitation to preach in the city of Zenith, although the support of realtor George Babbitt and most of the clergymen proves controversial. Bill doesn't feel she is ready for this big move, yet she proves otherwise. Her religious value, then under dispute by prominent newspaperman Jim Lefferts, causes her public disfavor.

Soon even Babbitt tries to withdraw his support until Gantry discovers that his properties include a speakeasy and brothel. Elmer helps Sharon's cause even more by revealing Lefferts as an agnostic who has used the Bible's writings as facts to attack her.

Babbitt is bamboozled by Gantry into buying radio time to counterattack Jim's reporting against Sharon. Elmer is dynamic with his radio preaching. At this point both Bill and Jim are impressed by Gantry, who is soon leading the police on vice raids. At one raid on a brothel, Elmer finds Lulu working as a prostitute. She lures him to her room and tricks Gantry into kissing her and giving her money with a photographer hiding outside the window.

Sharon, now romantically involved with Elmer, is blackmailed to buy the negatives. Instead, Lulu gives them to a newspaper (Lefferts had refused to use them for his own paper).

During a near-empty revival meeting, Gantry is belted by hecklers with eggs and vegetables. Lulu is regretful, but runs away from him.

When Lulu is being beaten by her pimp for not selling the pictures for big money, Elmer arrives, roughs him up, and comforts her. Later, Jim lets Elmer know that she admitted the photos were a frame-up; this big news, printed by Jim's paper, makes Sharon and Elmer even more popular.

However, Elmer has disappeared for a few days. When he returns Sharon is about to celebrate the opening of her very own tabernacle in Zenith. He now seems disillusioned with revivalism and wants her to give it up and marry him. But she goes before her congregation and actually believes she has the divine power to heal a deaf man. A fire then accidentally breaks out, burning down her tabernacle and killing her.

Elmer Gantry: **Burt Lancaster's most acclaimed performance.**

Afterward, Elmer and Sister Rachel lead Sharon's mourners in song. Although Bill wants him to continue with Sharon's work, Elmer feels that it's time to move on.

COMMENTARY: Richard Brooks and Burt Lancaster first met as screenwriter and actor during the making of 1947's *Brute Force*. Hollywood legend has it that even then Brooks mentioned to Lancaster the possibility of making *Elmer Gantry*, the Sinclair Lewis novel on revivalism in the 1920s, into a film one day. Richard tried to interest several film companies in the idea, but they were reluctant to explore the delicate subject matter.

Burt Lancaster and Jean Simmons in *Elmer Gantry*.

In 1955, Brooks bought the screen rights to the novel and began writing the screenplay. An extensive first draft was developed that even included Gantry as a 22-year-old (just as in the book). Lancaster was definitely interested in the project, but realized for him to be credible the story would have to center on Elmer's later years (with a reference to his past). For seven months, Burt involved himself with the story as Richard wrote the final draft. The title character was more humanized, and thus more likable, than Lewis's creation.

Gantry certainly had his faults—his slick charm was a facade for a bold opportunist—and the film version was a provocative look into his world as an evangelist. An honest attempt was made to show the pros and cons of revivalism. Brooks and Lancaster formed Elmer Gantry Productions to make this picture together for a 1960 United Artists release (the filming took place in the summer of 1959, mainly at the available studio facilities at Columbia Pictures in Burbank, California). Bernard Smith was chosen to produce, and Richard Brooks directed. *Elmer Gantry*, although costing over $3 million to make, was successful enough to reach number 13 on the year's list of top box office films, with earnings of $5.2 million.

Lancaster electrified audiences with his outrageous yet outstanding performance as Elmer Gantry (rightly considered his greatest role). He nearly jumps right out of the screen, his energy is so exuberant. His Gantry was surely a ham, who loved to hear the sound of his own voice, and Burt noted, "Some parts you fall into like an old glove. Elmer really wasn't acting. It was me."

Shirley Jones surprised everyone with her own riveting performance as prostitute Lulu Bains. Previously regarded for her wonderful singing in Hollywood musicals, producer Smith saw her playing a drunk on a *Playhouse 90* television drama and brought her to Burt's attention. Delightful support was also given by the always enchanting Jean Simmons as Sharon Falconer, Elmer's more tender counterpart, as well as a who's who of fine character actors.

Five Academy Award nominations were given to *Elmer Gantry*: Best Picture, Best Actor (Burt Lancaster), Best Supporting Actress (Shirley Jones), Screenplay Based on Material from Another Medium (Richard Brooks), and Music Scoring of a Dramatic or Comedy Picture (Andre Previn).

The Apartment took the Best Picture honor, and Ernest Gold the music award for *Exodus*. But Miss Jones, Brooks, and Lancaster won their Oscars. The other nominees for Best Actor were Jack Lemmon in *The Apartment*, Trevor Howard in *Sons and Lovers*, Laurence Olivier in *The Entertainer*, and Spencer Tracy in *Inherit the Wind*.

At the Oscar Awards on April 17, 1961: Peter Ustinov, Shirley Jones, Elizabeth Taylor, and Burt Lancaster.

At the 33rd Annual Academy Awards, on April 17, 1961, Burt was handed his Oscar by Greer Garson. He replied, "I want to thank all who expressed this kind of confidence by voting for me and right now I'm so happy I want to thank all the members who didn't vote for me." He also won a Golden Globe Award for *Elmer Gantry* and his second New York Film Critics Award.

REVIEWS: *New York Times:* "Sinclair Lewis's *Elmer Gantry*, which shocked, amused, confounded, but rarely bored readers back in 1927, has been lifted from the pages of the justifiably controversial novel and impressively transformed into an exciting film."

Commonweal: "Burt Lancaster gives his best performance to date as Elmer Gantry, the lecherous drummer who graduates with ease from vacuum cleaners to preaching when he meets the evangelist Sister Sharon."

The Young Savages

A Harold Hecht Production   A Contemporary Productions Inc. Picture   Released through United Artists   Released May 23, 1961   100 minutes   Black and White

CREDITS: John Frankenheimer (Director); Pat Duggan (Producer); Carter De Haven Jr. (Assistant Director); Harold Hecht (Executive Producer); Edward Anhalt and J.P. Miller (Screenplay); Lionel Lindon (Photography); Eda Warren (Editor); Burr Smidt (Art Director); James M. Crowe (Set Decorator); Jack Angel and Roselle Novello (Costumes); Robert Schiffer (Make-up); Harry Mills and Eldon Coutts (Sound); David Amram (Music Score). Based on Evan Hunter's novel *A Matter of Conviction*.

CAST: Burt Lancaster (Hank Bell); Dina Merrill (Karin Bell); Shelley Winters (Mary Di Pace); Edward Andrews (Dan Cole); Vivian Nathan (Mrs. Escalante); Larry Gates (Randolph); Telly Savalas (Lt. Richard Gunnison); Pilar Seurat (Louisa Escalante); Jody Fair (Angela Rugiello); Roberta Shore (Jenny Bell); Milton Selzer (Walsh); Robert Burton (Judge); David J. Stewart (Barton); Stanley Kristien (Danny Di Pace); John Davis Chandler (Arthur Reardon); Neil Nephew (Anthony Aposto); Luis Arroyo (Zorro); Jose Perez (Roberto Escalante); Richard Velez (Gargantua); Chris Robinson (Pretty Boy); William Sargent (Soames); Stanley Adams (Lt. Hardy); William Quinn (Capt. Larsen); Linda Danzil (Maria Amora); Rafael Lopez (Jose); Henry Norell (Pierce); Jon Carlo (McNally); Bob Biheller (Turtleneck); Harry Holcombe (Doctor); Helen Kleeb (Mrs. Patton); Thom Conroy (Mr. Abbeney); John Walsh (Lonnie); Irving Steinberg (Wohlman); Clegg Hoyt (Whitey); Joel Fluellen (Court Clerk); Robert Cleaves (Sullivan).

SYNOPSIS: In New York City's Harlem neighborhood, a blind youth belonging to a street gang known as the Horsemen is stabbed to death by three teenage boys from a gang called the Thunderbirds. The trio are caught by the police and charged with murder.

Assistant District Attorney Hank Bell is the prosecutor determined to find justice for the murder of the young man, Roberto Escalante, by Danny Di Pace, Arthur Reardon, and Anthony Aposto. Dan Cole, the district attorney, has ambitions to become governor and wants the three killers to receive the death penalty.

At first, Hank seems to favor the death penalty, although his wife, Karin, is against it. He grew up in the same neighborhood as the boys and Danny's mother, Mary, was an old girlfriend. Mary believes her son is innocent.

Hank undertakes a thorough investigation, causing trouble with Dan.

The Young Savages, with (left to right) Burt Lancaster, Telly Savalas, and Edward Andrews.

It is revealed that Roberto carried hidden weapons for his gang members and was a pimp for his sister's prostitution. Teenaged delinquents threaten Karin on an elevator and later savagely attack Hank on the subway to stop his investigation. Hank's fury when striking back at one of his assailants makes him realize how blind hatred can cause killing.

During the trial, Hank brings out the hatred that has built up in a conflicting society, thereby creating the violence between the rival street gangs of Italian and Puerto Rican descent. Hank is able to reveal that Danny never stabbed Roberto. Danny is given a light punishment, Arthur a severe prison sentence, and Anthony will receive care in a mental institution.

COMMENTARY: Burt Lancaster was receptive to portraying the social issue of juvenile delinquency with *The Young Savages*, his first released motion picture after winning an Academy Award. Director John Frankenheimer's first film with Burt was vivid in its violence. The very murder that sets up the story is chillingly reflected in the victim's dark glasses. The picture was made even more graphic by the director's insistence on filming on location in New York City (the area of East Harlem used was actually part of Burt's own neighborhood growing up).

By 1961 this material was a bit shopworn in films (although the same year's *West Side Story*, about New York street gangs, was a tremendous success with stunning choreography and songs). The more realistic if clichéd approach of *The Young Savages* was not especially receptive, however, with audiences.

Evan Hunter's 1959 novel, *A Matter of Conviction*, was the basis for this United Artists release. J.P. Miller was involved with rewriting the screenplay initially written by Edward Anhalt (with the latter also helpful in bringing director Frankenheimer to the attention of the film's executive producer, Harold Hecht). Pat Duggan produced *The Young Savages* (which originally was planned to use Hunter's own title).

Although the Hecht, Hill, and Lancaster production company officially ended in 1960, Harold's and Burt's obligations to United Artists united them on this film (and the later *Birdman of Alcatraz*). Lancaster's politically ambitious assistant district attorney was played in a dignified, resolute manner that saw his compassionate stance outweighing any other. Dina Merrill and Shelley Winters lent a welcome air of compassion throughout most of the heated story. As the teens up for murder, Stanley Kristien, John Davis Chandler, and Neil Nephew left indelible impressions (and they were given special coaching by the film's dialogue director, Sydney Pollack).

REVIEWS: *Saturday Review:* "Its flashes of savagery, while brutal and shocking, are always pertinent to the story, not added for their own sake; and the screenplay, prepared by Edward Anhalt and J.P. Miller from a novel by Evan Hunter, conscientiously explores liberal catchphrases to arrive at the hard core of truth that lies within every cliché."

New York Times: "Mr. Lancaster's performance is vigorous but colored with a soft romantic tinge, and the two leading actresses are hardly so pungent as their roles would permit."

Judgment at Nuremberg

A Stanley Kramer Presentation   A Roxlom Films Production   Released through United Artists   Released December 19, 1961   190 minutes   Black and White

CREDITS: Stanley Kramer (Director and Producer); Ivan Volkman (Assistant to the Director); Phillip Langner (Associate Producer); Abby Mann (Screenplay); Ernest Laszlo (Photography); Frederic Knudtson (Editor); Rudolph Sternad (Production Designer); George Milo (Set Decorator); Jean Louis (Miss Dietrich's Gowns); Joe King (Costumes); Robert Schiffer (Make-up); Ernest Gold (Music Score). Based on the *Playhouse 90* teleplay by Abby Mann.

CAST: Spencer Tracy (Judge Dan Haywood); Burt Lancaster (Ernst Janning); Richard Widmark (Col. Tad Lawson); Marlene Dietrich (Madame Bertholt); Maximilian Schell (Hans Rolfe); Judy Garland (Irene Hoffman); Montgomery Clift (Rudolph Petersen); William Shatner (Capt. Byers); Edward Binns (Senator Burkette); Kenneth MacKenna (Judge Kenneth Norris); Joseph Bernard (Maj. Abe Radnitz); Werner Klemperer (Emil Hahn); Torben Meyer (Werner Lammpe); Alan Baxter (Gen. Merrin); Virginia Christine (Mrs. Halbestadt); Otto Waldis (Pohl); Karl Swenson (Dr. Geuter); Ray Teal (Judge Curtiss Ives); Ben Wright (Halbestadt); Olga Fabian (Mrs. Lindnow); Martin Brandt (Friedrich Hofstetter); John Wengraf (Dr. Wieck); Howard Caine (Wallner); Paul Busch (Schmidt); Bernard Kates (Perkins); Sheila Bromley (Mrs. Ives); Jana Taylor (Elsa Scheffler); Joseph Crehan (Spectator).

SYNOPSIS: In Nuremberg, Germany, in 1948, American judge Dan Haywood heads the trial of four German judges. Colonel Tad Lawson, the American prosecutor, accuses the four men of aiding Adolf Hitler in the extermination of six million innocent Jewish people during World War II. The higher Nazi war criminals have already been put on trial and sentenced by the military courts.

Hans Rolfe is the German defense lawyer for the four judges; he feels that if they are guilty for following Hitler's mandates, then all of the German people should stand trial. Three of the accused—Emil Hahn, Werner Lammpe, and Friedrich Hofstetter—plead not guilty, but the last and most intelligent, Ernst Janning, refuses to recognize the court or speak on his own behalf.

Janning had believed in his native Germany; although going along with Hitler, he hated the dictator and eventually was removed from his post as Minister of Justice. A German aristocrat, Madame Bertholt, also was against Hitler, although her husband, a Nazi general, was executed by the American military. She is against the four judges being punished.

Prosecutor Lawson shows a film to the court about the German concentration camps and their victims. Like so many of her fellow Germans, Madame Bertholt had not known about the atrocities at the camps.

Two important witnesses are brought to the trial by the prosecution. The first is Rudolph Petersen, a mentally deficient Communist who had been ordered sterilized by one of the German judges. The other, Irene Hoffman, is a German falsely accused of having sexual relations with an elderly Jewish man (who was then ordered executed by Janning).

Irene is put through such anxiety in the cross-examination by defense counsel Rolfe that Ernst Janning finally speaks up. He admits to his guilt, proclaiming that he knew better but the cruelties became a way of life.

Judgment at Nuremberg: **Burt Lancaster (seated back left) with Maximilian Schell (seated front left) and players.**

The trial has extended over a period of months. Judge Haywood is urged to show leniency for the accused men because the American military may need the support of the German people in a dispute with the Russians.

Haywood shows understanding for Rolfe and the complexity of the trial, but concludes that the value of a single human life is the most important factor. The four judges are given sentences of life imprisonment. Haywood visits the broken Janning in his cell.

Out of the 99 defendants sentenced to imprisonment at the actual Nuremberg trials, not one is still in jail.

COMMENTARY: *Judgment at Nuremberg* focused on the theme of the Nazi war trials following World War II, but the particular case emphasized on the screen was fictitious. It was still a powerful motion picture on the very real conditions of inhumanity that existed. As a message film and as entertainment, the response was a great success following its 1961 release by United Artists. Producer and director Stanley Kramer was absorbed by the challenge of turning the original television drama (seen on *Playhouse 90*, April 16, 1959) into an even more extensive film. Both the teleplay and screenplay were written by Abby Mann.

Kramer's 1961 version was somewhat numbing because of the overwhelming length and disturbing material, but the filmmaker kept the movie flowing briskly with Frederic Knudtson's editing and Ernest Laszlo's photography of the actual German locations and the courtroom (filmed at Hollywood's Revue Studios). Kramer's enthusiasm for the project extended to a cast so big with Hollywood names that their presence was initially thought weighty enough to take away from the story. But the performers immersed themselves so deeply into their roles that the material became the weightier factor.

Judgment at Nuremberg: **Burt Lancaster as Ernst Janning.**

Spencer Tracy was the epitome of naturalism as the humane American judge searching for the answers to the inhumanity. This great actor felt that the film was his finest. The issue of human decency, with its complexity of exploration, ultimately was a simple thing to appreciate. This was not better conveyed than in the final sequence, when Tracy's judge visits the sentenced German judge, played by Burt Lancaster: "Judge Haywood, the reason I asked you to come ... those people, those millions of people ... I never knew it would come to that. You must believe it; you must believe it!" Tracy's reply: "Herr Janning, it came to that the first time you sentenced a man to death you knew to be innocent."

Although miscast and madeup to look like a 63-year-old man (a role initially slated for Laurence Olivier and played on television by Paul Lukas), Lancaster portrayed well the ruptured dignity of the cultured judge and ultimately the pity. Perhaps his acting was

a bit too calculated and forced, but his stirring, eight-minute speech relating the tragic truth to the court was the movie's climactic highlight.

Maximilian Schell (reprising his television role) and Richard Widmark lent vigorous frankness to their respective roles of defense counsel and prosecutor. Marlene Dietrich's aristocrat (a role created for the movie) was sophisticated yet naive regarding the terrible war crimes committed in her own Germany. Judy Garland and Montgomery Clift were most moving as unbearably sad victims of the Nazi plight.

Judgment at Nuremberg was nominated for 11 Academy Awards: Best Picture, Best Actors (Spencer Tracy, Maximilian Schell), Best Supporting Actor and Actress (Montgomery Clift, Judy Garland), Director (Stanley Kramer), Screenplay Based on Material from Another Medium (Abby Mann), Black and White Cinematography (Ernest Laszlo), Film Editing (Frederic Knudtson), Black and White

Costume Design (Jean Louis); and Art Direction and Set Decoration (Rudolph Sternad, George Milo). Mann's screenplay and Schell's acting both won Oscars and New York Film Critics Awards.

REVIEWS: *America:* "Considering the difficulties inherent in the subject, it is high praise indeed to say that everything the film presents is stamped by conviction and dramatic stature and a remarkable degree of objectivity."

Saturday Review: "Burt Lancaster's projection of power in restraint, Tracy's rock-ribbed integrity, Maximilian Schell's intellectual fire (artfully offset by a shocking, ticlike smile)—all of them, principals and supporting players alike, are unified by the direction into one shattering, devastating, illuminating whole."

Birdman of Alcatraz

A Harold Hecht Presentation A Norma Production Released through United Artists Released July 3, 1962 147 minutes Black and White
CREDITS: John Frankenheimer (Director); Stuart Millar and Guy Trosper (Producers); Dave Silver (Assistant Director); Harold Hecht (Executive Producer); Guy Trosper (Screenplay); Burnett Guffey (Photography); Robert Krasker (Co-photography); Edward Mann (Editor); Ferdie Carrere (Art Director); Robert Schiffer (Make-up); George Cooper (Sound); A.W. Kennard and Ray Berwick (Bird Handlers); Elmer Bernstein (Music Score). Based on the book by Thomas Gaddis.
CAST: Burt Lancaster (Robert Stroud); Karl Malden (Harvey Shoemaker); Thelma Ritter (Elizabeth Stroud); Neville Brand (Bull Ransom); Edmond O'Brien (Tom Gaddis); Betty Field (Stella Johnson); Telly Savalas (Feto Gomez); Hugh Marlowe (Roy Comstock); Whit Bissell (Dr. Ellis); Crahan Denton (Kramer); James Westerfield (Jess Younger); Leo Penn (Eddie Kassellis); Lewis Charles (Chaplain Wentzel); Arthur Stewart (Guard Captain); Raymond Greenleaf (Judge); Nick Dennis (Crazed Prisoner); William Hansen (Fred Daw); Harry Holcombe (City Editor); Robert Burton (Senator Ham Lewis); Len Lesser (Burns); Chris Robinson (Logue); George Mitchell (Father Matthieu); Edward Mallory (John Clary); Adrienne Marden (Mrs. Woodrow Wilson); Harry Jackson (Reporter).

SYNOPSIS: On a wharf in San Francisco, with a view of the island prison of Alcatraz, writer Tom Gaddis narrates his story about convict Robert Stroud. In 1912, with a trainload of other prisoners, Stroud is transferred from a federal prison in Washington to another in Leavenworth, Kansas. The warden, Harvey Shoemaker, reveals that in 1909 Stroud initially killed a man who was hitting a woman.

A guard, Kramer, warns Shoemaker that Stroud is dangerous after he gets into a scrap with an inmate. When Kramer refuses to let Stroud's mother, Elizabeth, visit him over an infraction, another fight breaks out. As the guard attempts to hit him with a club, Stroud kills him with a shiv.

After three trials, Stroud is sentenced to be hanged. However, Elizabeth visits President Woodrow Wilson's wife with a plea to save her son, and the sentence is changed to life imprisonment. Stroud is placed in solitary confinement. Very lonely, he finds a baby sparrow during an exercise period and is allowed to keep it by guard Bull Ransom.

When word reaches the other prisoners in solitary about the bird, the new warden, Jess Younger, lets canaries be sent to them by their families. After one inmate tires of his birds, he gives them to Stroud. Another, Feto Gomez, gives

BA-257-113

In *Birdman of Alcatraz* as Robert Stroud.

him a pregnant bird, and both men concern themselves with the hatching of the eggs.

Septic fever starts killing the birds, which have increased considerably; fortunately, Stroud finds a cure. To market his medicines, he goes into business with a bird lover named Stella Johnson. Younger's replacement as warden, Roy Comstock, states that new federal bureau rules stipulate no pets or businesses for prisoners.

Elizabeth and Stella help put together a petition with 50,000 signatures to allow Stroud to keep his birds (he even marries Stella to help him in the situation). Although these tactics work, Elizabeth and her son break off all communications because of his loyalty to Stella.

When Bull Ransom gives him a microscope, Stroud uses it for research in writing a book. It is called *Stroud's Digest of the Diseases of Birds*.

In 1942, Stroud is transferred without his birds to Alcatraz, now run by warden Shoemaker. Also there is Feto Gomez; aware of how his friend has served time over the years, then released only to return to prison, Stroud writes a book (opposed by Shoemaker) on the failure of penal reform. Stella follows her husband to Alcatraz, but he doesn't want her to waste her life waiting for him to be released. When a prison riot breaks out in 1946, Stroud's only participation is to attend to an injured inmate and turn over stolen weapons.

In 1959 Stroud is escorted to a prison hospital in Springfield, Missouri. Leaving Alcatraz, he meets Tom Gaddis.

COMMENTARY: A real person, Robert Stroud did kill two men and spend over half a century in prison (43 years were in solitary confinement). Although he became a self-taught authority on ornithology (with only a third-grade education), his defiant spirit was a source of irritation to the penal system for many years. Since 1937, he was denied parole 24 times. He died in prison in 1963 when he was 73 years old. Many aspects of his life were explored in the fascinating (if a bit overlong) 1962 film *Birdman of Alcatraz*, though other facts were ignored (such as a suicide attempt and his supposed homosexuality).

Burt Lancaster was sympathetic for Stroud's release at the time, but others were not (considering him too dangerous), including the attorney general at the time, Robert Kennedy. Yet Burt defended Stroud's story and said, "The fact that it dealt with the inadequacies of our penal system was important and worthy of being exploited, but the most compelling thing to me was the emotional story of this man and what he had gone through."

In his often heartbreakingly vulnerable portrayal of Stroud, Lancaster was called on to age over forty years (this was beautifully rendered by his longtime make-up artist, Robert Schiffer). That the performance—so hard, so precise, so tender—is one of his greatest leaves no doubt. It is stated that he put more of his soul into the role than any other. A third Academy Award nomination for Best Actor resulted, although he lost the prize to Gregory Peck in *To Kill a Mockingbird*; however, Burt did win the Best Actor Award at the 1962 Venice Film Festival and for Best Foreign Actor at the British Academy Awards.

Oscar nominations for Best Supporting Actor and Actress went to Telly Savalas and Thelma Ritter, as convict

Birdman of Alcatraz, with Karl Malden and Burt Lancaster.

Feto Gomez and Stroud's mother, Elizabeth, respectively. As with *Judgment at Nuremberg* before it, *Birdman* was filled with stunning performances, including Karl Malden as warden Harvey Shoemaker; Neville Brand as guard Bull Ransom; Betty Field as Stroud's wife, Stella; and Edmond O'Brien as Tom Gaddis (the author of the successful 1955 biography of Robert Stroud, on which Guy Trosper based his screenplay). An Oscar nomination also went to Burnett Guffey for Black and White Cinematography.

Lancaster resurrected Norma Productions for *Birdman of Alcatraz*, which was co-produced by its screenwriter and by Stuart Millar (with Harold Hecht in-

volving himself for the last time with Burt in the role of executive producer). Initially, Charles Crichton began directing *Birdman*, but three weeks into filming he was replaced by John Frankenheimer (who, ironically, had wanted to do Stroud's story earlier on as a CBS television program before the film was even planned).

Though filming was not allowed in the actual prisons depicted in the movie, interior reconstructions were built for $150,000 at Columbia Studios. Twenty-seven sparrows were used to play the one called Runty. Not, in Burt's words, "a great success" with audiences after its release by United Artists, *Birdman of Alcatraz* is nonetheless one of the best films ever made to show the loneliness and despair of prison life.

REVIEWS: *Time:* "The strange case of Robert Stroud has been fashioned into an absorbing film that is deceptively calm and emotionally powerful."

New York Times: "Granted that Mr. Lancaster is the virtual king of all he surveys in this saga, he does, however, contribute an outstanding performance marked by a restraint, vitality and honesty that make it one of his best."

A Child Is Waiting

A Stanley Kramer Presentation   A Larcas Production   Released through United rtists   Released February 13, 1963   102 minutes   Black and White

CREDITS: John Cassavetes (Director); Stanley Kramer (Producer); Lindsley Parsons Jr. and Douglas Green (Assistant Directors); Philip Langner (Associate Producer); Abby Mann (Screenplay); Joseph LaShelle (Photography); Gene Fowler Jr. (Editor); Rudolph Sternad (Production Designer); James Speak (Sound); Ernest Gold (Music Score). Based on the *Studio One* teleplay by Abby Mann.

CAST: Burt Lancaster (Dr. Matthew Clark); Judy Garland (Jean Hansen); Gena Rowlands (Sophie Widdicombe); Steven Hill (Ted Widdicombe); Bruce Ritchey (Reuben Widdicombe); Gloria McGehee (Mattie); Paul Stewart (Goodman); Elizabeth Wilson (Miss Fogarty); Barbara Pepper (Miss Brown); John Marley (Holland); June Walker (Mrs. McDonald); Mario Gallo (Dr. Lombardi); Fred Draper (Dr. Sack); Lawrence Tierney (Douglas Benham).

SYNOPSIS: A child, Reuben Widdicombe, is left at the Crawthorne State Mental Hospital by his father. Dr. Matthew Clark, a psychologist, heads the institution, which also houses a school for retarded children.

Accepting a job as the new music teacher, Jean Hansen becomes emotionally involved with Reuben. She learns that his parents, Ted and Sophie, do not visit him. Dr. Clark is against Jean's doting on the boy, and she does not understand his firm attitude toward the boy. The doctor feels that Reuben should learn to reach his fullest potential (which apparently has been a struggle in the two years he has been institutionalized).

Jean contacts Sophie (without Dr. Clark's approval) on the pretense that Reuben is sick. Sophie, who is now divorced from Ted, comes to the institution. Both Sophie and the doctor are upset with Jean because they feel even more harm will be done if the boy sees his mother. When Reuben does see Sophie, he becomes hysterical and soon runs away.

The next day, Reuben is found safe and picked up at a police station by Dr. Clark. Ted contemplates removing the boy from the state institution and putting him into a private school.

When teaching her students a song for a Thanksgiving play, Jean treats Reuben more firmly and he listens. Ted decides not to take Reuben out of the institution when he sees his son's improvement interacting as one of the children in the play.

COMMENTARY: *A Child Is Waiting* reunited Judy Garland, Burt Lancaster, Abby Mann, Stanley Kramer, and others who were involved on *Judgment at Nuremberg*. Producer Kramer certainly found them, as well as director John Cassavetes, eager participants in relaying the problems and treatment of mentally retarded children. The story was originally written by Mann, as with *Nuremberg*, as a CBS television

A Child Is Waiting, with Judy Garland and Burt Lancaster.

show (this time, however, for *Studio One* on March 11, 1957). Kramer and Lancaster felt somewhat at odds with the sometimes unconventional filming techniques of the younger Cassavetes, and the subject itself was considered unconventional at the time.

Indeed, the theme of mental retardation was regarded as taboo even in the early 1960s. *A Child Is Waiting* was commendable, even daring, for its honesty, but it found little favor with audiences on its United Artists release in early 1963. Its true success was in the sensitive work with the children, most of whom were actual patients at the Pacific

State Hospital in Pomona, California (some filming actually even involved this institution, along with the facilities at Revue Studios, where *Nuremberg* was made).

Although not really retarded, Bruce Ritchey gave a very believable performance in the title role; his scenes with Miss Garland are especially poignant. The actress was going through an apparently troubled personal life during filming, yet she managed to give perhaps her finest dramatic performance without the benefit of her great singing ability.

As with the earlier social drama *The Young Savages*, Burt portrayed a solid professional man, this time a doctor, with a firm yet compassionate demeanor. Equally skilled dramatic performances were given by Gena Rowlands and Steven Hill as the distraught parents bewildered by love for their retarded son. While the abandonment of their child may be understood better in the period surrounding the film, in an era of political correctness it seems rather unconscionable.

REVIEWS: *America:* "The picture, in any event, is a remarkably moving and illuminating account of how enlightened institutional care can help retarded children to achieve their maximum human potential."

Saturday Review: "Miss Garland as a teacher, and Lancaster as head of the institution radiate a warmth so genuine that one is certain that the children are responding directly to them, not merely following some vaguely comprehended script."

The List of Adrian Messenger

A Joel Production   A Universal Picture   Released May 29, 1963   98 minutes   Black and White
CREDITS: John Huston (Director); Edward Lewis (Producer); Anthony Veiller (Screenplay); Joseph MacDonald (Photography); Terry Morse and Hugh Fowler (Editors); Alexander Golitzen, Stephen Grimes, and George Webb (Art Directors); Oliver Emert (Set Decorator); Bud Westmore (Make-up Creator); John Chambers, Nick Marcellino, and David Grayson (Make-up Artists); Jerry Goldsmith (Music Score). Based on the novel by Philip MacDonald.
CAST: George C. Scott (Anthony Gethryn); Dana Wynter (Lady Jocelyn Bruttenholm); Clive Brook (Marquis of Gleneyre); Herbert Marshall (Sir Wilfred Lucas); Jacques Roux (Raoul Le Borg); Bernard Archard (Inspector Pike); Gladys Cooper (Mrs. Karoudjian); Walter Anthony Huston (Derek); John Merivale (Adrian Messenger); Marcel Dalio (Max); Anita Sharp-Bolster (Shopkeeper); Roland De-Long (Carstairs); Alan Caillou (Inspector Seymour); John Huston (Huntsman); Noel Purcell (Farmer); Richard Peel (Sgt. Flood); Bernard Fox (Lynch); Nelson Welch (White); Tim Durant (Hunt Secretary); Barbara Morrison (Nurse); Jennifer Raine (Student Nurse); Constance Cavendish (Maid); Eric Heath (Orderly); Delphi Lawrence (Airport Stewardess). Guest Stars: Tony Curtis (Italian); Kirk Douglas (George Brougham); Burt Lancaster (Woman); Robert Mitchum (Jim Slattery); and Frank Sinatra (Gypsy).

SYNOPSIS: At the estate of the marquis of Gleneyre, writer Adrian Messenger gives a list of 11 men to a retired British intelligence man, Anthony Gethryn, who is then to fathom whether they are alive or dead. Messenger is killed in an airplane explosion, and Gethryn learns from a survivor, Raoul Le Borg, that sabotage was involved. A man in disguise had planted a bomb aboard the plane.

Gethryn and Le Borg work together with the authorities to find Messenger's murderer. All of the names on the list turn up dead. Their deaths, as with Messenger's, reportedly were attributed at first to strange accidents; ironically as well, all were once POWs together in Burma.

It is reasoned out that another POW, who informed on their escape plans, is the actual killer of all the others (using a variety of disguises). His name is George Brougham, and he is a relative of the Bruttenholm family, who owns the Gleneyre estate.

Brougham had killed to dispel any incriminating history in his plan to do away with the marquis's young grandson, Derek, and thus inherit the Gleneyre property. At the estate, he charmingly wins the affection of his relatives, but Gethryn realizes Brougham's motives and decides to bring the situation to a head.

Gethryn purposely lets Brougham know that a murder investigation is taking place (without revealing the murderer). Brougham then sets a trap to kill him. However, Gethryn is prepared; during a fox hunt, Brougham, in the guise of a farmer, is exposed and killed in his own trap.

COMMENTARY: Joel Productions, a film company set up by Kirk Douglas and producer Edward Lewis, was responsible for the filming of *The List of Adrian Messenger* (and Kirk enjoyed a principal role as the disarming villain of many disguises). Douglas invited Frank Sinatra, Robert Mitchum, Tony Curtis, and Burt Lancaster to make cameo appearances heavily made up; their engaging unmasking at the end was more the film's novelty than the actual solution to the murder mystery. The Bud Westmore latex masks were quite realistic, and Burt was most deceptive as a brazen woman protesting the fox hunting.

George C. Scott held the prominent role as the sleuth, and director John Huston made fine use of his favorite Irish countrysides. Written by Anthony Veiller (from a 1959 Philip MacDonald novel), *The List of Adrian Messenger*, despite the amusing distraction of its guest stars, still proved an amply entertaining mystery after its release by Universal in 1963. Jerry Goldsmith's music was delightfully spooky.

REVIEWS: *Newsweek:* "It's nice while it lasts; Huston has had a good time, and he lets his audience in on it."

Commonweal: "During much of the action, Tony Curtis, Kirk Douglas, Burt Lancaster, Robert Mitchum and Frank Sinatra wear molded masks and disguises so complete that one cannot tell who they are or even if they are all the same person."

The Leopard (Il Gattopardo)

A Titanus Production   A 20th Century–Fox Release   Released August 12, 1963   205 minutes (Italian version)   165 minutes (English version)   DeLuxe Color, CinemaScope

CREDITS: Luchino Visconti (Director); Goffredo Lombardo (Producer); Luchino Visconti, Suso Cecchi D'Amico, Pasquale Festa Campanile, Enrico Medioli, and Massimo Franciosa (Screenplay); Giuseppe Rotunno (Photography); Mario Serandrei (Editor); Mario Garbuglia (Art Director); Giorgio Pes and Laudomia Hercolani (Set Decorators); Piero Tosi (Costumes); Alberto De Rossi (Make-up); Franco Ferrara (Music Director); Nino Rota (Music Score). Based on a novel, *Il Gattopardo,* by Giuseppe di Lampedusa.

CAST: Burt Lancaster (Prince Don Fabrizio Salina); Alain Delon (Tancredi); Claudia Cardinale (Angelica Sedara); Rina Morelli (Maria Stella); Paolo Stoppa (Don Calogero Sedara); Romolo Valli (Father Pirrone); Lucilla Morlacchi (Concetta); Serge Reggiani (Don Ciccio Tumeo); Ida Galli (Carolina); Ottavia Piccolo (Caterina); Pierro Clementi (Francesco Paolo); Carlo Valenzano (Paolo); Anna-Marie Bottini (Governess Dombreuil); Mario Girotti (Count Cavriaghi); Leslie French (Chevally); Olimpia Cavallo (Mariannina); Marino Mase (Tutor); Sandra Chistolini (Youngest Daughter); Brook Fuller (Little Prince); Giuliano Gemma (Garibaldino General); Giovanni Melisendi (Don Onofrio Rotolo); Howard Nelson-Rubien (Don Diego); Lola Bracciani (Donna Margherita); Ivo Garrani (Colonel Pallavicino).

Burt Lancaster and Alain Delon in *The Leopard*.

SYNOPSIS: In Palermo, Sicily, in 1860, Prince Don Fabrizio Salina (who represents the ruling class at the time) prays with his family in their palace. That evening, the prince goes into the city and spends time with a woman who is not his wife.

The next morning, Tancredi, the prince's nephew, goes off to war. He fights with Garibaldi's Red Shirts against the Bourbons in the revolution that will reorganize Sicily and Italy. This change will bring the middle class to rise above the aristocrats and create a new order.

When Tancredi returns from the war an officer, he joins the prince and his family for a time at their summer home in Donnafugata. A priest gives praise to the prince. Tancredi is soon acquainted with the mayor's daughter, Angelica, who has returned home from schooling in Florence. Her beauty proves intoxicating to Tancredi, as does her father's wealth.

Mayor Don Calogero who represents the new ruling class and Prince Fabrizio agree that a marriage between Tancredi and Angelica will unite the old order with the new. Meanwhile, Tancredi has returned to the revolution.

When he comes home again, Tancredi, having shown disfavor with the power collapse generated by the rebel

Garibaldi, is now a soldier in the Royal Army. He gives Angelica an engagement ring.

Eventually in the prince's life, a friend, Chevally, implores him to accept a position as a senator in the new kingdom. Refusing, however, the prince speaks of Sicily's state of turmoil and his wish for eternal sleep.

A grand ball is held at the estate of Don Diego. Although delighted to dance with Angelica, the prince is saddened by the somewhat bawdy affair which has brought the two classes of people together. He is all too aware that only the awe and color of his once privileged class remains. Later, walking home through the streets, he kneels in prayer to the morning star and acknowledges his own death wish.

In *The Leopard* as **Don Fabrizio.**

COMMENTARY: Italian filmmaker Luchino Visconti assuredly sought a film masterpiece from Giuseppe di Lampedusa's 1958 novel, *Il Gattopardo* (its English translation in 1960, *The Leopard*, was rendered by Archibald Colquhoun). Though the novel had enjoyed international acclaim, the film version in 1963 did not. The epic splendor of a bygone time in nineteenth-century Sicily (during an actual period in history called the *Risorgimento*), and of a particular nobleman's melancholy for his faded majesty (di Lampedusa based this aristocrat on his own great-grandfather), was faithfully presented in the motion picture. However, it was received far differently in the two versions made (an Italian one and a shorter English-language one).

Abroad, *The Leopard* was honored with the Palme d'Or (the main prize) at the 1963 Cannes Film Festival; it was also chosen one of the Best Foreign Language Films of the year by the National Board of Review. Its reception with audiences in Europe was regarded as successful. Under Visconti's meticulous direction (with four others, he was involved on the screenplay), and Giuseppe Rotunno's Technicolor photography, the film was beautifully realized (despite its length) for the foreign market.

The dazzling visuals were somewhat impaired for the English version because of the use of lower-quality prints in DeLuxe Color. Also hampered was the dubbing of the foreign performers (an arduous task entrusted by Visconti to Burt Lancaster, whose own voice was dubbed in the Italian version). Although the English version was edited by 40 minutes, the attention to detail (as well as the problems with dubbing) proved too exasperating for audiences, and it was not a financial success. Piero Tosi did earn the film an Academy Award nomination for Color Costume Design.

Producer Goffredo Lombardo had initially needed a major movie star for the film to receive financial support from its distributor, 20th Century–Fox. Lancaster was interested; although Visconti had some misgivings at first, he agreed to the actor's casting as the prince after seeing *Judgment at Nuremberg* (as with this earlier film, Laurence Olivier was to do the part but was committed elsewhere). Burt received mixed reviews for his reserved performance, yet he seemed physically perfect as the renowned nobleman caught in a changing world.

Actual locations in Sicily were utilized to create this world, including Palermo's Gangi Palace for the climactic ball. It is at this ball that Lancaster's prince looks into a mirror and cries over past memories. The aura of vulnerability that graced many of his performances perhaps was never more tenderly expressed than in *The Leopard*. He was given wonderful support by Alain Delon and Claudia Cardinale, in their prime as the young couple in love.

REVIEWS: *New Yorker:* "It has been criticized as being too beautiful, as having the 'ennui of perfect beauty,' as seeming like 'an animated painting,' and as being dominated by 'taste, the very best taste,' as if these were all cinematographic mistakes."

Commonweal: "Under Visconti's direction, Burt Lancaster is excellent in this lead role, displaying a sensitivity and strength he has never shown before."

Seven Days in May

A Seven Arts–Joel Production A Paramount Picture Released February 20, 1964 120 minutes Black and White
CREDITS: John Frankenheimer (Director); Edward Lewis (Producer); Rod Serling (Screenplay); Ellsworth Fredericks (Photography); Ferris Webster (Editor); Bill Brame (Assistant Editor); Cary Odell (Art Director); Phil Jeffries (Assistant Art Director); Edward G. Boyle (Set Decorator); Wes Jeffries, Sid Mintz, and Angela Alexander (Wardrobe); Art Jones (Make-up); Joe Edmondson (Sound); Jerry Goldsmith (Music Score). Based on the novel by Fletcher Knebel and Charles W. Bailey II.
CAST: Burt Lancaster (Gen. James M. Scott); Kirk Douglas (Col. Martin Casey); Fredric March (President Jordan Lyman); Ava Gardner (Eleanor Holbrook); Edmond O'Brien (Senator Raymond Clark); Martin Balsam (Paul Girard); George Macready (Christopher Todd); Whit Bissell (Senator Prentice); Hugh Marlowe (Harold McPherson); Bart Burns (Arthur Corwin); Richard Anderson (Col. Murdock); Jack Mullaney (Lt. Hough); Andrew Duggan (Col. Henderson); John Larkin (Col. Broderick); Malcolm Atterbury (White House Physician); Helen Kleeb (Esther Townsend); John Houseman (Admiral Barnswell); Collette Jackson (Bar Girl).

SYNOPSIS: During a week in May, two groups of protesters are picketing in front of the White House. One group is in favor of a nuclear disarmament treaty recently concluded by President Jordan Lyman with the Soviet Union; the other group, being followers of a certain General Scott, is against the treaty. The American military system is against the treaty, and the poll reflects that 71 percent of the population in the United States feels the same way.

A marine colonel, Martin Casey, stumbles onto a wild scheme in which air force general James Scott—the chairman of the Joint Chiefs of Staff—and several other military officers conspire to overthrow their government and set up a military rule. Although he is Scott's aide, Casey feels a duty to uphold the doctrines of the U.S. Constitution.

Casey informs the president of the proposed plan. Finding the story incredible, Lyman nonetheless sends Senator Ray Clark to Texas to investigate the existence of a secret military base. Presidential aide Paul Girard manages to get a signed confession from an Admiral Barnswell. Before the confession can be delivered to Lyman, Girard is killed in an airplane crash.

Given the thankless job of informer, Colonel Casey acquires a packet of incriminating love letters from Scott's former mistress, Eleanor Holbrook. When General Scott is called to the White House, he refuses Lyman's order to resign. The president cannot bring himself to use the letters as blackmail against the general.

President Lyman stands firm, although Scott thinks he is weak. At a press conference, Lyman asks for the resignations of the general and his supporters. When the admiral's confession is found in the plane wreckage, Scott realizes then that he must resign.

COMMENTARY: In 1962, the novel *Seven Days in May* was written by Fletcher Knebel and Charles W. Bailey II; a political thriller of immense popularity, it ran almost a year as a bestseller. Kirk Douglas was taken with the fictitious yet plausible theme of a military conspiracy and involved his production outfit, Joel (with producer

Seven Days in May **publicity pose with Burt Lancaster, Fredric March, and Kirk Douglas.**

Edward Lewis), on the film project. Rod Serling's suspenseful screenplay was as spine-tingling as the book.

Director John Frankenheimer was at first hesitant to do the picture when Burt Lancaster came aboard because of their arguing during the filming of *Birdman of Alcatraz*. Ironically, it was Kirk, not Burt, whom Frankenheimer had problems with on *Seven Days in May*; apparently Lancaster was given his choice of the two top roles by Douglas, who felt the renegade general was the better part.

Lancaster's portrayal of the general reflected a reserved fanaticism that made his performance an utterly frightening one because he felt his actions were the best thing for the United States. Actually, Douglas had the more amiable role as the colonel simply caught between two opposing sides who must decide where his loyalties lie.

The top-notch cast headed by Kirk and Burt included Fredric March, Ava Gardner, and Edmond O'Brien. For his colorful performance as an alcoholic bloodhound of a United States senator, O'Brien received an Academy Award nomination for Best Supporting Actor. The film's dramatic highlight was the showdown between March's sturdy commander in chief and Lancaster, both actors readily exhausting themselves by the tense confrontation.

John F. Kennedy, then president of the United States when filming began in the spring of 1963, openly approved of the picture being made and even allowed the opening scene to be filmed in Washington, D.C., outside the White House. The Paramount sets in Hollywood were made to resemble the White House interiors. A second Oscar nomination was given to Cary Odell and Edward G. Boyle in the category of Black and White Art Direction—Set Decoration. After its release by Paramount in 1964, *Seven Days in May*, as an absorbing entertainment with a valid message about the threat of the nuclear age, proved popular with critics and public alike.

REVIEWS: *Commonweal:* "Handsomely produced by Edward Lewis with an outstanding cast and some fine photography of Washington and other locales, and excellently directed by John Frankenheimer, who builds up a tremendous suspense along with all the realistic touches, *Seven Days* succeeds in giving its farfetched story an it-could-happen-here tone."

New York Times: "And all the actors in it—Fredric March as the President, Burt Lancaster as the Air Force general, Kirk Douglas as a vigilant colonel in the Marines who suspects something fishy is happening and first reports it to the President, Martin Balsam as the President's press secretary, Edmond O'Brien as a stalwart Senator, Ava Gardner as a Washington hostess and several others—are assortedly superb."

The Train

A Jules Bricken Presentation A Co-production of Les Productions Artistes Associes/Ariane/Dear Films Released through United Artists   Released March 17, 1965   133 minutes   Black and White

CREDITS: John Frankenheimer (Director); Jules Bricken (Producer); Bernard Farrell (Associate Producer); Franklin Coen, Frank Davis, and Walter Bernstein (Screenplay); Jean Tournier and Walter Wottiz (Photography); David Bretherton and Gabriel Rongier (Editors); Willy Holt (Production Designer); Jean Zay (Wardrobe);

Georges Bauban (Make-up); Lee Zavitz (Special Effects); Maurice Jarre (Music Score). From a story by Franklin Coen and Frank Davis based on the book *Le Front de l'art* by Rose Valland.

CAST: Burt Lancaster (Labiche); Paul Scofield (Colonel von Waldheim); Jeanne Moreau (Christine); Michel Simon (Papa Boule); Suzanne Flon (Miss Villard); Wolfgang Preiss (Herren); Richard Munch (Von Lubitz); Albert Remy (Didont); Charles Millot (Pesquet); Jacques Marin (Jacques); Paul Bonifas (Spinet); Jean Bouchaud (Schmidt); Donald O'Brien (Schwartz); Jean-Pierre Zola (Octave); Art Brauss (Pilzer); Jean-Claude Bercq (Major); Howard Vernon (Dietrich); Bernard La Jarrige (Bernard); Louis Falavigna (Railroad Worker); Christian Fuin (Robert); Roger Lumont (Engineer Officer); Gerard Buhr (Corporal); Christian Remy (Tauber); Max From (Gestapo Chief); Jean-Jacques LeComte (Lieutenant); Jacques Blot (Hubert).

SYNOPSIS: In 1944, during World War II, German Colonel von Waldheim confiscates the beautiful and valuable collection of paintings from a museum in Paris. He plans to ship them by train to Berlin, but the museum's curator, Miss Villard, implores the French railroad to help keep the artwork in France. Railroad inspector Labiche refuses to risk human lives for art, and he assigns the train's direct route to Germany to engineer Papa Boule.

The old engineer, sympathetic with the cultural importance of the paintings, sabotages the train. Colonel von Waldheim discovers the act and has Papa shot despite Labiche's objection. Ordered to drive the train, Labiche's affection for Papa makes him decide to keep it out of Berlin.

Lancaster in *The Train* as Labiche.

Part of the French Resistance, Labiche is aided by other members, including friends Didont and Pesquet. Colonel von Waldheim is tricked into believing the train is on course; actually it travels in a circle back to its starting point and crashes into another train purposely placed in the way. Trying to escape, Labiche is shot in the leg, and Pesquet is killed.

A woman, Christine, hides Labiche. Didont joins him and others to paint the top of the art train to safeguard it during a plane bombardment. When the Germans see them, Didont is also killed.

Labiche temporarily waylays the train by planting an explosive on the track. Ultimately he removes a section of track spikes, which forces the train to derail. A group of hostages aboard are then ordered shot by von Waldheim.

A truck convoy passing the disabled train picks up the colonel's soldiers, but there is no room for the paintings. Colonel von Waldheim stays behind to confront Labiche and is killed. Labiche limps away, leaving the paintings in crates strewn alongside the train.

COMMENTARY: After *Seven Days in May*, Burt Lancaster was eager to film *The Train*, and he convinced John Frankenheimer to direct. Initially, Arthur Penn was the director, but relations didn't work out with him and Lancaster or producer Jules Bricken; until Frankenheimer came aboard, associate producer Bernard Farrell helmed the film.

Frankenheimer enlisted two uncredited writers, Howard Infell and Ned Young, to help with the script. Rose Valland's 1961 book, *Le Front de l'art* (which was based on an actual incident in World War II France), was the basis for the story by credited writers Frank Davis and Franklin Coen. While Walter Bernstein also worked on the screenplay, only Coen and Davis were listed on the film's one Academy Award nomination for, ironically, Story And Screenplay—Written Directly for the Screen.

The Train, like *Seven Days in May*, was immensely suspenseful with a documentary feel, although it smacked of high adventure. Lancaster's last feature film (in which he starred) to use black and white photography, it was highly atmospheric in duplicating a dark, desperate picture of the war in Europe of 1944. Made in France, the production was actually allowed by the French Railway System to use train engines and no-longer-in-use cars for the thrilling collisions. Cinematographers Jean Tournier and Walter Wottiz, along with special effects expert Lee Zavitz, were not nominated for Oscars, but they easily could have been.

Lancaster had some regrets for not adopting a French accent to his Resistance fighter, but his energy was downright remarkable. Frankenheimer even admitted to being amazed by the actor's physical daring; at one point, Burt hurt his knee from a jump off a moving train, and the resulting limp was integrated into the story. Paul Scofield displayed his superb acting ability with his exacting German officer. Jeanne Moreau and Michel Simon headed up a strong contingent of French performers, all of whom were quite touching as courageous souls. Never lost amid the sometimes bedlam of the drama and action was the value of human life over that of the historic artwork.

A joint American-French-Italian effort, *The Train* was made for $5.8 million. The domestic earnings, after its

1965 release by United Artists, tallied $3.4 million, but the worldwide release made it a box office winner. The film was Frankenheimer and Lancaster's most commercial together (*Birdman* was their most prestigious).

REVIEWS: *America:* "The film that director John Frankenheimer has assembled around this incident is extraordinarily good in many of its parts but rather disappointing as a whole. Its greatest virtue is an almost overpowering physical realism."

Saturday Review: "Burt Lancaster is perhaps the only American star both physically and psychologically endowed to play the hard, knowledgeable and perdurable railroad man."

The Hallelujah Trail

A Mirisch-Kappa Picture   Released through United Artists   Released July 1, 1965   165 minutes   Technicolor   Ultra Panavision   Cinerama
CREDITS: John Sturges (Director and Producer); Robert E. Relyea (Associate Producer); John Gay (Screenplay); Robert Surtees (Photography); Ferris Webster (Editor); Cary Odell (Art Director); Hoyle Barrett (Set Decorator); Edith Head (Costumes); Wes Jeffries (Wardrobe); Robert Schiffer (Makeup); A. Paul Pollard (Special Effects); Robert Martin (Sound); Ernie Sheldon (Songs); Leo Shuken, Jack Hayes, and Fred Steiner (Orchestrations); Elmer Bernstein (Music Score). Based on the Bill Gulick novel *The Hallelujah Trail*.
CAST: Burt Lancaster (Col. Thadeus Gearhart); Lee Remick (Cora Massingale); Jim Hutton (Capt. Paul Slater); Pamela Tiffin (Louise Gearhart); Donald Pleasence (Oracle Jones); Brian Keith (Frank Wallingham); Martin Landau (Chief Walks-Stooped-Over); John Anderson (Sgt. Buell); Tom Stern (Kevin O'Flaherty); Robert J. Wilke (Five Barrels); Jerry Gatlin (Brother-in-law #1); Larry Duran (Brother-in-law #2); James Burk (Elks-Runner); Dub Taylor (Clayton Howell); John McKee (Rafe Pike); Helen Kleeb (Henrietta); Noam Pitlik (Interpreter); Carl Pitti (Phillips); Bill Williams (Brady); Marshall Reed (Carter); Caroll Adams (Simmons); Whit Bissell (Hobbs); Hope Summers (Mrs. Hasselrad); Ted Markland (Bandmaster); Buff Brady (Bilkins); Bing Russell (Horner); Billy Benedict (Simpson); Karla Most (Mary Ann); Elaine Martone (Loretta); Carroll Henry (Sergeant); Val Avery (Bartender). Narration by John Dehner.

SYNOPSIS: In 1867, the men of Denver, Colorado, are urged by prophet Oracle Jones to replenish their whiskey supply with the advent of a hard winter. Frank Wallingham agrees to deliver 40 wagons of liquor to Denver with military protection from army commander Colonel Thadeus Gearhart at Fort Russell. Wallingham wants an escort because of the threat of hostile Indians.

The colonel assigns Captain Paul Slater to escort Wallingham's wagon train to Denver; meanwhile, a temperance leader, Cora Massingale, has the women at the fort in an uproar over whiskey. Slater is in love with Gearhart's daughter, Louise, who supports Cora. Gearhart is coerced into taking the ladies to Denver to protest the whiskey. A band of Indians are after the whiskey, and the men from Denver, led by Oracle, set out to meet the wagon train.

Eventually all parties collide in what becomes known as the "Battle at Whiskey Hills." Unbelievably, not a soul is killed.

After the Indians kidnap several of the ladies in exchange for some whiskey, Gearhart agrees to let them have ten wagons. Wallingham is furious, but Gearhart takes full responsibility. Cora believes she has been wrong with her

The Hallelujah Trail, with John Anderson and Burt Lancaster (left to right).

interference, seeing that she may be injuring the colonel's career; they soon become fond of each other over a few sips of whiskey.

Oracle and Frank mark a trail through Quicksand Bottoms to speed up the trip to Denver. Told that the Indians are being given ten wagons of champagne, the ladies trick them into stampeding away. The champagne explodes in the frenzy, and the Indians agree to go home. The rest of Wallingham's wagons are lost in the quicksand after the ladies switch the markers.

Staking a claim to Quicksand Bottoms, Frank and Oracle wait for the whiskey kegs to bob to the surface. Back at the fort, Paul and Louise are married, as are Thadeus and Cora.

COMMENTARY: *The Hallelujah Trail* was originally released by United Artists in 1965 on a reserved-seat basis with an intermission. However, it did poorly; the outlandish length was edited, and it was released generally. Designed as a spoof of western epics and as a rousing family entertainment, the film fared unsuccessfully at the box office anyway it was put.

Burt Lancaster wanted to do what he hoped was a popular extravaganza, yet the comic capers proved more cumbersome than funny (although there were some nice moments). The 1963 Bill Gulick novel *Hallelujah Trail* was the basis for John Gay's screenplay. The big, concave Cinerama screens initially used for the film actually enhanced the plodding escapades (there was some striking footage filmed in Gallup, New Mexico). John Sturges directed and produced with a spirited hand, but the sometimes slapstick comedy was not his forte. The especially winsome score by Elmer Bernstein and songs by Ernie Sheldon may have been the most entertaining features.

The all-star cast really seemed to enjoy themselves with the show. Lee Remick and Burt were amusing, but rather prim and proper in their respective roles as the fiery temperance leader and crusty colonel. However justified their actions, perhaps they would have been better to follow the sillier behavior of their co-stars. Certainly Jim Hutton and Brian Keith were right at home with the broad comedy; usually quite reserved as an actor, Donald Pleasence was a real surprise as an old kook.

REVIEWS: *Newsweek:* "*The Hallelujah Trail* could well have entered movie annals as the first laughless comedy."

Time: "Lancaster, a commanding presence as always, looks permanently flabbergasted over his first venture into an out-and-out farce, though his attitude seems appropriate to the movie's funniest scene—pondering strategy after a fierce battle waged in a blinding sandstorm, he finds that there hasn't been a single casualty on any side."

The Professionals

A Pax Enterprises Production   A Columbia Picture   Released November 2, 1966   117 minutes   Technicolor Panavision

CREDITS: Richard Brooks (Director, Producer, and Screenplay); Tom Shaw (Assistant Director); Conrad Hall (Photography); Peter Zinner (Editor); Edward S. Haworth (Art Director); Frank Tuttle (Set Decorator); Jack Martell (Wardrobe); Robert Schiffer (Make-up); Jackie Bone (Hairdresser); Willis Cook (Special Effects); William Randall Jr. and Jack Haynes (Sound); Maurice Jarre (Music Score). Based on the novel *A Mule for the Marquesa* by Frank O'Rourke.

CAST: Burt Lancaster (Bill Dolworth); Lee Marvin (Henry Rico Fardan); Robert Ryan (Hans Ehrengard); Jack Palance (Jesus Raza); Claudia Cardinale (Maria Grant); Ralph Bellamy (J.W. Grant); Woody Strode (Jacob Sharp); Joe DeSantis (Ortega); Rafael Bertrand (Fierro); Jorge Martinez de Hoyos (Padilla); Marie Gomez (Chiquita); Jose Chavez and Carlos Romero (Revolutionaries); Vaughn Taylor (Banker); Eddie Little Sky (Captive Indian).

SYNOPSIS: Oil tycoon J.W. Grant hires four men for $10,000 each to rescue his kidnapped wife, Maria. She is being held in a Mexican stronghold by a bandit named Jesus Raza. Weapons tactician Henry Fardan is the leader of the four—the others are horseman Hans Ehrengard, tracker Jacob Sharp, and dynamiter Bill Dolworth. They are confronted with the elements of nature and by bandits during the trek into Mexico. Dolworth is captured by bandits and about to be killed until his partners rescue him.

From a hidden viewpoint, the four observe Raza and his gang attack a Mexican military train and kill every soldier aboard. Raza is caught up in the revolution against the Mexican government, not as a bandit but as a rebel. The professionals plan their attack on Raza.

Under cover of darkness, Fardan and Dolworth are able to sneak into Raza's camp and grab Maria when Sharp creates a diversion. It is revealed that Maria and Raza are lovers, and she

Top: The Professionals, with Burt Lancaster, Lee Marvin, Robert Ryan, and Woody Strode. *Bottom:* Burt Lancaster and Claudia Cardinale in *The Professionals*.

protects him when Dolworth tries to shoot him. But she is forced to go with the four men.

Ehrengard, keeping the train ready for a quick getaway, has been captured by Raza's men; he is wounded breaking free. Dolworth threatens to kill Maria unless the rebels let them all go. The men and Maria do escape on the train. When Raza finally catches up to it, he finds the train has been abandoned.

The professionals seal a canyon passage with dynamite and venture on into the desert on horseback. In another canyon, Dolworth stays behind to hold off Raza to allow Fardan and the others to fulfill the contract and bring Maria back to her husband. Raza is wounded in the ensuing fight with Dolworth, and a few of his followers are killed, including a female revolutionary named Chiquita.

Maria is taken safely to the border by Fardan, Sharp, and Ehrengard. Dolworth joins them and with him is Raza. Grant orders an aide to kill the rebel, but the professionals stop it. They know that Maria, trapped in an arranged marriage, left on her own to be with Raza; a ransom note initially sent to Grant was a ploy to extort money for the revolution. Grant himself turns out to be the actual kidnapper. The professionals, losing their contract payment, let Raza and Maria return to Mexico.

COMMENTARY: *The Professionals* was Burt Lancaster's most popular film of the 1960s. One of the great western adventures of any decade, it grossed $8.8 million at the box office after a 1966 release from Columbia Pictures. A pair of Academy Award nominations went to Richard Brooks for Best Director and for Screenplay—Based on Material from Another Medium. Another Oscar nom-

ination went to Conrad Hall for Color Cinematography.

The 1964 Frank O'Rourke novel *A Mule for the Marquesa* was the source for the riveting action of this film. Nevada's Valley of Fire State Park supplied a good deal of its breathtaking visuals with the backgrounds illuminating a powerhouse cast. Many of the scenes, played against Maurice Jarre's superb score, leave unforgettable impressions.

As the rogue with a twinkle in his eye, Lancaster gave a terrific performance with the same kind of glorious abandon as Vallo the pirate, Joe Erin the outlaw, and Starbuck and Elmer Gantry the con men. In fact, Burt even referred to his lusty character of Bill Dolworth as "Elmer Gantry out West"; it perhaps was made more so by joining forces again with *Gantry*'s director/writer Brooks (who was also listed as producer of *The Professionals*).

When Richard Brooks first interested Burt in the western, the actor thought it would be as the leader of the adventurers (the role that Lee Marvin played). However, Brooks felt Burt had too stiff of an upper lip as an authority figure (which was especially proven in *The Hallelujah Trail*), and so convinced him to do the flashier part of the dynamiter (a character actually not in O'Rourke's novel).

Despite the scene stealing that often occurred whenever Burt was on screen, *The Professionals* was first and foremost an ensemble piece. Marvin and Woody Strode, Robert Ryan, and Jack Palance stood their ground with Lancaster, oozing machismo, yet they all had degrees of vulnerability. The masculinity that prevailed was especially given credence by placing the action around the quest for the overwhelmingly sensuous lady in distress played by Claudia Cardinale.

REVIEWS: *Newsweek:* "Richard Brooks, who wrote the screenplay, shoots high and often hits clouds. Richard Brooks, who directed, fires away at stunning scenery, good faces and great action, and hits the bull's-eye almost every time. The best marksman in the cast is Burt Lancaster, who is one of four adventurers commissioned to rescue Claudia Cardinale from Jack Palance's band of Mexican revolutionists."

Life: "The result is pure joy for those who first learned to love the movies while riding vicariously down long dusty trails in pursuit of the bad guy and in defense of honor. *The Professionals* is smartly paced, tough-minded and pleasingly acted; it has no real depth, but it has the breadth of all outdoors."

The Scalphunters

A Levy, Gardner, Laven and Roland Kibbee Presentation   From Norlan Productions-Bristol Pictures   Released through United Artists   Released April 2, 1968   103 minutes   DeLuxe Color   Panavision
CREDITS: Sydney Pollack (Director); Jules Levy, Arthur Gardner, and Arnold Laven (Producers); Charles Scott Jr. and Kevin Donnelly (Assistant Directors); William Norton (Screenplay); Duke Callaghan and Richard Moore (Photography); John Woodcock (Editor); Frank Arrigo (Art Director); Joe Drury (Costumes); Gary Liddiard (Make-up); Herman Townsley (Special Effects); Jesus Gonzalez Gancy (Sound); Alex Ruiz (Choreography); Elmer Bernstein (Music Score).
CAST: Burt Lancaster (Joe Bass); Shelley Winters (Kate); Telly Savalas (Jim Howie); Ossie Davis (Joseph Winfield Lee); Armando Silvestre (Two Crows); Dan Vadis (Yuma); Dabney Coleman (Jed); Paul Picerni (Frank); Nick Cravat, John Epper, Jack Williams, Chuck Roberson, Tony Epper, Agapito Roldan, Gregorio Acosta, and Marco Antonio Arzate (Scalphunters'); Angela Rodriguez, Amelia Rivera, and Alicia del Lago (Scalphunters' Women); Nestor Dominguez, Francisco Oliva, Benjamin Ramos, Enrique Tello, Raul Martinez, Jose Martinez, Rodolfo Toledo, Jose Salas, Cuco Velazquez, Alejandro Lopez, Raul Hernandez, and Pedro Aguilar (Kiowas).

SYNOPSIS: Before the American Civil War, trapper Joe Bass comes out of the mountains with fur pelts. He is ambushed by a band of Kiowa Indians; stealing his pelts, they leave him a kidnapped black man named Joseph Winfield Lee. Taking Lee with him, Bass chases after the Indians to get the furs back.

Finding whiskey hidden in the furs, the Indians become drunk. A gang of scalphunters (collecting Indian scalps for their bounty) attack and kill all the Kiowas except for Two Crows, the chief. The scalphunters, led by Jim Howie, take the fur pelts. When Bass goes after these scavengers, Lee is captured by them and made a servant for Howie's mistress, Kate.

Bass tries sneaking into the enemy camp, sniping, landslides, and poisoning a waterhole to get his furs back. Slowly, he kills off the scalphunters.

When Howie abandons the packhorse with the pelts, Bass makes a move to collect his goods, but is surprised by the scalphunter and knocked down. Stopping Howie from killing Bass, Lee kills the scavenger.

Having always felt that Lee was inferior, Bass gets into a fistfight with him; ending up in a mud hole, both men are soon the same color. The remaining scalphunters are killed off by another group of Indians led by Two Crows. The

Fighting in *The Scalphunters* with Ossie Davis and Burt Lancaster.

Indians not only take the furs but also kidnap Kate. Realizing Lee's equality now as a man, Bass mounts his horse, offers him a hand up, and the two men slowly ride after the Indians.

COMMENTARY: *The Scalphunters* was last of the four films that Burt Lancaster needed to pay off his share of the debts owed to United Artists when he was part of the production team of Hecht-Hill-Lancaster (the other films were *The Young Savages*, *Birdman of Alcatraz*, and *The Train*). Made in Mexico (locations included the Durango area used for the final HHL picture starring Burt, *The Unforgiven*), *The Scalphunters* was produced by the outfit of Levy-Gardner-Laven and also involved a new production company set up by Lancaster called Norlan. The script was acquired by Burt from William Norton.

It was apparent from the opening credits with Burt jumping and smiling in an amusing series of animated shots to Elmer Bernstein's jolly score that *The Scalphunters* was destined to be enjoyable. Sydney Pollack directed the western tale with a flair for both the action and humor; its winsome adventure, however, received only a modest reception from audiences after its release in 1968.

Lancaster still brought back happy memories, as he did with the well-received *The Professionals*, of his earlier tongue-in-cheek and athletic heroes. His Joe Bass is a delightful character cut from the folklore dimensions of Pecos Bill or Paul Bunyan. Shelley Winters and Telly Savalas were in on the fun, which was a bit broad at times yet moved at a better clip than the antics in *The Hallelujah Trail*. Look closely and you'll recognize old circus pal Nick Cravat as one of the scalphunters.

Not lost in the film's novelty was the rather daring civil rights theme, although it may have been handled just a bit too heavy-handed. Nonetheless, costar Ossie Davis (who stole nearly the whole movie with his very engaging portrait of an enterprising if bumbling runaway slave) paid Burt a compliment with a reflection that only someone of his caliber could have gotten the subject matter off the ground.

REVIEWS: *Senior Scholastic:* "This film touches all bases without slowing down once, and makes a rousing home run. It takes important and weighty themes like brotherhood (freedom loving trapper forced to accept real meaning of freedom from an ex-slave) and individuality (using ingenuity and resourcefulness, lone trapper defeats gang of scoundrels), and incorporates them into a fast paced Western."

New York Times: "Mr. Lancaster's hair grows as straight up and free as alfalfa. It has, in fact, a kind of exuberance that matches his performance which, direct and robust, gives unifying style to otherwise ramshackle, eclectic moviemaking."

The Swimmer

A Columbia Picture and Horizon-Dover Picture Presentation Released May 15, 1968 94 minutes Technicolor **CREDITS:** Frank Perry (Director);

Frank Perry and Roger Lewis (Producers); Michael Herzberg (Assistant Director); Sam Spiegel (Executive Producer); Eleanor Perry (Screenplay); David L. Quaid (Photography); Michael Nebia (Additional Photography); Sidney Katz, Carl Lerner, and Pat Somerset (Editors); Peter Dohanos (Art Director); Anna Hill Johnstone (Wardrobe); Elizabeth Stewart (Swimwear); John Jiras (Make-up); Leo Shuken and Jack Hayes (Orchestrations); Marvin Hamlisch (Music Score). Based on a story by John Cheever.

CAST: Burt Lancaster (Ned Merrill); Janet Landgard (Julie Hooper); Janice Rule (Shirley Abbott); Diana Van Der Vlis (Helen Westerhazy); Tony Bickley (Donald Westerhazy); Marge Champion (Peggy Forsburgh); Richard McMurray (Stu Forsburgh); Kim Hunter (Betty Graham); Charles Drake (Howard Graham); Diana Muldaur (Cynthia); Keri Oleson (Vernon); Bernie Hamilton (Chauffeur); Nancy Cushman (Mrs. Halloran); House Jameson (Mr. Halloran); Michael Kearney (Kevin Gilmartin); Cornelia Otis Skinner (Mrs. Hammar); Louise Troy (Grace Biswanger); Dolph Sweet (Henry Biswanger); Joan Rivers (Joan); John Garfield Jr. (Ticket Seller); Jan Miner (Lillian Hunsacker); Bill Fiore (Howie Hunsacker); Rose Gregorio (Sylvia Finney); Jimmy Joyce (Jack Finney); Alva Celauro (Muffie).

SYNOPSIS: One summer day, a man in swimming trunks appears at a large house and announces to some friends that he is swimming home. The journey covers eight river miles with various pools along the way. The man, Ned Merrill, calls it the Lucinda River, named after his wife. Everyone seems impressed by Ned's charm and energy.

At another home, Ned convinces a teenage girl, Julie Hooper, to join him. He recognizes her as a previous babysitter for his two daughters, who he says are home playing tennis. Julie admits to once having had a crush on him. When Ned then becomes amorous towards her, she runs away.

The Swimmer, with Burt Lancaster and Diana Van Der Vlis.

He comes to an estate where the owners, two nudists, greet him with some apprehension. Ned asks that his name be added to a list for an upcoming engagement, but they scratch his name off after he leaves.

Climbing into an empty pool, Ned and a boy named Kevin Gilmartin pretend they are swimming by walking along the bottom. Ned believes Kevin would jump from the diving board, although the child does know better.

Crashing a pool party, Ned gets into a squabble over a food wagon he claims belongs to his wife. The owners inform him that his wife sold it and they tell him to leave.

Shirley Abbott's home is on Ned's route, and she is displeased at seeing him—she is his former mistress. When

he remarks that they had a good time the year before in Toronto, Shirley tells him that she had not gone there at all. Ned makes a desperate pass at her, and she treats him bitterly.

Ned crosses a highway to get to a public pool. A group of people there ridicule him and state that his daughters loathed him. Hurt by this, he runs off.

It is raining as Ned comes to another house. The front door is locked and it is empty inside. He slumps against the door in tears because it is his own home.

COMMENTARY: John Cheever originally wrote *The Swimmer*, a 13-page story that appeared in *The New Yorker* magazine, in 1964. It revealed a modern middle-class man's mental breakdown. Frank and Eleanor

Perry, then married independent film-makers, were quite eager to do the film version. Although he directed (and co-produced with Roger Lewis) and she wrote the script, it was another inde-pendent, Sam Spiegel, who had more control as executive producer.

The Perrys' work seemed espe-cially sensitive to the rather bizarre drama that was being played out. Filmed in 1966 (actually before *The Scalphunters*) in Westport, Connecticut, *The Swimmer* was released later. It had been shelved for nearly two years be-cause Spiegel was displeased with the end result. In the interim, a key se-quence was even reshot—the episode between the swimmer and his ex-mis-tress—and an uncredited Sydney Pol-lack directed it in California with Jan-ice Rule replacing Barbara Loden.

Burt Lancaster was intrigued by the challenge of the title role; it is per-haps his most unusual part, and he was impressive in it. However, director Perry felt that Burt lacked the full, emotional range deemed necessary. Although Burt even had misgivings about the artistic dimensions, he believed that he was fully capable of presenting the physical side of the character. The actor trained for three months for his swimming scenes at the University of California under the guidance of head coach Robert Horn. Seventeen pairs of blue swimming trunks made up his entire wardrobe for the film.

An underrated film with little re-sponse from audiences with its initial re-lease by Columbia Pictures in 1968, *The Swimmer*'s status has improved over the years. In 1972, a 17-minute short called *I Who Am, Who Am I?* used footage from the movie to explore questions on self-image. It was reflective of a series,

Searching for Values, made for schools by Columbia and the Learning Corpora-tion of America.

REVIEWS: *Saturday Review:* "It makes for a curious and ultimately un-satisfactory film that fails to capture the haunting quality of the Cheever story, in spite of moments of fine, even poetic di-rection by Mr. Perry."

Commonweal: "Burt Lancaster is excellent as Neddy, the once-athlete who refuses to give up as he swims, trots, and shows off before the girls. Per-haps Lancaster doesn't always convey the difficult mental problems and tor-tures through which Neddy is going, but he comes close—and physically in his running, jumping, swimming stints he is just right."

Castle Keep

A Columbia Picture In Association with Filmways Presentation A Martin Ransohoff Production Released July 23, 1969 105 minutes Technicolor Panavi-sion Rated R ("Restricted"—under 17 requires accompanying adult)

CREDITS: Sydney Pollack (Director); Martin Ransohoff and John Calley (Pro-ducers); Edward L. Rissien (Associate Pro-ducer); Daniel Taradash and David Rayfiel (Screenplay); Henri Decae (Photography); Tyler Camera Systems (Aerial Photogra-phy); Malcolm Cooke (Editor); Michele Robert (Assistant Editor); Rino Mondellini (Production Designer); Jacques Fonteray and Jack Martell (Costumes); Robert Schiffer (Make-up); Lee Zavitz (Special Effects); Dirk Sanders (Choreography); Michel Legrand (Music Score). Based on William Eastlake's novel.

CAST: Burt Lancaster (Major Fal-coner); Patrick O'Neal (Capt. Beckman); Jean-Pierre Aumont (Count Tixier); Peter Falk (Sgt. Rossi); Scott Wilson (Cpl. Clear-boy); Tony Bill (Lt. Amberjack); Astrid Heeren (Therese); Al Freeman Jr. (Pvt.

Benjamin); James Patterson (Pvt. Elk); Bruce Dern (Billy Bix); Michael Conrad (Sgt. De Vaca); Caterina Boratto (Red Queen); Bisera Vukotic (Baker's Wife); Harry Baird (Dancing Soldier); Dave Jones (One-eared Soldier); Jean Gimello (Puerto Rican); Karen Blanguernon, Marja Allanen, Elisabeth Teissier, Eya Tuli, Anne Marie Moskovenko, Elizabeth Darius, and Maria Danube (Red Queen Girls).

SYNOPSIS: During World War II in Belgium, eight weary American soldiers come on a castle called Maldorais. It is owned by Count Tixier and his wife, Therese. Deciding to use the castle as a point of defense against the advancing German army is Major Falconer, the leader of the soldiers. The men under him are Captain Beckman; Lieutenant Amberjack; Sergeants Rossi and De Vaca; Corporal and Privates Clearboy, Elk and Benjamin. Their story is narrated by the last private.

Tixier is against his home being threatened by warfare and urges Beckman to change Falconer's mind. Although Beckman is fascinated by the castle's historic value and priceless art collection, to convince the major proves futile.

Falconer kills several German soldiers in the nearby forest; Rossi and Amberjack come across a single enemy soldier, who bewilders them with kindness until the sergeant shoots him. An enemy plane is shot down from the castle parapet.

Four of the Americans go to a local village brothel and amuse themselves,

Castle Keep, with Burt Lancaster and Al Freeman Jr.

and Rossi begins living with a woman in a bakery. Falconer is enjoying the sexual favors of the young and beautiful Therese; her much older husband approves, for he is impotent and wants an heir.

When an enemy force approaches, Falconer has the brothel's girls throw handmade bombs at the tanks. Rossi even steals one of the vehicles. The major tries to recruit a group of shell-shocked American soldiers, led by one Billy Bix, but there is an explosion and only Falconer comes away unscathed.

The castle grounds are reinforced with barbed wire. Tixier is killed by the Germans in an attempt to bargain with them for the safety of his home. Beckman has stored many of the castle's art treasures in the cellar, but Falconer has the cellar's passageway blown up to keep the enemy out. The Germans are relentless, however, in their assault.

Rossi, Amberjack, and Clearboy meet death in the rose garden. De Vaca and Elk are killed within the castle. Under a roaring flame on the castle parapet Beckman and Falconer perish. Only Benjamin survives of the eight Americans and escapes with Therese.

COMMENTARY: Director Sydney Pollack and Burt Lancaster argued while making *The Scalphunters* in 1967 and again during the filming of *Castle Keep* in 1968. They may have had their own opinions on filmmaking to cause the arguments, but Burt in time reflected, "He was the man who worked me hardest and the man I best communicated with."

Filmed in Yugoslavia, *Castle Keep* proved to be an even more bizarre motion picture than *The Swimmer* in combining tragic realism with a near surrealism. Derived from the 1965 best-seller by William Eastlake, it was an intriguing if ambiguous translation on the big screen (as *The Swimmer* was). Martin Ransohoff and Daniel Taradash are credited as being a contributing producer and screenwriter, respectively, yet found their conception of the film not as important as that of its director and star. David Rayfiel (who initially shared the idea of a partnership with Pollack and Lancaster) did most of the screenwriting, and John Calley was also credited as a producer.

While castle interiors were filmed at Belgrade's Avala Film Studios, an actual replica of a tenth-century castle was constructed in the area for $1 million and destroyed for the climax. Seven hundred gallons of gasoline and 1,000 sticks of dynamite created an overwhelming inferno. The castle was a wondrous vision amid the power of a modern war. Most stupendous were Henri Decae's cinematography and Rino Mondellini's production design.

Artistically, *Castle Keep* was a gem, but it was highly unpopular at the box office after its 1969 release by Columbia Pictures; surely its ambiguity contributed to its downfall. The new rating system formed by the Motion Picture Association of America rated the film R because of the violence, language, and sex scenes between Lancaster and actress Astrid Heeren.

As the one-eyed American major, Burt was a solid enough presence to remain rather laid back in a male-dominant cast of veterans and relative newcomers, all highly talented. There were various degrees of madness and heroism throughout, revolving around the major's quest for glory. *Castle Keep* shared the same year and war in history as *The Train*, as well as the breathtaking special effects of Lee Zavitz.

REVIEWS: *New York Times:* "It's a sometimes funny and entertaining movie that accomplishes the dubious feat of being both anti and pro war at the same time.... The film, set in the Ardennes Forest during the winter of 1944, has the form and visual beauty of a dark fairy tale."

Life: "A word about the special excellence of the three leading men. Lancaster, O'Neal and Falk are, in different ways, highly mannered actors. Under Pollack's direction they lose themselves (or anyway their images of themselves) in their roles and each, as a result, gives his best performance in years."

The Gypsy Moths

A Metro-Goldwyn-Mayer Presentation A John Frankenheimer–Edward Lewis Production Released August 28, 1969 110 minutes Metrocolor Rated M ("Mature Audiences")—subsequently changed to R

CREDITS: John Frankenheimer (Director); Hal Landers and Bobby Roberts (Producers); Edward Lewis (Executive Producer); William Hanley (Screenplay); Philip Lathrop (Photography); Carl Boenisch (Aerial Photography); Henry Borman (Editor); George W. Davis and Cary Odell (Art Directors); Henry Grace and Jack Mills (Set Decorators); Bill Thomas (Costumes); William Tuttle (Make-up); Elmer Bernstein (Music Score). Based on the novel by James Drought.

CAST: Burt Lancaster (Mike Rettig); Deborah Kerr (Elizabeth Brandon); Gene Hackman (Joe Browdy); Scott Wilson (Malcolm Webson); William Windom (V. John Brandon); Bonnie Bedelia (Annie Burke); Sheree North (Waitress); Carl Reindel (Pilot); Ford Rainey (Stand Owner); John Napier (Dick Donford).

SYNOPSIS: Professional skydivers Mike Rettig, Joe Browdy, and Malcolm Webson come into a Kansas town to perform. They stay with Malcolm's aunt and uncle, Elizabeth and John Brandon. To rouse a little publicity, Rettig attends Elizabeth's club meeting and demonstrates his jumping gear.

During supper, Rettig pensively discusses the choice between life and death in his work. Malcolm takes a liking to Annie Burke, a college student boarding with the Brandons. Browdy spends the night with a waitress. Elizabeth is lonely because of a neglectful husband, and she makes love to Rettig.

Browdy is worried about the rainy skies the next day and gets into an argument with Malcolm. Rettig asks Elizabeth to leave with him after their skydiving show, but she refuses, apparently content to leave her life the way it is.

The trio of daredevils perform their exciting aerial routines before a moderate crowd. The highlight is the cape stunt, where one skydiver pulls his parachute at the last second. Rettig dons the winglike cape. Falling at a horrifying speed, he crashes into the ground. The crowd is stunned. Malcolm sees that the parachute is still intact and functional.

A memorial jump has to be made to pay for Rettig's funeral expenses. Malcolm agrees to do the cape stunt to remove the fear of it out of his life. An enormous audience watches Malcolm succeed. He then leaves the town and skydiving behind him. Browdy will stay to take care of the funeral and then go his own way.

COMMENTARY: The best quality about *The Gypsy Moths* was Carl Boenisch's thrilling aerial photography of the skydiving. Trained parachutists were used for the dynamic stunts. The Kansas locations (which included the

Burt Lancaster in *The Gypsy Moths* as Mike Rettig.

town of Abilene and the Nelson Air Field near Wichita) were utilized during the summer of 1968 and contrasted vividly with the aerial footage. The movie seemed at times like a quaint piece of Americana.

James Drought's 1955 book was the source for William Hanley's screenplay. The theme to choose between life and death, however, was made rather pretentious by its very symbolism—particularly when Burt Lancaster's troubled vagabond daredevil gazes at moths flickering to their deaths around a lighted lamppost.

Lancaster brought out his character's suicidal prognosis with an overly low-key demeanor that was not entirely persuasive and yet was somewhat reflective of his role in *Castle Keep*. The world-weariness attached to both these roles seemed to reflect a style that Burt would use with varying degrees of success throughout the 1970s. *The Gypsy Moths* was the actor's last and least successful film with director John Frankenheimer (who formed a partnership with executive producer Edward Lewis to make the film). Bobby Roberts and Hal Landers were the accredited producers.

Gene Hackman and Scott Wilson (the latter taking over for John Philip Law, who was injured during the filming) had very strong co-starring roles as Burt's buddies; their more extroverted performances certainly revealed the tension needed to be released to withstand the rigors of skydiving. Deborah Kerr was convincing as a gentle but sexually suppressed wife. But her love scene with Burt was far too explicit and a painful reminder of just how well their romantic attraction for each other was handled 16 years earlier in *From Here to Eternity*.

The nudity displayed in *The Gypsy Moths* was largely responsible for the film ultimately earning an R rating. When first released in 1969 by Metro-Goldwyn-Mayer, the film had a rating of M; however, after an opening engagement to less than enthusiastic audiences at the Radio City Music Hall in New York, it was pulled and then re-released with added material (which included a striptease by the waitress, played by Sheree North). Despite both ratings, the picture was far from popular.

REVIEWS: *The New Yorker:* "Frankenheimer has always been fine at films about men in specialized, rather simple disciplines; *The Gypsy Moths*, with a script by William Hanley from a novel by James Drought, is more complex and more subtly cast than anything else he has done."

Life: "As he has grown older Mr. Lancaster has developed a capacity, unique in established stars, to give away scenes that his status in the movie pecking order entitles him to dominate. He did it in *Castle Keep*, he does it again in *The Gypsy Moths* and he deserves full credit for his shrewd selflessness."

The 1970s

Airport

A Ross Hunter Production   A Universal Picture   Released March 5, 1970
137 minutes   Technicolor   Todd-AO
Rated G   ("General Audiences")
CREDITS: George Seaton (Director and Screenplay); Ross Hunter (Producer); Donald Roberts and Peter Price (Assistant Directors); Jacque Mapes (Associate Producer); Ernest Laszlo (Photography); Stuart Gilmore (Editor); Alexander Golitzen and E. Preston Ames (Art Directors); Jack D. Moore and Mickey S. Michaels (Set Decorators); Edith Head (Costumes); Bud Westmore (Make-up); Don W. Weed and James Gordon (Special Effects); Ronald Pierce and David Moriarty (Sound); Alfred Newman (Music Score). Based on the novel by Arthur Hailey.
CAST: Burt Lancaster (Mel Bakersfeld); Dean Martin (Vernon Demerest); Jean Seberg (Tanya Livingston); Jacqueline Bisset (Gwen Meighen); George Kennedy (Patroni); Van Heflin (D.O. Guerrero); Maureen Stapleton (Inez Guerrero); Barry Nelson (Anson Harris); Lloyd Nolan (Harry Standish); Dana Wynter (Cindy Bakersfeld); Barbara Hale (Sarah Demerest); Helen Hayes (Ada Quonsett); Gary Collins (Cy Jordan); John Findlater (Peter Coakley); Jessie Royce Landis (Harriet DuBarry Mossman); Larry Gates (Commissioner Ackerman); Peter Turgeon (Marcus Rathbone); Whit Bissell (Mr. Davidson); Virginia Grey (Mrs. Schultz); Eileen Wesson (Judy); Paul Picerni (Dr. Compagno); Robert Patten (Capt. Benson); Clark Howat (Bert Weatherby); Lew Brown (Reynolds); Ilana Dowding (Roberta Bakersfeld); Lisa Gerritson (Libby Bakersfeld); Jim Nolan (Father Lonigan); Patty Poulsen (Joan); Ena Hartman (Ruth); Malila Saint Duval (Maria); Sharon Harvey (Sally); Albert Reed (Lt. Ordway); Jodean Russo (Marie Patroni); Nancy Ann Nelson (Bunnie); Dick Winslow (Mr. Schultz); Lou Wagner (Schuyler Schultz); Janis Hansen (Sister Katherine Grace); Mary Jackson (Sister Felice); Shelly Novack (Rollings); Chuck Daniel (Parks); Charles Brewer (Diller).

SYNOPSIS: One evening during a blizzard, a jumbo jet trying to land is stranded in the snow and partially blocks a runway at Lincoln International Airport. Mel Bakersfeld, the airport's manager, asks a troubleshooter named Patroni to help free the disabled plane. Other problems, personal and professional, confront Mel—his wife, Cindy, wants a divorce because of their different lifestyles; protesters are upset that the airport is near their homes; and a commissioner wants to close the airport temporarily because of the blocked runway.

Trans Global Airlines needs the second runway for a flight to Rome with Vernon Demerest and Anson Harris the scheduled pilots. Vern is married to Mel's sister, Sarah, but he is having an affair with Gwen Meighen, a stewardess on his flight (who is also pregnant). Although Mel seems surprised to learn that Cindy is seeing someone else, he has developed a romance with Tanya Livingston, a passenger agent for Trans Global.

Tanya must deal with a stowaway named Ada Quonsett, who manages to slip aboard Vern's plane. One D.O. Guerrero is also aboard with a hidden bomb; customs inspector Harry Standish is suspicious and urges Tanya to make an inquiry. Guerrero's wife, Inez, believes her husband is leaving her and rushes to the airport. The plane is already airborne as Inez is taken to Mel and Tanya. It is discerned that Guerrero

Airport: **Burt Lancaster as Mel Bakersfeld.**

was a mental patient and a demolitions excavator (who stole some dynamite from his last job and left an enormous flight insurance policy payoff to his wife).

Vern and Anson are alerted of the danger, and they slowly turn their jet around without alarming the passengers and head back to Lincoln Airport.

Gwen is informed and relates that Guerrero is clutching an attaché case; sitting beside him is Ada, and she is asked to help distract the bomber. With Vern's assistance, the plan nearly succeeds. But Guerrero sets the bomb off in a rear bathroom.

At the high altitude and speed the plane is traveling, the bomber is instantly sucked out of the tear in the plane by the air pressure. Gwen is seriously injured. The passengers and crew put on oxygen masks until Anson can stabilize the plane. The damage then makes it essential for the jet to use the largest runway.

The stranded plane is still there. Mel has plows ready to push it aside when Patroni finally manages to taxi it through the snow and off the runway. Anson and Vern are then guided by the airport's control center to a safe landing. Gwen is taken to a hospital with Vern at her side. Ada is given a lifelong pass by Trans Global. Mel and Tanya decide to spend the day together away from their hectic duties.

COMMENTARY: Producer Ross Hunter saw what enormous potential Arthur Hailey's 1968 best-seller *Airport* had as big-screen entertainment and filmed it with Universal Pictures for $10 million. The film was dominated by an all-star cast in a soap opera fashion of colorful if clichéd plot twists and characterizations under the auspices of George Seaton's screenplay and direction. (Henry Hathaway, though uncredited, was the director for a couple of weeks when Seaton became ill at the beginning of production in January 1969.) Indeed, a colossally entertaining picture on its release in 1970 (the biggest for Universal then), *Airport* went on to take in over $45 million at the box office.

Airport was the spectacle that opened the gateway for the other big disaster films of the 1970s, including three more *Airport* movies (in 1974, 1977, and 1979, respectively, and with George Kennedy reprising his character in each). Ten Academy Award nominations were given to the original adventure: Best Picture, Best Supporting Actresses (Maureen Stapleton and Helen Hayes), Cinematography (Ernest Laszlo), Film Editing (Stuart Gilmore), Art Direction—Set Decoration (Alex-ander Golitzen, E. Preston Ames and Jack D. Moore, Mickey S. Michaels), Costume Design (Edith Head), Sound (Ronald Pierce and David Moriarty), Original Score (Alfred Newman), and Screenplay Based on Material from Another Medium (George Seaton).

Helen Hayes was the single Oscar winner for her charming playing of the pixyish stowaway. Despite the occasional predictability of the characters, the entire cast was truly remarkable, centering around a large yet fictitious airport in turmoil (location filming was done at Minneapolis–St. Paul International Airport in Minnesota). The on-screen heroics by Burt Lancaster, Dean Martin (one of his best performances), Barry Nelson, and George Kennedy were superbly rendered. Jean Seberg, Jacqueline Bisset, Dana Wynter, and Barbara Hale were all quite good in handling the romantic nature of the picture. Perhaps the finest acting, however, was supplied by Hayes, Maureen Stapleton, Lloyd Nolan, and Van Heflin.

Although Ross Hunter's first choice for the airport manager was Lancaster (because of his trademark masculine yet sensitive demeanor), the actor initially turned the role down. Under the impression that *Airport* was a bit of tripe, Burt nonetheless accepted the part when it was agreed that he would receive a percentage of the box office earnings. He made a few million dollars from the film; it was the most profitable deal from any of his films.

REVIEWS: *Newsweek:* "Burt Lancaster's harried airport manager, Dean Martin's veteran pilot and Van Heflin's bomber are all serviceable performances, but as you run down the list of performers after the show you realize that you've seen very little more than a list of performances."

Senior Scholastic: "All the same, *Airport* remains a comfortable, enjoyable, old-fashioned movie. You just can't help getting involved in its goings-on, or becoming as familiar with its characters as if you were trapped in an elevator with them for 137 minutes."

Airport, with Dean Martin and Burt Lancaster.

Valdez Is Coming

A Norlan–Ira Steiner Production   Released through United Artists   Released April 9, 1971   90 minutes   DeLuxe Color   Rated PG ("Parental Guidance Suggested")
CREDITS: Edwin Sherin (Director); Ira Steiner (Producer); Roland Kibbee (Executive Producer); Roland Kibbee and David Rayfiel (Screenplay); Gabor Pogany (Photography); James T. Heckert (Editor); Jose Maria Tapiador and Jose Maria Alarcon (Art Directors); Rafael Salazar (Set Decorator); Louis Brown (Costumes); Mariano Garcia Rey and Alberto Comenar (Make-up); Chuck Gaspar and Linc Kibbee (Special Effects); Bud Alper (Sound); Charles Gross (Music Score). Based on the novel by Elmore Leonard.

CAST: Burt Lancaster (Bob Valdez); Susan Clark (Gay Erin); Jon Cypher (Frank Tanner); Barton Heyman (El Segundo); Richard Jordan (R.L. Davis); Frank Silvera (Diego); Hector Elizondo (Mexican Rider); Phil Brown (Malson); Lex Monson (Rincon); Ralph Brown (Beaudry); Juanita Penaloza (Apache Woman); Roberta Haynes (Polly); Maria Montez (Anita); Marta Tuck (Rosa); Jose Garcia (Carlos); James Lemp (Bony Man); Werner Hasselman (Sheriff); Concha Hombria (Inez); Per Barclay (Bartender); Michael Hinn (Merchant); Vic Albert and Allan Russell (Ranchers); Rudy Ugland and Joaquin Parra (Trackers); Santiago Santos and Losardo Iglesias (Riders); Juan Fernandez (Mexican Buyer); Tony Epper (Bodyguard); Mario Barros, Raul Castro, Nick Cravat, Santiago Garcia, Jeff Kibbee, Linc Kibbee, Ian MacLean, Tom McFadden, Jose Morales, Mario Sanz, Lee Thaxton, Robin Thaxton, Julian Vidrie, and Manolin Vidrie (Gang Members).

SYNOPSIS: In 1890, along the border of Arizona and Mexico, a gang of

Valdez Is Coming: **Burt Lancaster as Valdez.**

men under rancher Frank Tanner are firing their guns at a sod hut. Inside is Rincon, a black man accused of killing a white man named James Erin. Mexican constable Bob Valdez tries to mediate in the situation. But a Tanner man, R.L. Davis, interferes and forces Valdez to kill Rincon in self-defense. Tanner now realizes that Rincon is the wrong man.

Valdez then tries to collect $200 for the dead man's Apache woman; the local townspeople agree to pay half if Tanner does the same. Instead of helping, Tanner has his men make a fool of Valdez. Trying again later, the constable is beaten and tortured by Tanner's men (a wooden cross is tied to Valdez's back; trying to break it only causes the wood to cut him badly). A friend, Diego, helps Valdez with his injuries. Afterward, Valdez takes his guns and rides to confront Tanner.

Breaking into Tanner's bedroom, Valdez demands the money for the Indian woman. When Tanner's right-hand man, El Segundo, enters, Valdez flees and kidnaps Tanner's woman, Gay Erin. Valdez believes Tanner killed James Erin, her husband.

Three trackers (Tanner's men) chase Valdez into a canyon and he shoots them; one lives long enough to tell Tanner of the distant mountain pass where Valdez will be. Diego is hurt by Tanner to lure Valdez into the open and he comes, killing two more men and capturing R.L. Davis. From a ledge nearly a thousand feet away, Valdez shoots down several more of Tanner's men with a buffalo rifle.

Davis is sent back to Tanner with the message that Gay will be killed unless the money is brought to the mountain pass. Valdez discovers that Gay killed her own husband; she realizes Valdez will not harm her and they are attracted to each other.

El Segundo rides ahead of Valdez to the pass and surprises him. However, Segundo has come to respect Valdez and cannot kill him. Tanner is then forced to face Valdez alone.

COMMENTARY: *Valdez Is Coming* was director Edwin Sherin's feature film debut. Burt Lancaster's Norlan Productions (initially set up for *The Scalphunters*) hired Sherin and made the western with producer Ira Steiner. The first selection for director was Sydney Pollack; Burt was to play the rancher and Marlon Brando was slated as Valdez. But this concept fell through when Burt became involved with filming *Airport*.

Lancaster took over the title role (with Jon Cypher cast as Tanner). At Los Angeles City College, Burt was helped with the linguistics in developing his Mexican mannerisms he used in the film. Sympathetic in his early scenes as the soft-spoken, vulnerable Mexican, he became adamant in the retribution following the abuse of his body and soul. It is quite an interesting character study—Burt divested from his more recognizable facial features to partake in the dialect and heavy make-up for the part.

The film's vengeance-seeking parable did not entirely justify Valdez's belligerence (anymore than it did Tanner's) despite the exciting bursts of action. The climax was especially notable in the calm exchange between Valdez and one of his pursuers, El Segundo (played by Barton Heyman), and their mutual understanding for all that took place. But the themes of revenge and racial intolerance found little favor with audiences domestically after the movie's 1971 release by United Artists (although in Great Britain it was a hit).

Filmed in Almeria, Spain, *Valdez Is Coming* had the distinctive brooding and violent profile of the then-trendy "spaghetti westerns" (filmed in Spain or Italy). Taken from Elmore Leonard's 1969 novel, the screenplay was accredited to both Roland Kibbee and David Rayfiel. Initially, when Pollack and Brando were involved, so was Rayfiel, who later realized that Kibbee's material was the preferred choice.

REVIEWS: *Time: "Valdez Is Coming* offers little besides its star. Continual editorials about racism give the film contrived relevance. Edwin Sherin's direction may best be described as functional: the members of the cast do not bump into each other."

New York Times: "Mr. Lancaster himself is simply beyond criticism, an enduring star whose screen personality—decent, liberal, tough, well-intentioned—provides the shape of the movies that are constructed around him."

Lawman

A Michael Winner Film   A Scimitar Film Production   Released through United Artists   Released August 4, 1971   99 minutes   DeLuxe Color   Rated PG

CREDITS: Michael Winner (Director and Producer); Michael Dryhurst (Assistant Director); Gerald Wilson (Screenplay); Bob Paynter (Photography); Freddie Wilson (Editor); Stan Jolley (Production Designer); Herbert Westbrook (Art Director); Ray Moyer (Set Decorator); Ron Beck (Costumes); Richard Mills (Make-up); Leon Ortega (Special Effects); Jerry Fielding (Music Score).

CAST: Burt Lancaster (Jered Maddox); Robert Ryan (Cotton Ryan); Lee J. Cobb (Vincent Bronson); Sheree North (Laura Selby); Robert Duvall (Vernon Adams); Albert Salmi (Harvey Stenbaugh); J.D. Cannon (Hurd Price); John McGiver (Mayor Sam Bolden); Joseph Wiseman (Lucas); Richard Jordan (Crowe Wheelwright); John Beck (Jason Bronson); Ralph Waite (Jack Dekker); William Watson (Choctaw Lee); Charles Tyner (Minister); John Hillerman (Totts); Robert Emhardt (Hersham); Richard Bull (Dusaine); Hugh McDermott (Moss); Lou Frizzell (Cobden); Walter Brooke (Luther Harris); Bill Brimley (Marc Corman).

SYNOPSIS: When a bunch of cowboys shoot up the western town of Bannock in drunken revelry, an old man is killed. The marshal, Jered Maddox, follows the cowboys to their own community of Sabbath after shooting one on the trail. Maddox vows to Cotton Ryan, the marshal of Sabbath, that he will get the rest.

Ryan rides out to rancher Vince Bronson's spread to inform him that the lawman is after some of his men. The rancher is sorry about the accidental killing and unsuccessfully tries to offer Maddox a bribe to ride back to Bannock.

At the hotel in Sabbath, Laura, an old girlfriend of the lawman's, also tries without success to convince him to leave alone her man, Hurd Price, one of the cowboys. Maddox points out that Price can give himself up for trial.

A close friend of Bronson's, Harvey Stenbaugh (also in Bannock during the killing), starts a gunfight with Maddox in town and is killed. Furious, Bronson threatens retaliation. Ryan tries to intervene, but it is apparent that he takes orders from the rancher. Bronson seems to own much of the town; led by merchant Luther Harris, the citizens protest Maddox's presence.

Lawman, with Robert Duvall and Burt Lancaster.

Crowe Wheelwright, a Bronson hand, confronts Maddox, but is talked out of a gunfight. When a sniper fires at the lawman, Ryan arrests the culprit, named Dekker (another of the cowboys). Maddox believes Crowe was working with the sniper; however, the younger man denies it. The two later come to an understanding, and Crowe is not one of the cowboys sought by Maddox.

A man named Adams is wanted and tries to assassinate the lawman with Hurd Price. Instead, Adams is wounded and then captured as Price escapes. Taking Adams back into Sabbath, Maddox stops at Laura's place. Although against his severe methods, Laura realizes she still loves Maddox.

The lawman decides to give up the manhunt and leave town with Laura, as Bronson and a few others (including Price) ride in to confront him. Trying to shoot Maddox, Luther Harris is shot down by Lucas, a brothel owner and old acquaintance of the marshal. A Bronson hand, Choctaw Lee, forces Maddox to draw his gun and kill him. Jason Bronson, the rancher's son, also stands against the marshal and is killed. Running away from him, Price is shot in the back by Maddox. Bronson shoots himself at the loss of his son. Jered Maddox then rides out of town alone.

COMMENTARY: Producer/director Michael Winner beat fellow filmmaker Howard Hawks to the draw by just one hour to use the location of Durango, Mexico, for the filming of *Lawman*

(Hawks wanted to shoot *Rio Lobo* there with John Wayne, but had to film in Tucson, Arizona, instead). Englishman Winner had no trouble adapting to the rigors of his selected site or to making an American western.

Lawman was a conventional-looking western (with a script by Gerald Wilson) differentiated by its theme of fanatical justice and graphic violence. The spaghetti westerns assuredly were leaving a mark on American entries with their deluge of bloody killings by steely anti-heros like Clint Eastwood and Charles Bronson. It was ironic that both *Lawman* and *Valdez Is Coming* received only a PG rating when they were released in 1971 by United Artists.

Burt Lancaster's tough lawman was particularly relentless in his code of justice (and perhaps more similar to the actual Wyatt Earp than the one he enacted in *Gunfight at the O.K. Corral*). Welcome traces of Burt's vulnerability made his character more fully rounded; most effective was a resolved conflict without gunplay between the marshal and the would-be gunman played by Richard Jordan (seen also in *Valdez*).

Quite a familiar cast of seasoned pros boosted the conventional American flavor of *Lawman*, although the film was even less responsive with audiences than *Valdez Is Coming*. Still, strong support was given Lancaster by, among others, Jordan, Robert Duvall, Lee J. Cobb, and Robert Ryan (the latter in an extremely sympathetic role as the marshal whose grit has diminished). Also formidable was Sheree North (in a much better role than she had in *The Gypsy Moths*); her frontier heroine, like Susan Clark's before her in *Valdez Is Coming*, lent a weathered yet attractive countenance in an otherwise grim tale.

REVIEWS: *Washington Post:* "Instead of being a coherent or exciting or handsome Western, *Lawman* is just the Western with all the weird talk and all the grisly little crotchets—the Western that doesn't avert the camera when the hero is putting a bullet in the head of his injured horse, for example."

New York Times: "Some cutting dialogue and boiling psychological tension are the most winning things about *Lawman*, a potent but curiously exasperating Western with those three hardies, Burt Lancaster, Robert Ryan and Lee J. Cobb."

Ulzana's Raid

A Carter De Haven–Robert Aldrich Production A Universal Picture Released November 15, 1972 103 minutes Technicolor Rated R

CREDITS: Robert Aldrich (Director); Carter De Haven (Producer); Malcolm R. Harding (Assistant Director); Alan Sharp (Associate Producer, Screenplay); Joseph Biroc (Photography); Michael Luciano (Editor); James D. Vance (Art Director); John McCarthy (Set Decorator); Cinematique (Cosmetics); Waldon O. Watson and Jim Alexander (Sound); Frank DeVol (Music Score).

CAST: Burt Lancaster (McIntosh); Bruce Davison (Lt. DeBuin); Jorge Luke (Ke-Ni-Tay); Richard Jaeckel (Sergeant); Joaquin Martinez (Ulzana); Lloyd Bochner (Capt. Gates); Karl Swenson (Rukeyser); Douglass Watson (Major Cartwright); Dran Hamilton (Mrs. Riordon); John Pearce (Corporal); Gladys Holland (Mrs. Rukeyser); Margaret Fairchild (Mrs. Ginsford); Aimee Eccles (McIntosh's Indian Woman); Richard Bull (Ginsford); Otto Reichow (Steegmeyer); Dean Smith (Horowitz); Larry Randles (Mulkearn); Hal Maguire, Ted Markland, R.L. Armstrong, John McKee, Tony Epper, Nick Cravat, Richard Farnsworth, Walter Scott, Jerry Gatlin, Fred Brookfield, and Bill Burton (Troopers); Henry Camargo,

Gil Escandon, Frank Gonzales, Larry Colelay, George Aguilar, Marvin Fragua, Benny Thompson, and Wallace Sinyella (Indian Braves).

SYNOPSIS: In the American Southwest of the 1800s, the Apache Ulzana leads eight of his braves in an escape from the San Carlos Indian Reservation. At Fort Lowell a cavalry unit is assigned to bring the renegades back commanded by Lt. DeBuin, with McIntosh and Ke-Ni-Tay the scouts.

This is the young lieutenant's first field assignment; his superior officer urges him to respect McIntosh's experience with Indians but to remember who is in charge. McIntosh believes the Indians are bent on murder and destruction.

A lone trooper warning the white settlers in the area of the danger is escorting a woman and her child to the fort when the Indians strike. To prevent the Apaches from raping her and torturing him to death slowly, the soldier shoots the woman and himself. The Apaches mutilate the dead man's body.

When the cavalry unit arrives at the scene, the Indians are gone and two soldiers take the unharmed child back to the fort. The child's father is found brutally murdered at his homestead. When asked by DeBuin why the Indians are so cruel, Ke-Ni-Tay, also an Apache, reflects on the power that is believed to be taken by killing another man.

Ulzana's Raid: In front row sitting (left to right) are John Pascal, Bruce Davison, Richard Jaeckel, and Jorge Luke. Back row standing (left to right), Tex Armstrong, Hal Maguire, Nick Cravat, Ted Markland, Richard Farnsworth, and Burt Lancaster.

Two of Ulzana's braves are leading their string of stolen horses while the others drop off into the hills. The two scouts realize the ploy and ride off in opposite directions to find the trail that the pair of Indians are using to circle back to the other Apaches. McIntosh finds the pair, killing one and badly wounding the other.

The soldiers catch up to McIntosh, and the sergeant and a trooper are dispatched by DeBuin to track down the wounded Apache (despite the scout's opinion that the Indian will only crawl away to die if left alone). In the interim, several of the troopers, to the lieutenant's disgust, mutilate the body of the brave killed by the scout. The sergeant returns with a dead trooper, shot down by the other Indian.

A woman survivor of the Apaches' devastation is found, and McIntosh and Ke-Ni-Tay realize that she was kept alive only to separate the cavalry unit because an escort will have to take her to the fort. The patrol plans a strategy in which the sergeant, McIntosh and several troopers feign taking the woman back; DeBuin and the remaining soldiers will follow once Ke-Ni-Tay has stopped one of the Indians from warning Ulzana of the plan.

The plan backfires, and McIntosh and the escort are attacked in the canyon by Ulzana. The escort soldiers are killed, including the sergeant; badly wounded, McIntosh is able to kill three of the Apaches. DeBuin's group arrives too late except to run off one of the braves. Yet Ke-Ni-Tay has managed to kill the remaining Indians, including Ulzana. As the patrol returns to the fort, McIntosh bids his farewells to DeBuin and Ke-Ni-Tay, for he has chosen to stay behind and die in the canyon.

COMMENTARY: Director Robert Aldrich and producer Carter De Haven captured the full scope of suspense and action in *Ulzana's Raid*. The elements of savagery were utterly overwhelming as drawn from the riveting screenplay by Alan Sharp (who was also associate producer of the film). The locations utilized in Arizona (Nogales) and Nevada (*The Professionals'* Valley of Fire State Park) added immeasurably to the haunting starkness of the film generated by Joseph Biroc's cinematography.

Feeling the initial script was one of the best he ever read, Burt Lancaster later elaborated about the Apaches: "The white man didn't understand them. We lacked the cultural exposure to know, so we forced the Indians into reservations where they

Ulzana's Raid, with Bruce Davison and Burt Lancaster.

lost their predatory ways, lived an unnatural existence and became a depressed people. We explain in *Ulzana's Raid* that while some of the Indians' acts seem terrible to us, they were rooted in the religious beliefs and culture which the white man didn't understand."

There was also a Vietnam War perspective (of a different culture being dominated by an imperialistic force), which was overlooked for the most part when the picture was released by Universal in 1972. *Ulzana's Raid* was a better western than *Valdez Is Coming* and *Lawman*, although a weighty western adventure was still not very popular with audiences then exposed to the more flamboyant spaghetti westerns. The R rating was certainly justified due to the violent content.

The role of the seasoned, grizzled frontier scout was one of Burt's strongest roles of the 1970s; it was a more successful changeover to the character parts the actor wanted as he grew older. Like Eli Wakefield in *The Kentuckian*, Ben Zachary in *The Unforgiven*, Joe Bass in *The Scalphunters*, his McIntosh was charged with the same larger-than-life folk hero qualities (vividly seen when he is riding like the wind on horseback after the Apaches, and he throws his rifle into the air from its scabbard and catches it and fires). His grit and gruffness, however, could only radiate the vulnerability and simple dignity in his performance to the highest plain; in the closing moments of the film, when he is dying, Burt is especially touching.

In *Dances with Wolves*, Kevin Costner played a young, idealistic soldier with mannerisms not unlike those projected by Bruce Davison's naive soldier. Jorge Luke's Ke-Ni-Tay shares a friendship with McIntosh that seems an affectionate nod to that between frontiersman Hawkeye and Indian Chingachgook (in the films based on the famous James Fenimore Cooper novel, *The Last of the Mohicans*). Richard Jaeckel's sturdy sergeant shared with Burt a touching death scene; this fine character actor was reunited with Lancaster for the first time since *Come Back, Little Sheba*, filmed nearly twenty years before.

REVIEWS: *New York Times:* "The weak spot of the film is the character of the lieutenant, not because of any failings on the part of Davison, but because the hero-heel (a recurring character in Aldrich films) is, as written, a lightweight, a man who is apt to behave badly or well more for immediate plot needs than from any convictions or lack of same."

Christian Science Monitor: "Mr. Lancaster plays the scout named McIntosh with his usual fierce energy. He does it in John Wayne style: a solid presence, sun-squinting eyes in mahogany face, tight-lipped under a bushy gray moustache although he could tell that brash young cavalry lieutenant how to handle Ulzana."

Scorpio

A Mirisch Corporation Presentation A Michael Winner Film   A Scimitar Films Production   Released through United Artists   Released April 19, 1973   114 minutes DeLuxe Color   Rated PG

CREDITS: Michael Winner (Director); Walter Mirisch (Producer); Michael Dryhurst (Assistant Director); David W. Rintels and Gerald Wilson (Screenplay); Robert Paynter (Photography); Freddie Wilson (Editor); Herbert Westbrook (Art Director); William Kiernan and Josie MacAvin (Set Dressers); Philippe Pickford (Wardrobe); Richard Mills and Marty Bell

(Make-up); Alan Gibbs (Stunts); Brian Marshall (Sound); Jerry Fielding (Music Score). From a story by David W. Rintels.

CAST: Burt Lancaster (Cross); Alain Delon (Laurier); Paul Scofield (Zharkov); John Colicos (McLeod); Gayle Hunnicutt (Susan); J.D. Cannon (Filchock); Joanne Linville (Sarah); Vladek Sheybal (Zemetkin); Melvin Stewart (Pick); Burke Byrnes (Morrison); William Smithers (Mitchell); James Sikking (Harris); Jack Colvin (Thief); Shmuel Rodensky (Lang); Howard Morton (Heck); Robert Emhardt (Man in Hotel); Frederick Jaegar (Novins); George Mikell (Dor); Mary Maude (Anne); Celeste Yarnall (Helen); Sandor Eles (Malkin).

SYNOPSIS: Cross is an agent and Laurier a contract killer for the CIA. After their involvement in the assassination of a marked Arab in Paris, the two men return home to Washington, D.C., where their agency is headquartered. The head of the CIA, McLeod, claims that Cross, who wants to retire, is a suspected double agent.

A plan to bring Cross in fails. With the code name of Scorpio, Laurier was assigned to eliminate Cross in France, but he failed to do so because he had misgivings about Cross being guilty; the older man was also Laurier's mentor.

Donning a disguise, Cross flees to Vienna, where an old friend, Zharkov, offers him protection. Zharkov is a retired Russian spy, and he is pressured by the KGB to bring Cross over to the other side.

Cross tries to bring his wife, Sarah, to Vienna; while under surveillance by the CIA in Washington, she is accidentally killed. The CIA use force to convince Laurier to hunt down Cross. In a wild chase on foot in Vienna, Scorpio does try to kill Cross, although he escapes.

Back in Washington, Cross kills McLeod for instigating his wife's death. Another, Filchock, becomes the new CIA head; he shows Laurier a film on Cross's alleged double-dealing. Also, Susan, Laurier's girlfriend, is accused of helping Cross as a courier.

Scorpio, **with Paul Scofield and Burt Lancaster.**

Scorpio follows Susan to an underground parking lot and finds her and Cross together. He guns them both down. Walking away, Laurier is killed by a hidden gun because, like Cross, he knows of too many shady dealings within the CIA.

COMMENTARY: Michael Winner's film *Scorpio* was an ugly, convoluted look at the spying game and especially of the CIA. The director was indulgent with his camera angles, trying every trick in the book to make the overall clichéd material as interesting as possible. David W. Rintels conceived the story line and initially worked on the screenplay, although much of the script was rewritten by Gerald Wilson. Given a screen credit as producer, Walter Mirisch actually stepped aside from the production when his ideas didn't gel with Winner's.

This cloak-and-dagger formula did not find especially receptive audiences (being an old-hat commodity by the time of its United Artists release in 1973), but there were several highlights. Most winning were the locations which included Paris, Washington, and Vienna. Director Winner, cinematographer Robert Paynter, and the purveyor of the stunts, Alan Gibbs, combined (with Alain Delon and Burt Lancaster) to make the chase sequence through Vienna's then-incomplete underground railway a great action piece.

Scorpio's single most distinctive scene, however, was when the old spies enacted by Lancaster and Paul Scofield get drunk reflecting on the glories of the past. Delon's cool assassin, while displaying the actor's customary charisma, nonetheless was a stereotype in the espionage genre.

Lancaster said of the film, "There's an awfully good cast, but it's pure entertainment, of no lasting significance." Yet Burt was undoubtedly susceptible to the film's theme of the veteran agent being subjected to the powerful machinations of the CIA; he conveyed a high level of energy to his worldly warrior caught in a diffuse situation.

REVIEWS: *Christian Century:* "Director Michael Winner has an unsteady hand, especially in his insistence on staying so far away from his characters that the viewer feels as though he is watching a play from the back row."

Time: "If *Scorpio* does little else, it proves that Lancaster, after all this time, still has an enviable store of vigor. At fifty nine, he is a little paunchier, a little slower, and he breathes harder on the run, but he can still haul himself up a scaffolding with the best of them."

Executive Action

An Edward Lewis Production   In Association with Wakeford/Orloff Inc.   A National General Pictures Release   Released November 7, 1973   91 minutes   In Color   Rated PG

CREDITS: David Miller (Director); Edward Lewis (Producer); Dan Bessie and Gary Horowitz (Co-producers); Dalton Trumbo (Screenplay); Robert Steadman (Photography); George Grenville (Editor); Irving Lerner and Melvin Shapiro (Associate Editors); Ivan Dryer (Documentary Editor); Kirk Axtell (Art Director); Steve Jaffe (Technical Consultant); Randy Edelman (Music Score). Based on the story by Mark Lane and Donald Freed.

CAST: Burt Lancaster (Farrington); Robert Ryan (Foster); Will Geer (Ferguson); Gilbert Green (Paulitz); John Anderson (Halliday); Paul Carr (Gunman Chris, Team A); Colby Chester (Tim); Ed Lauter (Operation Chief Team A); Walter Brooke (Smythe); Sidney Clute (Depository Clerk); Deanna Darrin (Stripper); Lloyd Gough (McCadden); Graydon Gould (TV

Commentator); Richard Hurst (Used Car Salesman); Robert Karnes (Man at Rifle Range); James MacColl (Oswald Impostor); Jacquin Martinez (Art Mendoza); Oscar Oncidi (Jack Ruby); Tom Peters (Sergeant); Paul Sorenson (Officer Brown); Sandy Ward (Policeman); William Watson (Technician Team B); Dick Miller, Hunter Von Leer, and John Brascia (Riflemen Team B); Richard Bull and Lee Delano (Gunmen Team A).

SYNOPSIS: On June 5, 1963, six influential and wealthy men assemble in a Virginia mansion to arrange an executive action—the assassination of President John F. Kennedy. These men include Farrington, Foster, Halliday, and Ferguson. Although they all feel that Kennedy's political policies are a threat to the country's security, only Ferguson is reluctant to carry out the plan and advises the others to wait.

Farrington nonetheless has set up training camps elsewhere with two rifle teams of three men and a trainer on each. One team will do the shooting and the other will be a backup. The gunmen are former CIA operatives; they were fired after the Bay of Pigs incident.

A man with a disreputable military history and political agenda—Lee Harvey Oswald—is chosen to be the fall guy. Foster believes Oswald's past is made up of shady compromises with both the American and Russian governments.

An impostor is used to further discredit Oswald by taking a rifle (just like the one Oswald owns) to a gun shop for repair. Public disturbances by the impostor at a used car lot and on a rifle range also occur.

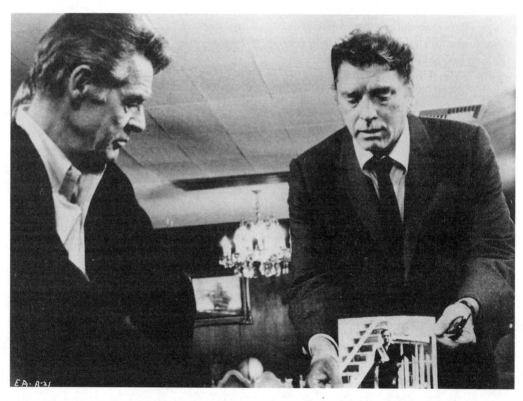

Executive Action, with Robert Ryan and Burt Lancaster.

When a television news report states that President Kennedy will have all the troops out of Vietnam in 1965 (thus leaving that country to the Communists), Ferguson agrees to the sanction. The operation chief of Team A is then notified that his team will do the shooting. Oswald's rifle is stolen; Chris, one of the gunmen, will use it with the same type going to his two associates.

On November 22, 1963, at 12:30 P.M., John Kennedy is traveling in his motorcade through Dallas, Texas. The three gunmen are positioned in Dealey Plaza—one is on the grassy knoll, one is on the roof of the Municipal Records Building, and Chris is in the School Book Depository, where Oswald is working. Several shots are fired as the president passes, three striking him. He later dies from his wounds.

Oswald's rifle is found at the depository; he is later taken to the Dallas Police Station, where he declares himself "a patsy." Farrington has an associate, Tim, contact Jack Ruby. Allowed in the police station basement, Ruby guns down Oswald. Foster receives a phone call from Tim that Farrington has died of a heart attack.

COMMENTARY: In 1973, a decade after President John F. Kennedy was assassinated supposedly by Lee Harvey Oswald, *Executive Action* was released by National General Pictures. Its theme that a conspiracy was involved was intriguing; although the film was a fictitious account of the tragedy, there is reputed proof based on documented material that a conspiracy in this case may actually not be so unrealistic.

Mark Lane wrote a book in 1966 called *Rush to Judgment*, which questioned the findings of the Warren Commission that Oswald acted alone. With

Donald Freed, Lane put together a screenplay on the conspiracy theory that found its way to producer Edward Lewis. Only when he researched the subject did Dalton Trumbo agree to do a rewrite of the script.

David Miller's direction of the documentary and business-like atmosphere was methodical in a hypothetical motion picture, yet this contrast was not wholly satisfying, nor was the film a major success. That it proved controversial, however, cannot be denied; even during filming an attempt to get a permit to shoot in Dallas was denied (although needed footage of the areas in Dallas was secretly acquired, the majority of the picture was made in Los Angeles).

Robert Ryan, Will Geer, and Burt Lancaster lent their respective professional statures to understated roles and low-key performances as a financier, oil tycoon, and ex–CIA man, and the film was Ryan's last before he died of cancer. *Executive Action*'s profile was a bit too delicate for the actors, with shadows of a disturbing part of American thinking where Kennedy must be killed because of his interests in the civil rights movement, a nuclear weapons test ban treaty with the Russians, and a proposal to withdraw American soldiers from Vietnam.

Lancaster had been supportive of Kennedy in reality and initially believed in the lone gunman theory; yet after his own research of the material, he was won over to the film's validity. He said, "There's no question that there was a conspiracy of some sort. That's why everyone has been so dissatisfied and why so many witnesses died afterwards." At the end of the film, there is a statement that there were one hundred thousand trillion to one odds of the eighteen material witnesses in the assassination dying (often horribly) within the following three years.

REVIEWS: *Commonweal:* "To make us accept its conspiracy theory, *Executive Action* must first try to refurbish Kennedy's radical image with newsreel footage…. This 'documentary' aspect of *Executive Action* is so shabbily handled and unpersuasive that, far from lending the whole film authenticity, it makes the patently fictitious plot look even more absurd."

New York Times: "Lancaster and Ryan appear as pensive, practical semi-academics, rationally planning an act as bloody as a small foreign invasion…. Both have the confidence and the casual class that we recall in many Kennedy appointees. Lancaster, looking miraculously young, overdoes the 'sincerity' at moments—an old habit of his."

The Midnight Man

A Norlan Production   A Universal Picture   Released June 14, 1974   117 minutes   Technicolor   Panavision   Rated R
CREDITS: Roland Kibbee and Burt Lancaster (Directors, Producers, and Screenplay); Brad Aronson and Warren Smith (Assistant Directors); Jack Priestley (Photography); Frank Morriss (Editor); James D. Vance (Production Designer); Joe Stone (Set Decorator); Melvin M. Metcalfe (Sound); David Grusin (Music Score). Based on the novel *The Midnight Lady and the Mourning Man* by David Anthony.
CAST: Burt Lancaster (Jim Slade); Susan Clark (Linda); Cameron Mitchell (Quartz); Morgan Woodward (Clayborn); Harris Yulin (Casey); Robert Quarry (Dr. Pritchet); Joan Lorring (Judy); Lawrence Dobkin (Mason); Ed Lauter (Leroy); Mills Watson (Cash); Charles Tyner (Ewing); Catherine Bach (Natalie); William Lan-

caster (King); Quinn Redeker (Swanson); Eleanor Ross (Nell); Richard Winterstein (Virgil); William T. Hicks (Charlie); Peter Dane (Metterman); Linda Kelsey (Betty); William Splawn (Lamar); Susan MacDonald (Elaine); Joel Gordon Kravitz (Pearlman); Nick Cravat (Gardener at College); Rodney Stevens (Jimmy); Weems Oliver Baskin III (Bartender); Jean Perkins (Nurse); Harold N. Cooledge Jr. (Collins); Gene Lehfeldt (Driver); William Clark (Deputy); Elizabeth Black (Bus Dispatcher); Rachel Ray (Parolee); David Garrison (Photographer); Hugh Parsons (Grocery Clerk); Lonnie Kay (Hostess); G. Warren Smith (Director); Lucille Meredith (Radio Evangelist); Mal Alberts (Basketball Announcer); Alan Gibbs, Jim Burke, Frank Orsatti, and Julie Johnson (Stunts).

SYNOPSIS: After serving prison time for killing his wife's lover, Jim Slade is released. He finds work as a night security guard at a small-town college in South Carolina. Linda is his parole officer. Slade is staying with Quartz, who heads the college's security unit.

As a former policeman, Slade shows a professional interest in one of the college girls when she breaks curfew. Her name is Natalie, and he escorts her back to her dorm. When she is later found murdered, Slade disagrees with Sheriff Casey that Ewing, a janitor, is responsible. The community is plagued by a series of calamities as Slade, to Casey's annoyance, does his own investigative work.

Slade does find out many things, risking his own life in the process. Among the dirt uncovered are that a gang of robbers are being backed by Deputy Virgil; Natalie had sexual relations with her father, a senator, and Linda as well; and that Linda and psychologist Dr. Pritchet are involved intimately and are blackmailing the senator

Susan Clark and Burt Lancaster in *The Midnight Man.*

over his incestuous conduct. Quartz is revealed to have killed Natalie. After all has been resolved, Casey offers Slade a job as deputy on the police force.

COMMENTARY: "When you reach my sort of age, and have done so much acting-wise, you begin to look around and wonder what to do next. I feel it's about time I made a move towards directing again." These words were spoken by Burt Lancaster in the early 1970s, and the movie chosen was instigated by Roland Kibbee. As producers, screenwriters, and directors, Lancaster and Kibbee collaborated on *The Midnight Man*, from David Anthony's 1969 mystery novel.

The two filmmakers had long been associated with several film projects over the years; and Kibbee convinced Lancaster to make this film for his Norlan Productions mainly for commercial reasons (with Burt doing most of the directing and Roland the writing). Though the film was certainly energized, it was highly confusing and was far from the financial success hoped for after its 1974 release by Universal. The convoluted proceedings, with the same profile as countless television crime dramas, made for just another potboiler.

In the title role, Lancaster mustered up enough of his diligent self to remain a respectable sleuth; there was a nice bit of rivalry between him and Harris Yulin's equally stalwart sheriff. Susan Clark and Cameron Mitchell, thoroughly commendable performers at all times, were among the many characters caught up in a web of deception.

The Midnight Man was filmed on location in South Carolina (at Clemson University and in the town of Anderson) in 1973, actually before *Executive Action* was made. Burt's son William and Nick Cravat had roles as other town locals—Bill as a boyfriend of Catherine Bach's college girl, and Nick as the gardener at the college.

REVIEWS: *Time:* "Unfortunately, the movie's good intentions are undone by a script that gets bogged down in a needlessly over-complex plot. What is good in the film is constantly lost in a tedious exposition."

New York Times: "Mr. Lancaster is an intelligent actor. He thinks about his characterizations. He makes choices. He moves through *The Midnight Man* with studied humility, saying 'yes, sir,' and 'no, sir,' more often than is always necessary, listening attentively when spoken to."

Moses, the Lawgiver

A Sir Lew Grade Presentation   An ITC/RAI Co-production   Broadcast on CBS Television on June 21 and 28, July 5, 12, and 16, and August 2, 1975   360 minutes   Released to theaters by Avco Embassy Pictures on March 26, 1976   141 minutes   Technicolor   Rated PG

CREDITS: Gianfranco De Bosio (Director); Vincenzo Labella (Producer); Francesco Cinieri (Assistant Director); Anthony Burgess, Vittorio Bonicelli, and Gianfranco De Bosio (Script); Marcello Gatti (Photography); Gerry Hambling, Peter Bolta, John Guthridge, Alberto Gallitti, and Freddie Wilson (Editors); Pierluigi Basile (Set Designer); Enrico Sabbatini (Costumes); Vittorio Biseo (Make-up); Mario Brava (Special Effects); Dov Seltzer (Additional Music, Songs, and Dances); Ennio Morricone (Music Score).

CAST: Burt Lancaster (Moses); Anthony Quayle (Aaron); Ingrid Thulin (Miriam); Irene Papas (Zipporah); Aharon Ipale (Joshua); Yousef Shiloah (Dathan); Marina Berti (Eliscba); Shmuel Rodensky (Jethro); Mariangela Melato (Princess Bithia); Laurent Terzieff (Mernefta); William Lancaster (Young Moses); Jacques Herlin (Magician); Galia Kohn (Young Miriam); Jose Quaglio (1st Minister); Umberto Raho (2nd Minister); Mario Ferrari (Pharaoh Ramses II); John Francis Lane (1st Consul); Dina Doronne (Yokebad); Melba Englander (Mernefta's Wife); Marco Steiner (Young Mernefta); Michele Placido (Caleb); Antonio Piovanelli (Koreh); Yossi Warjansky (Eleazar); Haim Banai, Haim Bashi, and Amos Talshir (Dathan's Henchmen). Narrated by Richard Johnson.

SYNOPSIS: In ancient times, the Israelites are in bondage to the Egyptians. Ramses, the pharaoh of Egypt, decrees that all baby boys of the enslaved people be drowned in the Nile River to stop a fear of overpopulation. An infant boy, Moses, is placed in a basket by his sister, Miriam, and he floats to safety down the river. Found by the Egyptian princess Bithia, Moses is raised in her royal household.

Growing into manhood, young Moses kills an Egyptian mistreating a slave, and he learns his true heritage. Moses is forced to flee into the desert.

As the years pass, Moses is a shepherd and is married to a woman named Zipporah. Ramses has died, and his son, Mernefta, the new pharaoh, wishes for Moses to return to a royal position. Declining this offer, Moses does go back to Egypt after communicating with God's spirit on a sacred mountain in the land of Sinai.

Moses, the Lawgiver: Burt Lancaster in the title role (1975). The sincerity projected into a role was by now a trademark fixture in many of Burt Lancaster's films.

With brother Aaron, Moses meets with the pharaoh, but without success tries to convince him of God's will to free the Israelites. Only after the ten plagues are brought down on the Egyptians and ultimately the death of his son does Mernefta let Moses lead the Israelites into the desert for a three-day pilgrimage. When they do not return, the pharaoh chases after them with his soldiers. The Israelites escape when the Red Sea parts to let them cross to the distant shore. Many of the Egyptian soldiers are killed when the sea comes crashing down.

Leading the exodus is an overwhelming task for Moses. When he returns to the sacred mountain with two tablets to receive God's laws, many of the people begin sinning despite the pleas of Aaron and Miriam. Those who have sinned are later punished with horrible deaths, as are two men stoned for working on the Sabbath. Dathan, one of the main antagonists, is killed by an earthquake.

For their lack of faith, the Israelites are ordained by God to wander through a series of holy wars for 40 years. Only then are they allowed to cross the River Jordan to their promised land. With Miriam and Aaron dead, another, Joshua, leads the people. For his inner conflict with God, Moses, before he dies, is only allowed to see the new land from a mountain.

COMMENTARY: When shown on CBS-TV, *Moses, the Lawgiver* ran in six one-hour installments over the summer of 1975. As simply *Moses*, it was edited drastically, to Burt Lancaster's dismay, and released by Avco Embassy to theaters in the spring of 1976.

Produced by Vincenzo Labella and directed by Gianfranco De Bosio, it was a highly ambitious production for its day, costing $6 million and taking six months to make. In August 1973, filming started and included use of Rome's Cinecitta Studio and location sites in Israel.

As a television miniseries (Burt's first), *Moses* was deemed a success, with some 25 million viewers watching each telecast in the United States (it was successful in Italy as well). Yet the condensed movie version found little mass-market appeal. Its spectacle seemed realistic and its story a down-to-earth human drama, but as a whole the film was cumbersome and episodic. The scenario, derived from the biblical book of Exodus, was written by director De Bosio, Vittorio Bonicelli, and Anthony Burgess.

Lancaster was not initially interested in playing Moses until he received Burgess's outline from Sir Lew Grade (whose ITC production company in England collaborated on the project with RAI Television of Italy). Although he himself admitted to being an atheist, Burt was won over by the human elements presented by Burgess and reflected on the writer, "He saw God as a very tough customer. That appealed to me immediately—me fighting God!"

The actor's performance in the title role was well rounded, expressing authority yet self-doubt, anger yet humility. Despite not having as richly defined roles, a cast of international players offered commendable support—including Anthony Quayle as Aaron, Ingrid Thulin as Miriam, Irene Papas as Zipporah, and Laurent Terzieff as Mernefta. William Lancaster, then 27, did very well with his portrayal of the young Moses; a most striking resemblance to his father was seen in the first odyssey in the desert.

Burt Lancaster showing the fury of Moses, in *Moses, the Lawgiver*.

REVIEWS: *New York Times:* "Mr. Lancaster, no longer in his first youth, has the elemental physical and emotional strength to make a fine Moses, if this were a better film."

New York Post: "It is never what one would call an inspired picture, despite all the heavenly intervention, but it does plod through the years without false-stepping into excessive theatrical gimmickry."

Conversation Piece (Gruppo di Famiglia in un Interno)

A Rusconi Film and Gaumont International Production   Presented at the New York Film Festival on September 26, 1975   A New Line Cinema Release   Released in February 1976   122 minutes   Technicolor   Todd-AO   Rated R
CREDITS: Luchino Visconti (Director); Giovanni Bertolucci (Producer); Giorgio Treves (Assistant Director); Suso Cecchi D'Amico, Enrico Medioli, and Luchino Visconti (Screenplay); Pasqualino De Santis (Photography); Ruggero Mastroianni (Editor); Mario Garbuglia (Art Director); Dario Simoni (Set Decorator); Piero Tosi and Vera Marzot (Costumes); Alberto De Rossi and Eligio Trani (Make-up); Franco Mannino (Music Score). From an idea by Enrico Medioli.
CAST: Burt Lancaster (Professor); Silvana Mangano (Bianca Brumonti); Helmut Berger (Konrad); Claudia Marsani (Lietta); Stefano Patrizi (Stefano); Elvira Cortese (Erminia); Dominique Sanda (Mother); Claudia Cardinale (Wife).

SYNOPSIS: A retired American professor is living in seclusion in an apartment building in Rome that was inherited from his mother's family. He is captivated with his exquisite collection of books and paintings and the dreams of his past.

Countess Bianca Brumonti, wife of a right-wing industrialist, coerces the professor to rent her an apartment on the floor above his. The apartment is redecorated in a contemporary style in contrast to the professor's more refined tastes. Bianca uses the apartment as a haven for her lover, Konrad, who is bisexual and intimate with her daughter, Lietta, and the girl's boyfriend, Stefano.

The professor is disturbed as well as fascinated with their self-indulgent lifestyles. When Konrad is beaten up for his involvement with drug smuggling, the professor cares for him.

After Bianca's husband is informed on by Konrad for an attempt to assassinate the Communists in the Italian government, the young man is killed in an oven explosion that is rigged to look like suicide. Although he had come to regard Konrad and the others in the apartment as his family, the professor has been put through a great deal of anxiety. Taken to a hospital, he dies of heart failure.

COMMENTARY: *Conversation Piece* was Italian filmmaker Luchino Visconti's next-to-last film before his death in 1976. He was apparently intrigued with the aristocracy in a changing society and was meticulous in indulging in both the splendor and tragedy of this social class. This film was a personal expression not unlike that earlier Visconti classic *The Leopard* about the influence of change on a man of wealth and culture (once again, the filmmaker involved himself on a script with Suso Cecchi D'Amico and Enrico Medioli).

Yet without *The Leopard*'s epic sweep, *Conversation Piece* seemed an

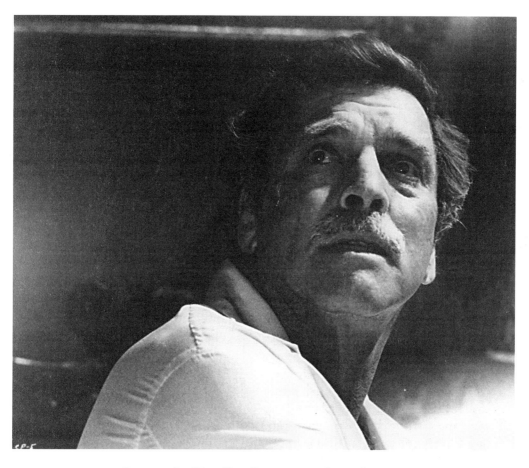

Conversation Piece: **Burt Lancaster as the professor.**

awkward presentation of the turbulence within a modern society (as compared to the artistry mastered using a nineteenth-century one in the 1963 film). Having suffered a stroke in 1973, Visconti directed nobly from a wheelchair in 1974 at the De Paolis and Dear Studios in Italy; perhaps the awkwardness of the picture can be jointly attributed to its sexual theme and to being studiobound. Rusconi Film (of Rome) and Gaumont International (of Paris) shared in the making of the production (which was produced by Giovanni Bertolucci).

The film was a success when initially shown in both Italy and France—the Italian version was called *Gruppo di Famiglia in un Interno* (*Family Group from Inside*), while the French one was called *Violence et Passion* (*Violence and Passion*). But *Conversation Piece*, the American title, was not appreciated at all when it opened the 13th New York Film Festival in 1975; in an English-language version, it was laughed at.

In finding international support, *Conversation Piece* was certainly disappointing. New Line Cinema, an American-based distributor, did try to improve its chances (with the Italian version using English subtitles) in London in 1976, New York in 1977, and Los

Angeles in 1978. Still, the film seemed flawed, even though Visconti's style for pictorial antiquities was touchingly rendered, particularly through the lifestyle of the leading character.

The true strength of the film came from Lancaster's sensitive playing of the reclusive professor. This sensitivity was made even more so because of Visconti having the professor observe, as if he was the director, the conflicting lifestyles around him (as well as a slant toward bisexuality). Silvana Mangano and Helmut Berger must be credited along with Lancaster for their bravura acting in delicate roles. Dominique Sanda and Claudia Cardinale were seen in brief flashbacks as the professor's mother and wife, respectively.

REVIEWS: *Sight and Sound:* "The center of it all is Burt Lancaster's performance. He makes those familiar gestures with his open hands, which here seem to be attempts at policing the chaos of events.... His clipped style, his voice and carriage somehow expressing the control of a barely containable force, gives back to the film the solemnity and dignity which elsewhere is dissipated."

Film Information: "Cinematically, the film is static. Here Visconti's preoccupation with death is not even illumined with the visual dream-like beauty of his *Death in Venice*, so the film's poor script and inane dialogue become unbearable."

Buffalo Bill and the Indians, or Sitting Bull's History Lesson

A Dino De Laurentiis Presentation   A David Susskind Production   A Robert Altman Film   Released through United Artists   Released July 4, 1976   123 min-

utes   DeLuxe-General Color   Panavision   Rated PG

CREDITS: Robert Altman (Director, Producer); Tommy Thompson (Assistant Director); David Susskind (Executive Producer); Alan Rudolph and Robert Altman (Screenplay); Paul Lohmann (Photography); Peter Appleton and Dennis Hill (Editors); Tony Masters (Production Designer); Jack Maxsted (Art Director); Anthony Powell (Costumes); Monty Westmore (Make-up); Jim Webb and Chris McLaughlin (Sound); Richard Baskin (Music Score). Suggested by Arthur Kopit's play *Indians*.

CAST: Paul Newman (William F. Cody); Joel Grey (Nate Salsbury); Kevin McCarthy (Major John Burke); Harvey Keitel (Ed Goodman); Allan Nicholls (Colonel Prentiss Ingraham); Geraldine Chaplin (Annie Oakley); John Considine (Frank Butler); Robert Doqui (Oswald Dart); Mike Kaplan (Jules Keen); Bert Remsen (Crutch); Bonnie Leaders (Margaret); Noelle Rogers (Lucille DuCharmes); Evelyn Lear (Nina Cavalini); Denver Pyle (McLaughlin); Frank Kaquitts (Chief Sitting Bull); Will Sampson (William Halsey); Ken Krossa (Johnny Baker); Fred N. Larsen (Buck Taylor); Jerri and Joy Duce (Trick Riders); Alex Green and Gary MacKenzie (Whip and Fast Draw Act); Humphrey Gratz (Old Soldier); Burt Lancaster (Ned Buntline).

SYNOPSIS: In the 1880s, William "Buffalo Bill" Cody has a Wild West Show in which he is the star performer. Annie Oakley is another of the star attractions, performing in a sharpshooter act with her husband/manager, Frank Butler.

Butler informs Cody that writer Ned Buntline is in their camp at the bar. To all who will listen, Buntline brags on how he invented Buffalo Bill. Annoyed by the writer's presence, Cody sends Nate Salsbury, his show business partner, to ask him to leave. Ned will stick around, he says, until Bill pays him a visit.

Chief Sitting Bull is escorted into camp by Major John Burke, Cody's

Buffalo Bill and the Indians, or Sitting Bull's History Lesson, **with Burt Lancaster and Paul Newman.**

publicist, and Indian agent McLaughlin to perform in the show. Cody mistakes the tall Indian interpreter, William Halsey, for the much shorter chief. Ed Goodman, Cody's nephew, reports that Sitting Bull wants to live across the river from the camp; this is laughed at because of the hardship of crossing over, but the chief easily reaches the far shore.

Halsey relates that the chief will stay only until President Grover Cleveland visits; more laughs break out, as there are no plans for this to happen. Sitting Bull wants blankets sent to his people, and he refuses to be in an act showing his cowardly treatment of the late General Custer. Instead, the chief wants to reenact a cavalry attack on the Indians. Cody gets angry and fires him.

Only when Annie threatens to quit over the matter does Bill rehire the chief.

In the bar, Buntline mentions that Buffalo Bill took credit for heroic feats he did not do. But the showman is greeted with applause at the season's first show; however, he is surprised when the audience applauds Sitting Bull. Later on, Cody, who has had too much whiskey, errs in thinking that the chief is trying to escape and fails to track him down.

President Cleveland does visit the Wild West Show. During her performance, Annie accidentally wings Frank (although she had been told by Ed of her husband's dalliance with another woman). Cody likes to romance opera singers; at a party after the show, he is rebuffed by the First Lady's singer, Nina Cavalini. Sitting Bull is rebuffed trying to make a request to the president.

Bill Cody finally visits the bar and has a drink with Ned Buntline. Ned then jumps a horse over a fence and disappears into the night.

After Sitting Bull's return to his people on the reservation and his reported killing by guards, Cody is haunted by the chief. Buffalo Bill may be a fraud, but his show is a rousing success.

COMMENTARY: A film by Robert Altman suggested an attack on any subject in a seriocomic fashion. *Buffalo Bill and the Indians, or Sitting Bull's History Lesson* was just a jocular exercise released by United Artists in the bicentennial summer of 1976. It was Altman's contribution to America's mythologizing process, which was shown as being a bit tarnished in glorifying this particular famous western hero as being more than simply a grand showman.

Paul Newman's charisma made him an ideal choice to play the star of the Wild West Show; his dynamic acting ability fully realized the essence of the character's soul. Burt Lancaster was the exiled legend maker in a much smaller role (which was filmed in four days at the film's location in Alberta, Canada, on the Stoney Indian Reserve). Yet each actor conveyed a bluster and melancholy that was very touching.

Geraldine Chaplin was especially charming as Annie Oakley, as historic a figure as Newman's Buffalo Bill and Lancaster's Ned Buntline. Will Sampson and Frank Kaquitts represented the Indians—the latter's enactment of Sitting Bull (also a historic personage) was a stunning contrast in his stoic delivery

of the truth to the lies of Bill Cody. Though a bit overdrawn, the point of the film was that it was better to have dignity than not.

Buffalo Bill and the Indians reflected on both the sentiments and ironies with its images. As well as being the producer and director, Robert Altman also wrote the screenplay with Alan Rudolph (suggested from a 1969 play by Arthur Kopit). But the humorous escapades that resulted were not at all appreciated by audiences at the box office. Still, its satire did earn the film the Golden Bear Award for Best Picture at the Berlin Film Festival, July 6, 1976.

REVIEWS: *New York Times:* "It's a sometimes self-indulgent, confused, ambitious movie that is often very funny and always fascinating."

Time: "Buffalo Bill Cody (superbly played by Paul Newman) was a legend created out of flimsy cloth by a pulp writer and promoter named Ned Buntline (impersonated by Burt Lancaster), who lurks around the fringes of the film."

Victory at Entebbe

A David L. Wolper Production Broadcast on ABC Television on December 13, 1976   180 minutes   Released to theaters by Warner Communications in December 1976   119 minutes   Color

CREDITS: Marvin J. Chomsky (Director); Robert Guenette (Producer); David L. Wolper (Executive Producer); Albert J. Simon (Associate Producer); Ernest Kinoy (Script); James Kilgore (Photography); Jim McElroy and Mike Gavaldon (Editors); David Saxon (Supervising Editor); Edward Stephenson (Production Designer); Charles Fox (Music Score).

CAST: Helmut Berger (German Terrorist); Theodore Bikel (Yakov Shlomo);

Linda Blair (Chana Vilnofsky); Kirk Douglas (Hershel Vilnofsky); Richard Dreyfuss (Colonel Yonatan Netanyahu); Stefan Gierasch (Mordecai Gur); David Groh (Benjamin Wise); Julius Harris (President Idi Amin); Helen Hayes (Mrs. Wise); Anthony Hopkins (Yitzhak Rabin); Burt Lancaster (Shimon Peres); Christian Marquand (Captain Dukas); Elizabeth Taylor (Edra Vilnofsky); Jessica Walter (Nomi Haroun); Harris Yulin (General Dan Shomron); Allan Miller (Natan Haroun); Bibi Besch (German Woman); David Sheiner (Aaron Olav); Severn Darden (Moshe Meyer); Ben Hammer (Yaakobi); Anthony James (Gamal Fahmy); Victor Mohica (Jaif); Samantha Harper (Nan Peyser); Philip Sterling (Colonel Baruch Bar-Lev); Erica Yohn (Belgian Woman); Lilyan Chauvin (French Nun); Miriam Byrd-Nethery (Nun's Ward); Zitto Kazann (Peruvian); Jessica St. John (Parisienne); Kristina Wayborn (Claudine); Austin Stoker (Dr. Ghota); Dimitri Logothetis (Young Soldier); Jenny Maybrook (Captain Abi); Than Wyenn (Rabin's Aide); Eunice Christopher (Israeli Intelligence Worker); Pitt Herbert, Barbara Carney (Passengers); Michael Mullins (Aryeh); Vera Mandell (Young Mother).

SYNOPSIS: An Air France jet is hijacked by terrorists working for a Palestinian organization. The plane is taken to Entebbe Airport in Uganda, Africa, and the passengers and crew are held hostage at gunpoint in the terminal. Those who are not Jewish are released.

Idi Amin, the Ugandan president, does nothing to help the hostages except to act as an intermediary. The Israeli prime minister, Yitzhak Rabin, meets with his cabinet of advisors, including Defense Minister Shimon Peres, to discuss how to rescue their people.

Rabin is hard pressed by the public to negotiate with the terrorists for the release of the Jewish hostages. The terrorists want Israel to free other Arab terrorists who have been imprisoned, but Peres reminds Rabin that the military policy is not to give in to terrorism in any form.

Hershel and Edra Vilnofsky plead with Rabin to negotiate because their daughter, Chana, is one of the hostages. Benjamin Wise is a hostage with his mother; she becomes ill and is taken to a local hospital.

A bold plan is worked out to send Israeli commandoes to Entebbe to stop the terrorists and rescue the hostages. Peres assigns the operation to General Dan Shomron and Colonel Yonatan Netanyahu.

During the raid, the terrorists are killed; in the confusion, several hostages are also slain. Netanyahu is the only commando to die in the brief fighting. The remaining hostages are also freed, except for Mrs. Wise. It is revealed that she has been murdered in the hospital.

COMMENTARY: *Victory at Entebbe* was based on a true event that took place between June 27 and July 4, 1976. The actual raid, which took 90 minutes, stunned the world. This event overflowed with human drama and adventure, and two major television networks quickly sensed the value of these ingredients for an exciting entertainment. ABC was the first with their videotaped program seen on December 13, just a little more than five months after the actual event. NBC presented its telecast, *Raid on Entebbe*, on January 9, 1977.

Though the ABC reenactment of the daring commando raid was moderately exciting, the more exacting emphasis was on the human relationships. Particularly fleshed out in Ernest Kinoy's Emmy-nominated teleplay was the struggle between Israel's Yitzhak

Victory at Entebbe, with Richard Dreyfuss, Harris Yulin, Burt Lancaster and Stefan Gierasch.

Rabin and Shimon Peres over how to handle the dilemma.

Burt Lancaster was forthright and stern as Peres, who conscientiously strives to help the hostages without compromising military doctrine (as with *Buffalo Bill and the Indians*, Burt's part only took a few days to do, this time at the Warner Bros. Studio in Burbank). Anthony Hopkins's Rabin carried the burden of whether to use force against force with even more thoughtfulness. The onscreen tension between the two actors was engrossing (Jack Warden and Peter Finch played Peres and Rabin quite respectably in the later television film, but with less friction).

Nonetheless, *Victory at Entebbe* also abounded with clichés (mainly in regard to its stereotyping of the hostages) and was not considered as good as *Raid on Entebbe* or a later theatrical film in 1977 called *Operation: Thunderbolt*, which dealt with the same subject matter. Harris Yulin's Shomron and Richard Dreyfuss's Netanyahu, the raid's co-leaders, were solid enough; Kirk Douglas and Elizabeth Taylor were less so as the distraught parents of a hostage (Linda Blair), because of their brief appearances.

The original three-hour telecast of *Victory at Entebbe* (directed by Marvin J. Chomsky and produced by Robert Guenette) was also made into a theatrical film for overseas distribution. Warner Communications handled these rights to the David L. Wolper production, and the film's theme created several problems. Five Arab ambassadors protested the picture in Tokyo on December 17, 1976, proclaiming that it might disturb relations between some Arab countries and Japan. A terrorist organization, the Palestinian Combatants for Arab Revolution, caused minor disturbances at four theaters in Rome. Demonstrations against the film were also made in Norway.

REVIEWS: *TV Guide: "Victory at Entebbe* boasts a dozen stars—Helen Hayes, Burt Lancaster and Elizabeth Taylor among them—to glitter in Ernest Kinoy's dramatization."

Washington Post: "The show bears watching ... and remembering."

The Cassandra Crossing

A Sir Lew Grade and Carlo Ponti Presentation   For Associated General Films   An Avco Embassy Release   Released February 9, 1977   127 minutes   Color-Prints by CFI   Panavision   Rated R

CREDITS: George Pan Cosmatos (Director); Carlo Ponti (Producer); Antonio Gabrielli (Assistant Director); Giancarlo Pettini (Executive Producer); Tom Mankiewicz, Robert Katz, and George Pan Cosmatos (Screenplay); Ennio Guarnieri (Photography); Tazio Secciaroli (Special Photography); Francois Bonnot and Roberto Silvi (Editors); Aurelio Crugnola (Art Director); Andriana Berselli (Costumes); Carlo Palmieri (Sound); Jerry Goldsmith (Music Score). From a story by Robert Katz and George Pan Cosmatos.

CAST: Sophia Loren (Jennifer); Richard Harris (Chamberlain); Martin Sheen (Navarro); O.J. Simpson (Father Haley); Lionel Stander (Conductor); Ann Turkel (Susan); Ingrid Thulin (Elena); Lee Strasberg (Kaplan); Burt Lancaster (MacKenzie); Ava Gardner (Nicole); Lou Castel (Driver); John Philip Law (Stack); Ray Lovelock (Tom); Alida Valli (Mrs. Chadwick); Stefano Patrizi (Attendant); Carlo De Majo (Patient); Fausta Avelli (Katherine).

SYNOPSIS: Three members of a Swedish terrorist movement fail in their task to sabotage an American-controlled biological lab at the International Health Organization in Geneva, Switzerland. However, exposing himself to deadly plague germs, one man escapes aboard the Transcontinental Express train, which is carrying 1,000 people.

An American army intelligence officer, Colonel MacKenzie, tries to restrict the plague from spreading outside the train. Basing his headquarters at the health building, he contacts a Dr. Chamberlain aboard the train to warn of the danger. The plague-carrying terrorist is captured, but not before spreading the germs to others. Father Haley and Jennifer, Chamberlain's ex-wife, help the doctor isolate those infected. An infected dog is removed by helicopter for observation.

A force of soldiers in protective gear are waiting at a train station. No one is allowed off the train; one passenger, Kaplan, is wounded trying to get away and later takes his own life. With the soldiers now aboard, the train is relocated by MacKenzie to a quarantine center, which can only be reached by going over an insecure bridge—the Cassandra Crossing.

Although Chamberlain warns MacKenzie about the bridge, he does not listen. A couple, Navarro and Nicole, are aboard, and Father Haley is actually a narcotics agent trying to bust the man. But Haley, agreeing that the train must be stopped, lets Navarro try to climb outside past the soldiers to the engine. The soldiers kill Navarro and later Haley, who gets into a gun battle with the doctor against them.

Due to receiving a large dose of oxygen, the exposed dog as well as the infected people on the train are slowly getting better. MacKenzie will still not listen, feeling things are too uncertain; the passengers are apparently worth any sacrifice to save even more lives from the threat of the plague. As the train speeds toward the bridge, Chamberlain unhooks part of it and is able to save Jennifer, Nicole, himself, and many others. The rest of the train hurtles across the bridge, which collapses and sends the trapped people to their deaths.

COMMENTARY: During 1977, Burt Lancaster appeared in three motion pictures classified as thrillers, although none were successful at the box office domestically. Avco Embassy's release of *The Cassandra Crossing* came in the midst of other disaster films in the 1970s that began with *Airport* (combining exciting, life-threatening situations with all-star casts).

The excitement in this adventure began, interestingly enough, with its ironic theme on the dangerous biological experiments secretly going on. There

The Cassandra Crossing, with John Philip Law, Ingrid Thulin, and Burt Lancaster.

is an especially chilling sequence in which the soldiers, in their bizarre apparel, guard the train like robots. Yet the film ran off in so many directions that the exciting moments turned into foolish ones. The all-star cast ultimately paled.

Richard Harris and Lancaster were the protagonists pitted against each other, each believing in his own sense of duty. However, Harris was clearly the heroic one as the good doctor (a role originally pegged for Lancaster, yet rejected because it would have been far more time consuming). The role of the colonel was played by Burt with that hard stoicism seen in other films; this portrayal bore a certain resemblance to his general in *Seven Days in May*, but, filmed in but ten days' time (at the Cinecitta Studio in Rome), it was not nearly as well executed.

Other notable stars entangled in the mishmash included Sophia Loren, Martin Sheen, and Ava Gardner (both Burt and Gardner received special billing). Carlo Ponti (Loren's husband) produced the picture, and George Pan Cosmatos directed. The story for *The Cassandra Crossing* initially came from Cosmatos and Robert Katz, both of whom were given credit for the screenplay along with Tom Mankiewicz (although uncredited as a writer, Lancaster also was involved on the script).

REVIEWS: *Los Angeles Times:* "The premise isn't really any better or worse than for many other formula films, but it's done in by its silly chatter, except for the most undemanding audiences. Even so, it's fun in a so-bad-it's-good-way, thanks to the driving energy of its Greek-born director George Pan Cosmatos."

New York Times: "Burt Lancaster bears his totally incomprehensible role as if it were a toothache. His jaw is clamped so tight that it looks swollen."

Twilight's Last Gleaming

A Lorimar-Bavaria Presentation   A Geria Production   An Allied Artists Pictures Release   Released February 9, 1977   146 minutes   Technicolor   Rated R

CREDITS: Robert Aldrich (Director); Merv Adelson (Producer); Wolfgang Glattes (Assistant Director); Helmut Jedele (Executive Producer); Ronald M. Cohen and Edward Huebsch (Screenplay); Robert Hauser (Photography); Michael Luciano and Maury Weintrobe (Editors); Rolf Zehetbauer (Production Designer); Werner Achmann (Art Director); Tom Dawson (Costumes); Henry Millar and Willy Neuner (Special Effects); John Wilkinson and James Willis (Sound); Jerry Goldsmith (Music Score). Based on Walter Wager's novel *Viper Three*.

CAST: Burt Lancaster (Lawrence Dell); Roscoe Lee Browne (James Forrest); Joseph Cotten (Arthur Renfrew); Melvyn Douglas (Zachariah Guthrie); Charles Durning (President David Stevens); Richard Jaeckel (Capt. Stanford Towne); William Marshall (William Klinger); Vera Miles (Victoria Stevens); Gerald S. O'Loughlin (Michael O'Rourke); Richard Widmark (Gen. Martin MacKenzie); Paul Winfield (Willis Powell); Burt Young (Augie Garvas); Charles Aidman (Col. Bernstein); Leif Erickson (Ralph Whittaker); Charles McGraw (Peter Crane); Morgan Paull (1st Lt. Louis Cannellis); Simon Scott (Phil Spencer); William Smith (Hoxey); Bill Walker (Willard); Ed Bishop (Maj. Fox); Phil Brown (Rev. Cartwright); Gary Cockrell (Capt. Jackson); Don Fellows (Gen. Stonesifer); Werton Gavin (Lt. Wilson); Garrick Hagon (Alfie); Elizabeth Halliday (Secretary); David Healy (Maj. Winters); Thomasine Heiner (Edith); Bill Hootkins (Sgt. Fitzpatrick); Ray Jewers (Sgt. Domino); Ron Lee (Sgt. Rappaport); Robert Sherman

(Maj. Le Beau); John Ratzenberger (Sgt. Kopecki); Robert MacLeod (Chambers); Lionel Murton (Col. Horne); Pamela Roland (Sgt. Kelly); Mark Russel (Mendez); Rich Steber (Capt. Kincaid); Drew W. Wesche (Lt. Witkin); Kent O. Doering (Barker); Roy E. Glenn (Servant); Alan Moore, Phil Senini, and Rich Demarest (Sharpshooters).

SYNOPSIS: Lawrence Dell is a former American air force general. For his radical opposition to his country's involvement in the Vietnam War, he was framed on a manslaughter charge and sent to prison. He escapes, however, with three other convicts, Hoxey, Garvas, and Powell. They then break into a nuclear missile silo; when Hoxey proves to be a vicious killer, Dell eliminates him.

In the silo, the convicts hold hostage two air force men, Captain Towne and 1st Lieutenant Cannellis. Dell's one-time superior, General Mackenzie, is made aware of the situation as is the president of the United States, David Stevens.

At the White House, the president brings together his most valuable political and military people to deal with the problem and Dell's demands. Dell threatens to set off nine Titan missiles unless several things are done—$10 million must be handed over, safe passage must be provided aboard Air Force One with the president as hostage, and President Stevens must read a secret military document to the American people. The document reveals that the military sacrificed lives in the Vietnam War to show the Russians that the insanity was there to use nuclear force against Russia if needed.

Although the president is disturbed by this revelation, he allows MacKenzie to send men and try a takeover of the silo by force. In the skirmish that results, Garvas is killed and Dell prepares to launch the missiles into Russia.

Powell is able to keep Dell from this course of action. Reluctantly, President Stevens agrees to come to the silo as their hostage. He has the secretary of defense, Zachariah Guthrie, promise to release the document if anything should happen to him.

Unfortunately it does; Stevens is gunned down with Dell and Powell by sharpshooters under MacKenzie's command. As he dies, the president finds Guthrie not heeding the promise.

COMMENTARY: As in *The Cassandra Crossing*, Burt Lancaster was involved with a sly military force in *Twilight's Last Gleaming*. This time it was the other side of the coin, as he was seen as a disillusioned and bitter man whose resentment of America's actions against Vietnam and Russia incited him to action against the very structure that he was part of in the first film. Who better to guide Burt than director Robert Aldrich, one of the great action filmmakers, in their fourth and last film together.

It was Aldrich's idea to expand on Walter Wager's 1971 novel, *Viper Three* (which dealt with criminals taking over a missile complex), by initiating one of the criminals' discrepancy with the U.S. military in Vietnam. Edward Huebsch and Ronald M. Cohen came up with a screenplay in under three weeks. *Twilight's Last Gleaming*, though intriguing, must bear enormous scrutiny over flaws in logic. It was not given approval by the U.S. military. Although set in the United States, the film, produced by Merv Adelson, was shot at the Bavaria Studio in Munich, Germany.

Leading a strong cast, Lancaster offered a forceful, commanding performance as the fool's hero carrying out a gutsy (but stupid) move. Richard Widmark was also commanding as the crafty general opposing Lancaster (in a role very similar to Burt's in *Cassandra Crossing*, even right down to the name). A very distinguished roster of supporting actors included Melvyn Douglas, Paul Winfield, and Richard Jaeckel. However, none gave better support than Charles Durning as an all-too-human president of the United States.

Vera Miles's brief role as the First Lady was cut from the film despite the fact that she still received billing in advertisements at the time of the film's release in 1977 by Allied Artists (it may have been felt that her character held up the suspense). Despite the film's high profile for suspense and action, it was not well received by the public. Even Burt was disappointed with the end result. Jerry Goldsmith composed music scores for *Twilight's Last Gleaming* and *Cassandra Crossing*, and both pictures were actually brought out on the same day.

Twilight's Last Gleaming, with Burt Young, Paul Winfield, and Burt Lancaster.

REVIEWS: *Women's Wear Daily:* "Everything about *Twilight* ... is preposterous. Though the screenplay seems to understand the intricacies of gaining access to a missile site it has absolutely no understanding of things like politics or how human beings talk. As in *Cassandra* the basic impulse is to manipulate the audience."

Film Information: "Burt Lancaster, as the idealistic general, and Charles Durning, as the president of the United States, give such believable performances they make the plot's weaknesses—including an overemphasis on sensationalism—less noticeable."

The Island of Dr. Moreau

A Samuel Z. Arkoff Presentation   A Skip Steloff/Sandy Howard/Major Production   An American International Pictures Release   Released July 13, 1977   98 minutes   Movielab Color   Rated PG
CREDITS: Don Taylor (Director); John Temple-Smith and Skip Steloff (Producers); Bob Bender (Assistant Director); Samuel Z. Arkoff and Sandy Howard (Executive Producers); John Herman Shaner and Al Ramrus (Screenplay); Gerry Fisher (Photography); Marion Rothman (Editor); Philip Jefferies (Production Designer); James Berkey (Set Decorator); Emma Porteus and Rita Woods (Costumes); John Chambers, Dan Striepeke, and Tom Burman (Creative Make-up); David Hildyard (Sound); Ralph D. Helfer (Animal Stunt Coordinator); Laurence Rosenthal (Music Score). Based on the novel by H. G. Wells.
CAST: Burt Lancaster (Dr. Moreau); Michael York (Andrew Braddock); Nigel Davenport (Montgomery); Barbara Carrera (Maria); Richard Basehart (Sayer of the Law); Nick Cravat (M'Ling); The Great John L (Boarman); Bob Ozman (Bullman); Fumio Demura (Hyenaman); Gary Baxley (Lionman); John Gillespie (Tigerman); David Cass (Bearman).

SYNOPSIS: Two sailors, lost at sea in a rowboat, land on a tropical island. One man is dragged away to his death by mysterious creatures, while the other falls into a trap and loses consciousness.

The surviving seaman, Braddock, comes to inside a compound. Braddock meets Montgomery, the compound's foreman, and its owner, Dr. Moreau. Maria, a beautiful young woman, is also on the island; in time she and young Braddock fall in love.

Braddock is told by Moreau not to venture outside the compound at night. But during daylight hours, Braddock finds M'Ling, a servant of the doctor's, drinking like an animal from a jungle stream. When M'Ling is brought back into the compound, Braddock is further surprised to see that he now *looks* like an animal as well.

Dr. Moreau informs the curious Braddock that he has been turning the jungle beasts into humanlike creatures. It is done by injecting a serum into the creatures, thereby altering their cell structure. The process is not always perfect, as the creatures revert back to their animal characteristics.

Intrigued by the distant animal howls from the jungle, Braddock enters their cave and is attacked. Moreau arrives to save him and instill a fear into the creatures that the law forbids attacking and shedding the blood of man. One of the creatures, called the Sayer of the Law, leads the others in actually saying Moreau's dictates.

Another of the strange beasts, the Bullman, rebels against Moreau and kills a tiger. Afraid to be injected again with

The Island of Dr. Moreau, with David Cass (left) and Burt Lancaster.

the serum, the Bullman is chased down and pleads with Braddock to shoot him and put him out of his misery. This Braddock does, to the anger of the other creatures.

In retaliation, Moreau punishes Braddock by injecting him with the serum, which slowly is turning him into an animal. Trying to stop it, Montgomery is shot by the doctor. Montgomery's body is left outside the compound by M'Ling; when the creatures realize that Moreau has broken the law, they maul him to death.

Braddock hangs Moreau's body above the compound, hoping the creatures will believe the doctor is still alive and not attack. It doesn't work for long,

and the creatures destroy the compound and are destroyed in the process. After a struggle with the last of the creatures, Braddock, the serum now out of his system, escapes from the island with Maria.

COMMENTARY: *The Island of Dr. Moreau* had all the ingredients for perfect summer of 1977 entertainment—fantasy, adventure, romance—combined into one colorful package. However, the film did not secure the holiday crowds expected (with the big summer movie being *Star Wars* instead); it actually lost money (its production costs were $6 million) after its release by American International Pictures.

Director Don Taylor and producers John Temple-Smith and Skip Steloff may have actually kept the horror in the story too restrained for its own good. Nonetheless, the strangeness of the scenario supplied by Al Ramrus and John Herman Shaner took elements from both H. G. Wells's 1896 novel and a 1933 motion picture called *The Island of Lost Souls.*

Charles Laughton delivered a hammy but distinguished performance as the renegade Dr. Moreau in the actually more chilling earlier film. In the 1977 version, Burt Lancaster also distinguished himself but was more subdued (although his forcefulness was quite evident when provoked). Still more subdued was Marlon Brando (although casting a bizarre physical appearance) as Moreau in the 1996 version.

Lancaster's words on his own interpretation included this statement, "I am playing Dr. Moreau as a dedicated scientist who, before he goes mad, feels that what he is doing is a noble thing. I don't think he is a heroic man, but he is unusual, strange. He believes it is the duty of science to investigate all things."

For *The Island of Dr. Moreau,* Michael York clearly had the heroic role as the seaman and displayed a most adventurous spirit. Barbara Carrera's dark, radiant mystique was fascinating as the island beauty; the film's ending leaves it up to the viewer to speculate whether or not she is one of Moreau's creations (the character seems disturbed by a facial change that takes place). Also beautifully visualized were the exotic landscapes filmed on St. Croix in the Virgin Islands.

Yet the most fascinating aspect of this thriller were the masks of the so-called Humanimals created by John Chambers, Tom Burman, and Dan Striepeke. Among the striking creatures were Nick Cravat as a servant and Richard Basehart as the Sayer of the Law (this latter role was played in the 1933 film by that great horror film star Bela Lugosi).

REVIEWS: *Senior Scholastic:* "It has dignity, sincerity, good performances, and startling make-up and special effects. But in spite of all the spooky goings-on and brooding atmosphere, it lacks real tension. Even the spectacular action sequences between real animals and the beast men don't set the pulses pounding."

New York Times: "Mr. Lancaster is a very benign madman, courtly, gentle-mannered, a perfect host to the uninvited guest until Mr. York goes poking around and stirring up trouble with the homemade help."

1900 (Novecento)

An Alberto Grimaldi Presentation   In Association With PEA Cinematografica/ Artistes Associates/Artemis   A Bernardo Bertolucci Film   A Paramount Release Presented at the New York Film Festival on October 8, 1977   248 minutes   Technicolor   Rated R

CREDITS: Bernardo Bertolucci (Director); Alberto Grimaldi (Producer); Gabriele Polverosi and Peter Shepherd (Assistant Directors); Franco Arcalli, Giuseppe Bertolucci, and Bernardo Bertolucci (Screenplay); Vittorio Storaro (Photography); Franco Arcalli (Editor); Ezio Frigerio (Art Director); Gitt Magrini (Costumes); Claudio Maielli (Sound); Ennio Morricone (Music Score).

CAST: Robert De Niro (Alfredo Berlinghieri, Grandson); Gerard Depardieu (Olmo Dalco); Dominique Sanda (Ada Fiastri Paulhan); Francesca Bertini (Desolata); Laura Betti (Regina); Werner Bruhns

(Ottavio); Stefania Casini (Neve); Sterling Hayden (Leo Dalco); Anna Henkel (Anita, Olmo's Daughter); Ellen Schwiers (Amelia); Alida Valli (Signora Pioppi); Romolo Valli (Giovanni Berlinghieri); Stefania Sandrelli (Anita Foschi); Donald Sutherland (Attila); Burt Lancaster (Alfredo Berlinghieri, Grandfather); Anna-Maria Gheradi (Eleonora); Pippo Campanini (Don Tarcisio); Paolo Branco (Orso); Giacomo Rizzo (Rigoletto); Antonio Piovanelli (Turo); Liu Bosisio (Nella); Maria Monti (Rosina); Paolo Pavesi (Alfredo as a Child); Robert Maccanti (Olmo as a Child); Tiziana Senatore (Regina as a Child); Jose Quaglio (Aranzini); Edoardo Dallagio (Oreste); Salvator Mureddu (Chief of Guards); Allen Midgette (Vagabond).

SYNOPSIS: Italy, 1945, Liberation Day. A boy holds a man at gunpoint, while another man and woman are attacked by a group of people.

Going back to the year 1901, two boys are born on the same day—one is the grandson and namesake of Alfredo Berlinghieri, the *padrone* of an estate; the other is named Olmo and is the bastard grandson of Leo Dalco, who heads the peasants that work the farm on the estate.

The two boys play together as children, despite the class differences between the bourgeoisie and peasants. Grandfather Alfredo, now a bit senile, loves his grandson, but loathes Giovanni, his own son. After attempting sex with an adolescent peasant girl, old Alfredo hangs himself in his shame and impotence.

When a hailstorm damages half of the farm, Giovanni, the new *padrone*, reduces the salary of the workers. They strike, and old Leo passes away sitting under a tree as the landowners take to the fields.

World War I is ending and Olmo, now a young man, returns home from being a soldier. The new foreman on the farm is called Attila, who is part of the rising Fascist movement under Mussolini.

Giovanni breaks a labor contract with his workers, which is opposed by the now grown Alfredo. As a Communist, Olmo struggles to help his fellow peasants.

Through his Uncle Ottavio, Alfredo meets and falls in love with a French girl, Ada. Olmo has wed Anita, a teacher, and she dies giving birth to their daughter. Giovanni dies; Alfredo is now *padrone* and marries Ada. His cousin Regina is jealous and takes up with Attila.

Olmo urges Alfredo to send Attila away because he is a killer, but Alfredo resists. He is torn between the conflicting forces of Communism and Fascism that are suppressing his bourgeois life. Ada is disturbed by Alfredo's resistance and becomes an alcoholic.

During World War II, Alfredo finally fires Attila. But Ada has already left him. Attila massacres a group of workers.

Liberation Day, 1945. The man held at gunpoint is Alfredo; the man and woman being attacked by the peasants are Attila and Regina. Olmo helps Alfredo, but Attila is shot in the head.

Many years pass. Now old men, Olmo slumps beneath a pole while Alfredo lies across a railroad track with a train approaching.

COMMENTARY: *1900* was an epic motion picture from filmmaker Bernardo Bertolucci. His goal was to make his audience see Italy's past, which he felt was vital, and important; Bertolucci not only directed but also collaborated on the screenplay (with his brother, Giuseppe, and Franco Arcalli).

Burt Lancaster as Grandfather Alfredo in *1900*.

Alberto Grimaldi was the producer. The film was a fascinating lapse into an insurgent past, and the violence was shocking. The idealism Bertolucci felt for the working people could be discerned even through the turmoil of events depicted.

1900 was well received at the 1976 Cannes Film Festival in its original Italian version of over five hours (entitled *Novecento*), but it was not so well received when a shortened English-language version was seen at the New York Film Festival in 1977. Paramount Pictures wanted the shorter, four-hour showing. In actuality, the film lacked a cohesive strength to make it a total success; it sagged heavily in its political overtones. As with *The Leopard* and *Conversation Piece* before it, the English dubbing proved to be a problem. Visu-

ally, like *The Leopard*, *1900* was stunning.

Production costs were initially shared by companies in Rome (PEA), Paris (Artistes Associates), and Berlin (Artemis). Distribution of the picture was shared by Paramount (which had rights in Canada and the United States) with 20th Century–Fox (which had the European rights) and United Artists (which had the rights in the rest of the world).

Burt Lancaster spoke of his participation during 1974 in Parma, Italy: "Bertolucci asked me to do *1900*, but there was no way he could meet my usual salary so I worked for nothing. I wasn't doing anything at the time and it was only two weeks' work." He added, "I found the aging character I play a very rich, exciting part."

Lancaster's moments with Sterling Hayden, where the two robust bulls drink to their new grandsons, are among the film's best. Never one to keep from revealing a vulnerable side, Burt must be especially commended for daring to reflect the breakdown of his character in trying to have intercourse with a child (a sequence not shown in the Italian version).

Dominique Sanda was lovely and amusing as the picture's main heroine, and Donald Sutherland had a field day as the villain. Especially good were Gerard Depardieu and Robert De Niro in the main roles as the respective grandsons. Depardieu seems to fare better because of his peasant's more volatile nature. De Niro was perhaps in a more difficult part as the last *padrone* because he was not called on to show the same passion.

In the spring of 1991, a restored five-hour-and-eleven-minute version of *1900* was re-released to theaters in the United States. Mildly received (as the domestic 1977 showing had been), the extended length only served to increase the existing problems with plot and characters regarding continuity.

REVIEWS: *Time:* "This $8 million epic, Bertolucci's first effort since *Last Tango in Paris*, is a fabulous wreck. Abundantly flawed, maddeningly simple-minded, *1900* nonetheless possesses more brute poetic force than any other film since Coppola's similarly operatic *Godfather II.*"

America: "The cinematography by Vittorio Storaro is simply magnificent. His long, uninterrupted tracking shot through a World War I army camp should become a textbook classic. Gerard Depardieu, as the young peasant, Burt Lancaster, as the first padrone, and

Stefania Sandrelli, as the Marxist evangelist, are fine."

Go Tell the Spartans

A Spartan Productions/Mar Vista Productions Presentation   An Avco Embassy Pictures Release   Released June 14, 1978   114 minutes   CFI Color   Rated R

CREDITS: Ted Post (Director); Allan F. Bodoh and Mitchell Cannold (Producers); Jesse Corallo and Michael Kane (Assistant Directors); Michael F. Leone (Executive Producer); Wendell Mayes (Screenplay); Harry Stradling Jr. (Photography); Millie Moore (Editor); Jack Senter (Art Director); Ron Dawson (Costumes); Bill Randall (Sound); Dick Halligan (Music Score). Based on the novel *Incident at Muc Wa* by Daniel Ford.

CAST: Burt Lancaster (Major Asa Barker); Craig Wasson (Cpl. Stephen Courcey); Marc Singer (Capt. Al Olivetti); Jonathan Goldsmith (Sgt. Oleonowski); Joe Unger (Lt. Raymond Hamilton); Dennis Howard (Cpl. Abraham Lincoln); David Clennon (Lt. Finley Wattsberg); Evan Kim (Cowboy); John Megna (Cpl. Ackley); Hilly Hicks (Signalman Toffer); Dolph Sweet (Gen. Harnitz); Clyde Kasatsu (Col. Minh); James Hong (Cpl. Oldman); Denice Kumagai (Butterfly); Tad Horino (One-Eyed Charlie); Phong Diep (Minh's Interpreter); Ralph Brannen (Minh's Aide-de-camp); Mark Carlton (Capt. Schlitz).

SYNOPSIS: In July 1964, a group of American military advisors are teamed with their Vietnamese allies in Vietnam. Major Asa Barker is an experienced and cynical American army officer. His executive officer is the ambitious Captain Al Olivetti.

A General Harnitz orders Major Barker (who was caught in a sexual situation with the general's wife) to send a team of advisors to secure a garrison outpost at Muc Wa. Barker and Olivetti, at Penang, then interview a

As the commanding officer in *Go Tell the Spartans*, Burt Lancaster (far left) gives orders to his troops (left to right): Dennis Howard, John Megna, Craig Wasson, Evan Kim, Jonathan Goldsmith, Joe Unger, and Marc Singer.

number of men—American and Vietnamese alike—for the assignment, which the major is against. The Americans include Lt. Hamilton, Sgt. Oleonowski, and draftee Cpl. Courcey; and the Vietnamese leader is a mercenary called Cowboy.

Lt. Hamilton is dispatched as the group's commander when they go to Muc Wa. The Viet Cong are relentless in their attacks on the garrison. Proving to be naive with his first mission, Hamilton is killed. Sgt. Oleonowski is a world-weary soldier, and the pressures of his responsibility become too much for him under the Viet Cong assault.

Barker is upset with the total disintegration of this operation; by the time General Harnitz decides to do anything about it, it is too late. A helicopter brought by Barker to Muc Wa only has enough room to rescue the Americans. Objecting to this, Cpl. Courcey remains behind to help the Vietnamese allies. Inspired to do the same, Barker is among those killed in the fighting.

COMMENTARY: *Go Tell the Spartans* begins at a time in history when the first American fighting men were yet to be officially deployed in Vietnam (that came in 1965, some nine months after so-called military advisors were dispatched to the troubled region of Muc Wa). The French were there before the United States, but they were suppressed in 1954 in the struggle against the Communist influence.

Daniel Ford's 1967 novel, *Incident at Muc Wa*, was the source for the screenplay by Wendell Mayes. Muc Wa originally had been the site for a French fort that still stood. There was a French cemetery near this outpost, and, according to the story, part of an ancient Greek poem was written on an arch reflecting on all fighting men. This noble reference—"Go tell the Spartans, thou who passest by, That here, obedient to their laws, we lie"—originated from Simonides' elegy mourning the brave force of Spartan warriors who gave their lives in 480 B.C. at the Battle of Thermopylae.

Produced by Allan F. Bodoh and Mitchell Cannold, the film was shot in Southern California (in Valencia) under Ted Post's astute direction. Basically an old-fashioned war movie when soldiers were caught up in their duties and pressures under combat, *Go Tell the Spartans* brought out the waste of war with the misguided venture of the United States in Vietnam. The simple power of the film was in its concern for the fighting man.

Although thought very well of by critics, the film had little response at the box office after its 1978 release by Avco Embassy. In all probability his finest performance of the 1970s, Burt Lancaster played the veteran commander, Asa Barker, with strength, compassion, and even humor that may have very well been echoing his own aging years at the time. He was well supported by a predominately young cast; especially solid were Marc Singer and Craig Wasson.

Lancaster, who put up $150,000 of his own money for the project, commented, "It's extremely difficult for Americans to accept the idea that they can be beaten in any way. Nobody else would put any money into our film. It was a struggle for us to bring it out. But what we finally achieved was excellent. I'm very pleased with it, and very proud of it."

REVIEWS: *New Republic:* "Spartans is no earth-shaking masterpiece, but in its small-scale way it's strong, hard, forthright—very much more incisive about its subject than the star-laden, flabby *Coming Home.* The final effect of *Spartans* is as if a war movie had actually gone to war."

Saturday Review: "It is also admirably acted. Burt Lancaster has been as reliable a professional in life as Major Barker is in the movie, and he conveys superbly the weary integrity of a soldier committed to what he knows to be a worthless war."

The 1980s

Zulu Dawn

A Lamitas Presentation   A Samarkand Production   An American Cinema Release   Released February 1980   98 minutes   A New World Pictures Release   Released July 1982   117 minutes   Technicolor   Panavision   Rated PG

CREDITS: Douglas Hickox (Director); Nate Kohn (Producer); John O'Connor (Assistant Director); Dieter Nobbe (Associate Producer); Cy Endfield and Anthony Storey (Screenplay); Ousama Rawi (Photography); Malcolm Cooke (Editor); John Rosewarne (Production Designer); Peter Williams (Art Director); Bob Simmons (Action Sequences/Stunt Coordinator); Elmer Bernstein (Music Score). Based on a story by Cy Endfield.

CAST: Burt Lancaster (Col. Anthony Durnford); Peter O'Toole (Lord Chelmsford); Simon Ward (William Vereker); John Mills (Sir Bartle Frere); Nigel Davenport

Zulu Dawn, with (seated) John Mills, Peter O'Toole, (standing) Burt Lancaster and Simon Ward.

(Col. Hamilton-Brown); Michael Jayston (Col. Crealock); Peter Vaughan (Quartermaster Sgt.); James Faulkner (Lt. Melvill); Denholm Elliott (Col. Pulleine); Ronald Lacey (Norris Newman); Freddie Jones (Bishop Colenso); Christopher Cazenove (Lt. Coghill); Ronald Pickup (Lt. Harford); Donald Pickering (Major Russell); Anna Calder-Marshall (Fanny Colenso); Graham Armitage (Capt. Shepstone); Bob Hoskins (Sgt. Major Williams); Dai Bradley (Pvt. Williams); Paul Copley (Pvt. Storcy); Chris Chittell (Lt. Milne); Nicholas Clay (Lt. Raw); Patrick Mynhardt (Major Harness); Brian O'Shaughnessy (Major Smith); Midge Carter (Lt. Cavaye); Phil Daniels (Boy Soldier Pullen); Raymond Davies (Sgt. Murphy); Ken Gampu (Kambula); Simon Sabela (Cetshwayo).

SYNOPSIS: In 1879, the British empire has thrust its military colonization into South Africa. At Isandhlwana, Lord Chelmsford, the commander in chief of the British forces, contemplates the massacre there of 1,323 soldiers by 25,000 native Zulu warriors.

The Zulu people were once content to simply live on their lands in peace. Chelmsford and Sir Bartle Frere, the high commissioner, have convinced England to send them more soldiers to protect the colonies. In the colony of Natal, at Pietermaritzburg, among the officers is a veteran campaigner, the one-armed Colonel Anthony Durnford. A volunteer is William Vereker, an aristocrat farm owner.

An ultimatum is sent to the Zulu king, Cetshwayo, and the African is prepared to fight for his lands. Frere then signs the declaration of war.

Chelmsford leads his troops to Isandhlwana. With his own command, Durnford is chosen to assist another colonel, Pulleine, while Chelmsford rides on to Ulundi, the Zulu capital. On a scouting mission, Vereker and a small troop come across the bulk of the Zulu warriors and are forced to flee back to Durnford.

The Zulu warriors sweep over a ridge and into the British. The sheer number of Zulus make them invincible. Durnford, in a brave but futile move, attempts to build a line of defense. He is slain with an enemy spear.

The fighting is merciless, and all the British soldiers are killed. Vereker is the last to die. The conquering Zulu warriors then sing of their victory on the journey home.

COMMENTARY: *Zulu Dawn* was filmed in 1978 on location in Africa, at the site of the historic battle between the native warriors and the British soldiers. The battle occurred January 22, 1879, at a time when Victoria was queen of England and Benjamin Disraeli was prime minister. Colonel Durnford was unjustly blamed for the massacre, and a new man, Wolseley, was sent by Disraeli to take over as both high commissioner and commander in chief. Lord Chelmsford's army managed to defeat the Zulus at Ulundi, and Cetshwayo was taken prisoner. Wolseley divided Zululand into eight areas, each with its own chief.

Cy Endfield, who was involved with the screenplay (with Anthony Storey) from his own story, died prior to the film's production. Initially, Endfield had shown his interest in this phase of African history in 1964 when he directed and co-wrote the script for the film *Zulu*, which showcased another encounter the British had with the native warriors. English director Douglas Hickox was at the helm of *Zulu Dawn* (with producer Nate Kohn) to convey the full vim and vigor of its valiant adventure.

Cutting a heroic figure in *Zulu Dawn*, Burt Lancaster often played a man of courage.

Although there may be some misgivings about his Scottish accent, Burt Lancaster seemed a most suitable choice to reflect the gallantry of the courageous Col. Durnford. His stand at the end against the enemy warriors is riveting. "This is an honest film," Burt said, "full of action and courage. It is very realistic with an almost documentary approach that follows the course of history accurately."

An esteemed British cast of actors were also well in form. Displaying the high bearings of Lord Chelmsford and Sir Bartle Frere to perfection were Peter O'Toole and John Mills, respectively. Simon Ward played the honorable William Vereker, while Nigel Davenport (Burt's co-star from *The Island of*

Dr. Moreau) was on hand as one of the British officers. As the Zulu ruler, Simon Sabela did a proud turn.

Originally previewed at the 1979 Cannes Film Festival (and shown that same year in London), *Zulu Dawn*'s distribution went from being handled by Orion Pictures to American Cinema Pictures. In 1980, a try-out period in the United States met the same poor reception from audiences as the British opening.

Apparently the film's aura as an old-fashioned battle piece and the theme of British imperialism were just not what people wished to see at the time. A longer version, released in the United States in 1982 by New World Pictures, was likewise not a success. But, domestically, there were openings to place *Zulu Dawn* into high schools and colleges as a historical source, as well as being on cable and video, improving its marketability.

REVIEW: *Variety:* "The action sequences are superbly handled, as are the scenes in which the men and material are assembled and maneuvered. For sheer scope and numbers of people being manipulated for the cameras, *Zulu Dawn* is positively DeMillesque in scale."

Atlantic City

An I.C.C.–International Cinema Corporation Presentation   A John Kemeny–Denis Heroux Production   A Canada-French Co-production   A Louis Malle Film   A Paramount Picture   Released April 3, 1981   105 minutes   Color   Rated R

CREDITS: Louis Malle (Director); Denis Heroux (Producer); John Board (Assistant Director); Justine Heroux and Larry Nesis (Associate Producers); John Guare (Screenplay); Richard Ciupka (Photography); Suzanne Baron (Editor); Federico Salzmann (Assistant Editor); Anne Pritchard (Production Designer); Wendell Dennis (Set Dresser); Francois Barbeau (Costumes); Rita Ogden (Make-up, Hair Stylist); Jean-Claude Laureux (Sound); Michel Legrand (Music Score).

CAST: Burt Lancaster (Lou Pasco); Susan Sarandon (Sally); Kate Reid (Grace); Michel Piccoli (Joseph); Hollis McLaren (Chrissie); Robert Joy (Dave); Al Waxman (Alfie); Robert Goulet (Singer); Moses Znaimer (Felix); Angus MacInnes (Vinnie); Sean Sullivan (Buddy); Wally Shawn (Waiter); Harvey Atkin (Bus Driver); Norma Dell'Agnese (Jeanne); Louis Del Grande (Mr. Shapiro); John Mc-

Curry (Fred); Eleanor Beecroft (Mrs. Reese); Cec Linder (President of Hospital); Sean McCaan (Detective); Vincent Glorioso (Young Doctor); Adele Chatfield-Taylor (Florist); Tony Angelo (Poker Player); Sis Clark (Toll Booth Operator); Gennaro Consalvo (Casino Guard); Lawrence McGuire (Pit Boss); Ann Burns, Marie Burns, and Jean Burns (Singers in Casino); Connie Collins (Connie Bishop); John Allmond (Police Commissioner); John Burns (Anchorman).

SYNOPSIS: A packet of cocaine, meant for the Philadelphia underworld, is stolen by a young man named Dave. With his pregnant girlfriend, Chrissie, he hitchhikes to Atlantic City. They share quarters with Chrissie's sister, Sally, who was once Dave's wife. Sally works at an oyster bar in one of the new casinos, but she is studying to become a blackjack dealer under the training of Joseph, a croupier.

Lou Pasco is a neighbor of Sally's in the old hotel where they live, and he is a numbers runner for the local hoodlums. Lou also supplements his small income by running errands for a bedridden neighbor, Grace, who seems full of self-pity missing her younger, glory years.

Atlantic City, with Susan Sarandon and Burt Lancaster.

In a bar, Lou finds Dave trying to sell the cocaine. Dave convinces Lou to deliver the goods to a buyer. Not knowing Lou has the dope, two Philadelphia thugs, Felix and Vinnie, murder Dave.

Selling some of the cocaine to a buyer named Alfie, Lou arranges Dave's funeral. His kindness attracts Sally, who is unaware of the dope, and they make love. The thugs feel that Sally knows something, and they rough up her and Lou.

Lou gets a gun after feeling his manhood has suffered for failing to protect Sally against Vinnie and Felix. She learns all about the cocaine from Chrissie, who has become friends with Grace. Chrissie's kindness helps Grace out of her self-pity, so Grace makes an offer to send the younger woman home to have her baby.

Having lost her chance to be a croupier at the casino because of Dave bringing the dope into town, Sally is upset and goes after Lou. She finds him at the casino pretending to be a big shot in the underworld with the money from selling the cocaine. The two are confronted by the thugs again, and Lou shoots them both dead.

Overwhelmed by his nerve and chance to strut like the old gangsters from the past, Lou shares a festive night outside town with Sally. He asks her to go to Florida with him so he can show her off to his friends, but Sally's dream is to go to Monaco and become a croupier.

Sally takes a share of the money from the cocaine deal to follow her dream. Lou returns to Atlantic City and to Grace, the golden moment reflected in a smile.

COMMENTARY: Originally entitled *Atlantic City, U.S.A.*, when previewed at the Venice Film Festival in September 1980, the film shared the Golden Lion Award as Best Picture. For years the seacoast resort in New Jersey was an illegal den for gambling; during Prohibition in the 1920s, it was the central intake point for rum. By 1978, the state had legalized the gambling, and the old facade of its Boardwalk buildings began to be demolished. Resorts International was the first of the big casinos to emerge, and it played a significant role in the movie. *Atlantic City* was filmed on the actual site of its romantic and dangerous tale instead of on a duplicate.

Director Louis Malle, the celebrated French filmmaker, made his American film debut with *Pretty Baby* in 1977. Malle built a career expressing the dire emotions of people in his pictures; with his second American movie, he and writer John Guare made manifest these passions and ironies. Denis Heroux produced the joint American-Canadian-French venture.

Made especially moving were the characters' hopes and dreams within the setting's nostalgic and mythmaking elements. The gangster influence into this scenario added immeasurably to the mystique; everything came together as a telling and riveting piece of Americana.

Burt Lancaster gave a tour de force performance as Lou, the small-time hoodlum who finally realizes his dreams after living in the shadows of Atlantic City's underworld for 40 years. It is indeed shocking to see Burt looking so old and with white hair, yet he also appears distinguished. Malle chose him for the part over Robert Mitchum (just as Fred Zinnemann had in 1953 for *From Here to Eternity*). Both men were famous for playing strong heroes.

Atlantic City: **Burt Lancaster as Lou Pasco.**

Vividly reflected was a bold contrast with Lancaster's indomitable image; the charm and vulnerability displayed in many past films, reached its zenith with this one. Susan Sarandon nearly contributed as much as Burt with her portrayal of the ambitious Sally; her wide-eyed beauty and vitality never masking an equally vulnerable nature. Both were very touching, as were Kate Reid and Hollis McLaren. Robert Joy made a striking film debut.

Upon its release by Paramount in 1981, *Atlantic City* was a critical success, albeit not a financial one; it only grossed $3 million by year's end. But the film earned five Academy Award nominations: Best Picture, Best Actor (Burt Lancaster), Best Actress (Susan Sarandon), Best Director (Louis Malle), and Screenplay Written Directly for the Screen (John Guare).

Lancaster's Oscar nomination was his fourth, but he lost to Henry Fonda in *On Golden Pond*. The British Academy Award was awarded to Burt for Best Actor and one to Louis Malle for Best Director. The New York Film Critics, Los Angeles Film Critics, and National Society of Film Critics bestowed their awards on *Atlantic City* as well— the first group for Burt as Actor and John Guare for Screenplay; the second group for Best Film, and Lancaster and Guare; and the third group for Best Picture, Burt, Malle, and Guare.

REVIEWS: *New York Times:* "*Atlantic City*, Louis Malle's fine new movie, may be one of the most romantic and perverse ghost stories ever filmed, set not in a haunted castle but in a haunted city, the contemporary Atlantic City, a point of transit where the dead and the living meet briefly, sometimes even make love, and then continue on their individual ways."

Newsweek: "Sarandon is touching and funny—a truly fresh performance. But the movie's sweet, elegiac heart belongs to Lancaster. Lou may be the role of his lifetime, and he carries it gently, obviously cherishing the gift."

Cattle Annie and Little Britches

A King-Hitzig Production   A Universal Release   Released May 15, 1981   97 minutes   CFI Color   Rated PG
CREDITS: Lamont Johnson (Director); Rupert Hitzig and Alan King (Producers); David Anderson (Assistant Director); John Daly and Derek X. Dawson (Executive Producers); David Eyre and Robert Ward (Screenplay); Larry Pizer (Photography); Robbe Roberts and William Haugse (Editors); Stan Jolley (Production Designer); Dick Purdy (Set Decorator); Rita Riggs (Costumes); Manuel Topete (Sound); Sanh Berti and Tom Slocum (Music Score). Based on a story by Robert Ward from his novel.

CAST: Burt Lancaster (Bill Doolin); Rod Steiger (Tilghman); John Savage (Bittercreek Newcomb); Amanda Plummer (Annie); Diane Lane (Jenny); Scott Glenn (Bill Dalton); Redmond Gleeson (Red Buck); William Russ (Little Dick Raidler); Ken Call (George Weightman); Buck Taylor (Dynamite Dick); John Quade (Morgan); Perry Lang (Elrod); Steven Ford (Deputy Marshal); Mike Moroff (Deputy); John Hock (Bank Teller); Roger Cudney Jr. (Fireman); Michael Conrad (Engineer); Chad Hastings (Conductor); Yvette Sweetman (Mrs. Sweetman); Tom Delaney (Ned's Father); Matthew Taylor (Ned); John Sterlini (Corey); Roger Cudney (Capps); Jerry Gatlin (Cop); Russ Hoverson (Guard).

SYNOPSIS: Ned Buntline's tales of the Old West are the inspiration for two teenaged girls, Annie and Jenny, to seek out their heroes. The West of their dreams is not what they quite imagined when they are picked up by a bumbling outlaw gang led by one of the heroes, Bill Doolin.

The gang leader takes under his guidance the younger Jenny, nicknamed Little Britches because of the pants she wears. Called Cattle Annie because she stirs up a herd of cattle to give the outlaws a getaway, Annie shares a brief romance with fellow outlaw Bittercreek Newcomb.

Hot on their trail is a resourceful Marshal Tilghman. The gang becomes fed up with their rotten luck and disband. Doolin, captured by the marshal, shares a mutual respect with his adversary and quips, "It's been a grand chase."

Jenny and Annie's spunkiness helps bring the sparkle back to the outlaws. The sly old rogue, Doolin, is rescued.

But the girls are caught by the marshal, spanked, and returned home.

COMMENTARY: Filmed in 1979 (before *Atlantic City*), *Cattle Annie and Little Britches* was to have been distributed by Hemdale Pictures; the company, however, had financial problems and the property was then picked up by Universal. Rupert Hitzig and Alan King were the producers.

Western movies were not popular going into the 1980s, perhaps because of the disillusionment of their heroes brought on by self-mockery, whether intentional or unintentional. Yet Universal, gambling with *The Legend of the Lone Ranger*, released both films almost simultaneously in 1981. Neither western was a box office success; *Cattle Annie* was not even initially shown in theaters outside of New York City.

Cattle Annie and Little Britches: **Bill Doolin (Burt Lancaster) is a prisoner of U.S. marshal Big Bill Tilghman (Rod Steiger, left). Both were real-life figures.**

Although director Lamont Johnson expressed a brisk humor and sentiment, they may have been the film's reward as well as drawback. A detached look seemed to prevail. An irony in the tale (from David Eyre and Robert Ward's script, based on the latter's own story and 1977 novel) was the fascination the title heroines had for Ned Buntline's stories; Burt Lancaster portrayed the nineteenth-century writer Buntline in *Buffalo Bill and the Indians*.

Burt's playing of outlaw Bill Doolin was with a world-weariness mixed with a twinkle in his eye. One particular incident stands out: After being captured and taken to town in handcuffs, the amiable renegade is scrutinized by the townsfolk, and he harbors a deep frown, which turns to a delightfully wicked grin. This western was Burt's last (and fourth one made in Durango, Mexico).

Nice performances were turned in by Rod Steiger and the two leading actresses, Diane Lane and Amanda Plummer. Sometimes a very showy actor, Steiger was surprisingly subtle as Marshal Tilghman, and the young ladies nearly matched Lancaster's charm with their own.

REVIEWS: *Variety:* "*Cattle Annie and Little Britches* is as cutesy and unmemorable as its title. If oaters were currently being made as regularly as they were in the past, there might be room for this sort of fanciful marginalia."

New York Times: "It's a funny, very good-natured sort of movie that has, in addition to Mr. Lancaster at his politely comic best, a very fine debut performance by Amanda Plummer."

La Pelle (The Skin)

An Opera Film Produzione and Gaumont-Italia Production   A Gaumont Release   Presented at the Cannes Film Festival on May 22, 1981   131 minutes   Technicolor

CREDITS: Liliana Cavani (Director); Renzo Rossellini (Producer); Manolo Bolognini (Executive Producer); Robert Katz and Liliana Cavani (Screenplay); Armando Nannuzzi (Photography); Ruggero Mastroianni (Editor); Dante Ferretti (Production Designer); Piero Tosi (Costumes); Renato Marinelli (Sound); Lalo Schifrin (Music Score). Based on the novel by Curzio Malaparte.

CAST: Marcello Mastroianni (Curzio Malaparte); Burt Lancaster (General Mark Cork); Claudia Cardinale (Princess Caracciolo); Ken Marshall (Jimmy Wren); Carlo Giuffre (Eduardo Mazzullo); Alexandra King (Deborah Wyatt); Yann Babilee (Jean-Louis); Jacques Sernas (General Guillaume).

SYNOPSIS: It is Naples, Italy, in 1943. World War II has left the city occupied by allied liberation troops under the command of American general Mark Cork.

Curzio Malaparte, the general's Italian liaison officer, negotiates with local gangster Eduardo Mazzullo for the sale of German prisoners of war to Cork's Fifth Army. Helping with the negotiations is Jimmy Wren, who is in love with an Italian woman named Maria Concetta.

An ex-mistress of Malaparte's is Princess Caracciolo. Malaparte is used by Cork to prevent a colonel, Deborah Wyatt, from trying to steal the general's glory.

Although the city has been liberated, the struggle to live again is marred by chaos and degradation among the victorious Allies and the conquered Italians. Eruptions from Mt. Vesuvius only add to the devastation.

COMMENTARY: Burt Lancaster made several films in Italy during the

1980s; having an apartment in Rome made it convenient to work on a project that interested him. *La Pelle* was his first film for a female director, Liliana Cavani, and Lancaster felt she was "strong and creative." The communication during filming between the two was as if they had worked together for years, unlike the occasional flare-ups between Burt and his previous directors, Lamont Johnson and Louis Malle.

Energetically was how Burt played the ambitious American general, representing the victors, who leads the Fifth Army into Naples, the first city to be liberated during World War II, and then into Rome. Various cast listings referred to Lancaster's character as either Mark Cork or Mark Clark (the latter was the historic figure the part was drawn from).

Receiving billing over Lancaster was Marcello Mastroianni as Curzio Malaparte, representing the vanquished and whose novel was the basis for this joint Italian-French production (the French title was *La Peau*). It was the fourth film in which Burt co-starred with Claudia Cardinale. Sites in Naples and Rome were among those used for filming.

La Pelle was previewed at the 1981 Cannes Film Festival, but was received with more criticism than not. However, Liliana Cavani's forcefulness as a filmmaker was apparent (she also co-wrote the script with Robert Katz), and the film was deemed successful with audiences in Italy after its release by Gaumont. Renzo Rossellini produced.

The overpowering depiction of bleakness in the aftermath of war was not considered marketable in America. It was the first of Lancaster's motion pictures not to be released theatrically in the United States. The English-language title was *The Skin*, and, ironically, overseas it was seen with the Americans speaking English and the Italians their own native tongue.

REVIEW: *Variety:* "*La Pelle* is mostly a poorly staged creepshow travesty with little to redeem it. Performances, dialogue and especially direction are embarrassingly inadequate. Seasoned performers like Burt Lancaster and Claudia Cardinale are trapped by indulgent helming and rendered vulnerable by unrewarding dialogue."

Marco Polo

Supplied by RAI-TV, Proctor & Gamble, and Chinese Cinematographic Company   Broadcast on NBC-TV from May 16 to May 19, 1982   Color   600 minutes

CREDITS: Giuliano Montaldo (Director); Vincenzo Labella (Producer); Giovanni Bertolucci (Executive Producer); John A. Martinelli (Associate Producer); David Butler, Vincenzo Labella, and Giuliano Montaldo (Script); Pasqualino DeSantis (Photography); Luciano Ricceri (Art Director); Enrico Sabbatini (Costumes); Ennio Morricone (Music Score). Based on *The Travels of Marco Polo* by Marco Polo and Rustichello of Pisa.

CAST: Ken Marshall (Marco Polo); Denholm Elliott (Niccolo Polo); Tony Vogel (Matteo Polo); F. Murray Abraham (Jacopo); Anne Bancroft (Marco's Mother); Kathryn Dowling (Monica); John Gielgud (Doge of Venice); James Hong (Phags-Pa); John Houseman (Patriarch of Venice); Burt Lancaster (Teobaldo/Pope Gregory X); Tony LoBianco (Brother Niccola); Ian MacShane (Ali Ben Youssuf); Leonard Nimoy (Achmet); Beulah Quo (Chaibi); Ying Ruocheng (Kublai Khan); Sada Thompson (Aunt Flora); David Warner (Rustichello); Mario Adorf (Giovanni); Hal Buckley (Brother William); Agnes Chan (Mei-Lei); Rosella Como (Donna Laura); Bruno Corazzari (Agostino); Riccardo Cucciola (Uncle Zane); John Dix (Brother Philip);

Unighi Ishida (Chinkin); Andrew Keir (The Immortal); Zao Khan (Nayan); Lao Li (Bayan); Antonella Murgia (Zorah); Soon-Teck Oh (Wang Zhu); Alexander Picolo (Marco as a Child); En He Sen (Bektor); Georgia Slowe (Caterina); Marilu Tolo (Fiammetta); Jack Watson (Sailor); Bruno Zanin (Giulio).

SYNOPSIS: In 1298, Marco Polo is captured commandeering a ship against the Genovese in a trade war. His many past travels as trader and emissary are dictated to Rustichello of Pisa while he is imprisoned.

As a child in Venice, Marco waits for his father, Niccolo Polo, and Uncle Matteo Polo to return from a trading journey to Persia. Marco's mother dies leaving him in the care of his Aunt Flora.

Years pass, and Marco joins his father and uncle on their journeys. They meet with the Doge and Patriarch of Venice before traveling to the Holy Land in Palestine.

Pope Gregory X gives the three Polos greetings in the Holy Land to take to Kublai Khan, Mongol founder and emperor of China. A conflict in the Armenian Desert between the Mongols and Moslems involves Marco.

In Persia, Marco fights the plague. Journeying on to the court of Khan, he runs afoul of the turmoil within the Chinese empire and the struggles with Japan. Marco is befriended by the emperor's son, Prince Chinkin, yet must contend with the villainy of regent Achmet.

A romance takes place between Marco and Monica, an orphan with ties to rebels opposing Kublai Khan. In the battle against the emperor, Marco is part of the opposition. Ultimately, Marco Polo returns to Venice.

COMMENTARY: In November 1980, the Italians, the Americans and the Chinese began production on *Marco Polo*. Thirty million dollars and thirteen months were spent on the arduous project, which included location filming in Italy, Morocco, and the Peoples Republic of China. It became a ten-hour miniseries shown by NBC-TV over four nights in 1982. Vincenzo Labella (the producer of *Moses, the Lawgiver*) produced, Giuliano Montaldo directed, and the teleplay was written by them both along with David Butler.

Over 200 sources were drawn from for the historic story. Given particular basis was an apparent account by 13th century writer Rustichello of Pisa as told by Marco Polo. Yet many liberties were taken interpreting actual events with the script. The essence of the Venetian's wanderlust, however, was magnificently visualized in his journey to the realm of the great Khan as sanctioned by the pope to open new vistas of trade and communication.

An international cast was splendid overall. Perhaps Ken Marshall, in the title role, may have been a little too boyish, but he was still very appealing. Denholm Elliott and Tony Vogel portrayed his father and uncle, David Warner was Rustichello, Leonard Nimoy was Achmet, and Ying Ruocheng played Kublai Khan. Among performers seen in smaller roles were Anne Bancroft, as Marco's mother and Burt Lancaster as the pope.

Both Lancaster and Marshall joined the production in Italy (where all Burt's scenes were filmed in three weeks) after working on *La Pelle*. Of his lively performance (actually a cameo), *Newsweek* elaborated, "despite being imprisoned in eighty pounds of papal

In *Marco Polo*, as Teobaldo/Pope Gregory X.

regalia, Burt Lancaster appears so delighted to be playing Pope Gregory X that one can almost hear a heavenly chorus every time he parades onscreen."

Marco Polo averaged a twenty-point rating for each telecast, making it a success with viewers. It went on to win an Emmy Award for Outstanding Limited Series. Another Emmy was awarded for Outstanding Costume Design. Enrico Sabbatini designed 4,200 costumes worth $2 million for the miniseries.

REVIEWS: *Christian Science Monitor:* "It is as much a dazzling voyage into fantasy as into reality. If there are flaws, well, there are flaws in most of the world's largest diamonds. But it must be appraised as a huge, spectacular, ostentatious, although reasonably authentic jewel."

Variety: "Burt Lancaster's natural authority constitutes an international acting treasure, and despite the fact that he looks like no Pope that ever existed, his moments on the screen were overwhelming and unforgettable."

Local Hero

An Enigma Production for Goldcrest Released by Warner Bros. Released February 17, 1983 111 minutes Color Rated PG
CREDITS: Bill Forsyth (Director and Screenplay); David Puttnam (Producer); Jonathan Benson, Joel Tuber, Melvin Lind, and Matthew Binns (Assistant Directors); Iain Smith (Associate Producer); Chris Menges (Photography); Michael Bradsell (Editor); Roger Murray-Leach (Production Designer); Richard James, Adrienne Atkinson, Frank Walsh, and Ian Watson (Art Directors); Wally Veevers (Special Effects); Louis Kramer (Sound); Mark Knopfler (Music Score).
CAST: Peter Riegert (Mac MacIntyre); Denis Lawson (Gordon Urquhart); Fulton MacKay (Ben); Burt Lancaster (Felix Happer); Peter Capaldi (Danny Oldsen); Jenny Seagrove (Marina); Norman Chancer (Moritz); Jennifer Black (Stella); Rikki Fulton (Geddes); Alex Norton (Watt); Christopher Rozycki (Victor); Christopher Asante (Rev. MacPherson); John Jackson (Cal); Dan Ammerman (Donaldson); Tam Dean Burn (Roddy); Luke Coulter (Baby); Karen Douglas (Mrs. Wyatt); Kenny Ireland (Skipper); Harlan Jordan (Fountain); Charles Kearney (Peter); David Mowat (Gideon); John Poland (Anderson); Anne Scott Jones (Linda); Ian Stewart (Bulloch); Tanya Ticktin (Russian); Jonathan Watson (Jonathan); David Anderson (Fraser); Caroline Guthrie (Pauline); Ray Jeffries (Andrew); Willie Joss (Sandy); James Kennedy (Edward); Buddy Quaid (Crabbe); Edith Ruddick (Old Lady); John Gordon Sinclair (Ricky); Sandra Voe (Mrs. Fraser); Jimmy Yuill (Iain); Betty Macey, Michele McCarel, and Anne Thompson (Switchboard Operators); Mark Winchester, Alan Clark, Alan Darby, Roddy Murray, Dale Winchester, and Brian Rowan (Ace Tones).

SYNOPSIS: In Houston, Texas, a board meeting is taking place at Knox Oil. Chairman Felix Happer is napping through it. Big on astronomy (he has his own private planetarium) Happer decides that the constellation Virgo offers a favorable outlook for building a new oil refinery.

The place selected is Ferness, Scotland, a fishing village with strange starry happenings. Happer chooses a younger executive, Mac MacIntyre, to go buy the village because he thinks the man is Scottish; Mac, however, is actually Hungarian.

Mac is met in Scotland by one Danny Oldsen, and they ride over a rabbit while motoring toward Ferness. They are forced to spend the night in the car because of the fog, and in the morning find the rabbit doing well.

At the inn in Ferness, Mac finds lodging. Innkeeper Gordon Urquhart cooks the rabbit and serves it to Mac. Gordon also acts as the village spokesman when it comes to talking of selling property for the refinery.

The villagers are agreeable to a sale, except for Ben, an old beachcomber who actually owns the shoreline. While Mac negotiates for its sale, Danny becomes infatuated with Marina, a marine biologist, whose webbed feet are believed to be those of a mermaid.

Mac sees the aurora borealis showering the sky with wonder, and he telephones Happer about this phenomenon. Happer is busy back in Texas with a psychiatrist he has hired to insult him as a reminder of his mortality.

But when Mac fails to buy the land from Ben, Happer flies in by helicopter and lands on the beach. Ben and Happer powwow, and decide to build a sea and sky study center instead. Returning home, Mac finds that his memories of the quaint little village make him melancholy.

COMMENTARY: Scottish director/writer Bill Forsyth's *Local Hero* was a charming satire combining a contemporary lifestyle with an older one. Everything about this endearing little movie easily provoked a smile because of its gentle whimsies. The idea for the film was developed from a newspaper article read by producer David Puttnam, dealing with an American oil company buying an island from a Scotsman.

After its release in 1983 by Warner Bros., *Local Hero* proved a hit in England. However, it moved a bit slowly for American audiences to fully appreciate, even though it was one of the best films of the year. Forsyth's screenplay was voted the year's best by the New York Film Critics.

As a collection of eccentric characters in the enchanting Scottish village, Denis Lawson, Fulton MacKay, Peter Capaldi, Jenny Seagrove, and all the others contributed greatly to the spirit of the story. The local hero was played by

Local Hero, with (left to right) Peter Riegert, Burt Lancaster, and Peter Capaldi.

The cast of *Local Hero*, front row: Denis Lawson and Jennifer Black; center row: Peter Capaldi, Peter Riegert, Christopher Rozycki; standing in rear: Burt Lancaster, Fulton MacKay.

Peter Riegert with a deadpan manner never masking the joy he was slowly feeling for the folks and their town. Burt Lancaster spent only a couple of weeks or so working on the film (in both Houston and the Scottish town of Pennan, which doubled for the fictitious Ferness). Yet Burt's small role of the tycoon stargazer may have captured the film's spirit more than anything else.

It was a sweet performance that Burt gave (and one for which an Oscar nomination for Best Supporting Actor would have been justified). He spoke admiringly of the experience making the film with Forsyth: "There's so much gentle, ironical humor in *Local Hero*.

Bill pokes fun at people gently. He always knew a little bit better than I did what ought to be done. It was very refreshing."

REVIEWS: *New York Times:* "Genuine fairy tales are rare; so is filmmaking that is thoroughly original; Bill Forsyth's disarming *Local Hero* is both. A funny movie, it demonstrates Mr. Forsyth's uncanny ability for making an audience sense that something magical is going on."

Baltimore News American: "No one but Burt Lancaster could have been the sly, half-mad, half conniving oil baron with his wounded ego, impish humor and commanding presence."

The Osterman Weekend

A Michael Timothy Murphy and Guy Collins Presentation   A Davis-Panzer Production   A 20th Century–Fox Release   Released October 21, 1983   104 minutes   DeLuxe Color   Rated R
    CREDITS: Sam Peckinpah (Director); Peter S. Davis and William N. Panzer (Producers); Win Phelps and Robert Rooy (Assistant Directors); Michael Timothy Murphy, Larry Jones, and Marc W. Zavat (Executive Producers); Alan Sharp (Screenplay); Ian Masters (Adaptation); John Coquillon (Photography); Edward Abroms and David Rawlins (Editors); Robb Wilson King (Art Director); Keith Hein (Set Decorator); Richard Bryce Goodman and Bayard Carey (Sound); Lalo Schifrin (Music Score). Based on the novel by Robert Ludlum.
    CAST: Rutger Hauer (John Tanner); John Hurt (Lawrence Fassett); Craig T. Nelson (Bernard Osterman); Dennis Hopper (Richard Tremayne); Burt Lancaster (Maxwell Danforth); Chris Sarandon (Joseph Cardone); Meg Foster (Ali Tanner); Helen Shaver (Virginia Tremayne); Cassie Yates (Betty Cardone); Sandy McPeak (Stennings); Christopher Starr (Steve Tanner); Cheryl Carter (Marcia); John Bryson and Anne Haney (Honeymoon Couple); Kristen Peckinpah (Secretary); Jan Triska (Mikalovich); Hansford Rowe (Gen. Keever); Merete Van Kamp (Zuna); Bruce Block (Manager); Buddy Joe Hooker (Kidnapper).

SYNOPSIS: A woman is murdered by two men. Lawrence Fassett, her husband, is an American CIA operative, and the killers are reportedly Russian KGB agents.
    The CIA chief, Maxwell Danforth, uses Fassett's grief to help apprehend a supposed group of Russian agents. The group of suspects are friends of a television journalist named John Tanner.
    Fassett shows incriminating videotapes of the friends to Tanner, hoping to get his help in disclosing them. Tanner agrees, but with the stipulation that Danforth allow himself to be interviewed on television.
    Every year, Tanner and his friends gather for a festive weekend named after one of them, Bernard Osterman. The others are couples Richard and Virginia Tremayne and Joseph and Betty Cardone. Also present are Tanner's wife, Ali, and son, Steve.
    Complications arise with the bugging equipment set up in the Tanner home by Fassett. Everyone learns of the surveillance. Fassett kills the two couples when they try to leave. Osterman denies that anyone is a Russian agent.
    In the struggle that ensues, Ali slays several of Fassett's agents with a crossbow. But Fassett captures her and Steve and exclaims that Danforth had his wife killed. Tanner's family will be freed if he helps destroy Danforth.
    Tanner has his own television footage (for the Danforth interview) prerecorded, while Danforth is being interviewed live. Fassett breaks into the channel denouncing him as a murderer and for instigating the plot against Tanner's friends. Still on the air, Danforth is forced to try to explain away these accusations. Rescuing his wife and son, Tanner kills Fassett.

COMMENTARY: *The Osterman Weekend* was director Sam Peckinpah's first film in five years (it was also his last one). Peckinpah's intense and violent style was evident and should have worked well with a spy thriller, but the movie was not a success after its 1983 release by 20th Century–Fox.
    The complexity of the film actually bordered on incoherence. Based on Robert Ludlum's 1972 best-seller, the story even then was considered

Lancaster with Rutger Hauer in *The Osterman Weekend*.

hackneyed regardless of any suspense or excitement. The adaptation of the novel was by Ian Masters and the screenplay by Alan Sharp. Peckinpah even had qualms about it all and tried, unsuccessfully, with producers Peter S. Davis and William N. Panzer to have changes made.

Rutger Hauer, John Hurt, and Craig T. Nelson were at the head of a creditable cast. In his third small role in a row, Burt Lancaster's manipulating CIA chief was elusive (perhaps symbolic of the whole film); his reserved, calculating performance was reminiscent of his roles in *Seven Days in May* and *The Cassandra Crossing*, and the subject of CIA double-dealing of *Scorpio*.

Lancaster was generally given special billing when his parts were shorter, sometimes with "and" before his name or "as" after it. As had *Local Hero* that same year, *The Osterman Weekend* followed this pattern. Though both were notorious for having bad tempers, Peckinpah and Lancaster apparently only had the deepest respect for each other in the ten days or so the actor was involved on the film.

REVIEWS: *Washington Post:* "The issues here are invasion of privacy and media manipulation. *The Osterman Weekend* is intriguing, but perplexing."

Baltimore News American: "Poor Burt. He looks good, sounds strong— but he's far away from *Atlantic City*."

Scandal Sheet

A Fair Dinkum Production   Broadcast on ABC Television on January 21, 1985   120 minutes   Color by Keylite PSI
   CREDITS: David Lowell Rich (Director); Roger Birnbaum (Producer); Henry Winkler (Executive Producer); Howard Rodman (Script); Jacques Marquette (Photography); Peter Berger (Editor); George Chan (Art Director); Travis Nixon (Set Decorator); Randy Edelman (Music Score).
   CAST: Burt Lancaster (Harold Fallen); Lauren Hutton (Meg North); Pamela Reed (Helen Grant); Robert Urich (Ben Rowan); Peter Jurasik (Simon McKey); Bobby DiCicco (Platte); Max Wright (Stan Clark); Susan Peretz (Mrs. Hunt).

SYNOPSIS: Actor Ben Rowan is released from a hospital after being treated for alcoholism. A reporter, Simon McKey, bribes a hospital attendant to admit that Ben is a drunk.

Simon is praised for his work on the Rowan story by publisher Harold Fallen, who puts out a weekly tabloid for *Inside World*. When Fallen learns that freelance writer Helen Grant is a friend of Ben and his actress wife Meg North, he attempts to coerce her into working for the tabloid.

Helen at first refuses to become involved, calling Fallen's newspaper garbage. But when a deal with a publisher named Stan Clark for an article is put on hold, she accepts the offer from Fallen to provide for her son.

The first assignment for Helen with *Inside World* is to impose on parents who have just lost their sons—Siamese twins—during surgery. Her next task is to cover Ben and Meg's new film together; she refuses, but Fallen insists as part of her contract.

When Helen visits Meg and Ben at home and informs them of her new job,

the actor demands that she leave. Meg tells Helen that she is just being used by Fallen to hurt them.

McKey manages to get a copy of Ben's insurance premium, secretly paid for by Meg to protect the film company's investment against his risky health. After Fallen sends the couple a bogus tabloid headline revealing the matter, Ben gets so upset that he has a fatal heart attack.

Ordered to take Ben's picture in his coffin, Helen confronts Meg with the headline deception. But Meg will have nothing to do with her because Fallen put Helen's byline on it. Helen resigns herself to a future with *Inside World*.

COMMENTARY: *Scandal Sheet* was a hard-hitting ABC-TV movie in early 1985 on the rather unscrupulous world of tabloids. *Inside World* was a fictitious newspaper, but Howard Rodman derived his teleplay on an article written by Paul Corkery for the very real *Enquirer*. The film's executive producer, Henry Winkler, wanted the people who read this sensationalism to be more aware of all the hype involved; ironically, however, the film could be accused of sensationalizing as well.

The best thing about *Scandal Sheet* was its impressive cast under the direction of David Lowell Rich. The producer was Roger Birnbaum. Seen in strong co-starring roles were Lauren Hutton and Robert Urich, while Pamela Reed actually held the most pivotal part as the writer who sells her soul.

Winkler (Fonzie of *Happy Days* television fame) personally sought out Burt Lancaster for the role of the devilish publisher. The actor liked the subject matter, although his first really starring role in a few years and his age (he was 71) sometimes played havoc

Scandal Street: Burt Lancaster and Pamela Reed in a publicity pose.

Charming even as a villain, in *Scandal Sheet*.

with his memorization skills. His portrayal of the cool, charming viper was assuredly a delicious throwback to his nasty columnist in *Sweet Smell of Success*.

In 1955, Lancaster had had a real experience with a tabloid—*Confidential* published a story of the actor and accused him of trying to rape a woman in his office. He wanted to sue, but his lawyers advised not to because it would only spread the story and give it circulation.

REVIEWS: *Baltimore Sun:* "*Scandal Sheet* probably could have been a powerful film if it had stayed credible and played it dead straight about the tabloid press. As a polemic it seems shrill and less interesting."

New York Daily News: "In all other respects, the show is a strong one—the performances are commendable, especially by Lancaster and Pamela Reed, and the information is apparently on target."

Little Treasure

A Vista Films/Herb Jaffe Production A Tri-Star Pictures Release   Released May 1, 1985 95 minutes Metrocolor Rated R

CREDITS: Alan Sharp (Director and Screenplay); Herb Jaffe (Producer); Ramiro Jaloma and Jose Luis Ortega (Assistant Directors); Joanna Lancaster and Richard Wagner (Executive Producers); Alex Phillips (Photography); Garth Craven (Editor); Jose Rodriguez, Granada Estevez, and Enrique Estevez (Production Designers); Laurencio Cordero (Special Effects); Joanne Divito and Chea Collette (Choreography); Claude Hitchcock (Sound); Leo Kottke (Music Score).

CAST: Margot Kidder (Margo); Ted Danson (Eugene Wilson); Burt Lancaster (Delbert Teschemacher); Joseph Hacker (Norman Kane); Malena Doria (Evangelina); John Pearce (Joseph); Gladys Holland (Sadie); Bill Zuckert (Charlie); James Hall (Chuck).

SYNOPSIS: A young woman named Margo comes to a town in Mexico to meet her father, Delbert Teschemacher. When he doesn't show up, a follow American, Eugene Wilson, offers to drive her to her father's cabin.

Teschemacher is laid up in bed with a bad ax wound on his foot. He refuses to see a doctor. Eugene returns to town because he shows movies to the locals out of his van.

Margo hasn't seen her father since she was a child and he ran off. Teschemacher confides to her that he was once a bank robber, stealing $18,000 and then burying it under a cottonwood tree in some ghost town. He wants her to have the money, but she has to find it.

With his foot gangrenous, Teschemacher becomes delirious. With Eugene's help Margo tries to take her father to a doctor, but he dies in the van from blood poisoning.

Deciding to stay together, Margo and Eugene search for the buried money. Knowing it will take time to find the right ghost town, they find work, Margo as a stripper and Eugene as a bartender.

Eventually they find what Margo feels is the right town and tree; while digging, Eugene is skeptical the money exists. Arguing with each other over it, Margo accidently shoots him in the shoulder. An old couple tends to Eugene's wound.

Eugene goes back alone to the dig site and finds the sack of money. On his way to get Margo, he drops a handful of the cash off to the old couple.

COMMENTARY: Filmed in Mexico (Durango and Cuernavaca), *Little Treasure* was produced by Herb Jaffe and directed by Alan Sharp. The latter, who was making his debut as a director, wrote the screenplay as well. Tri-Star Pictures did not give the film much of a release in the spring of 1985 perhaps because as a whole it was quite pedestrian.

Although a tame affair, the film's R rating was for the bawdy language from Margot Kidder as well as her nude flashes (dancer Chea Collette doubled for the actress in some of the shots). Detached yet likable enough performances were given by Kidder, Ted Danson, and Burt Lancaster.

Looking particularly grizzled, Burt was mildly amusing as the stubborn old codger (the part was done in two weeks' time, actually before *Scandal Sheet*). His own daughter Joanna was one of *Little Treasure*'s executive producers.

A publicized on-the-set donnybrook between Kidder and Lancaster—where she pulled him and he struck her over their frustration on how a scene should be played—may have been given

Burt Lancaster, Margot Kidder, and Ted Danson in *Little Treasure.*

more attention than the actual film. She filed suit, but director Sharp felt both were to blame; ultimately, the matter was settled out of court.

REVIEWS: *Variety:* "Pic, though well photographed in seldom seen locales, is painfully slight in terms of story and not likely to attract any but the curious."

New York Times: "Mr. Lancaster is on and off the screen much too fast, but he's an interesting if brief presence."

On Wings of Eagles

From Edgar J. Scherick Associates/In Association with Taft Entertainment Television   Broadcast on NBC Television on May 18 and 19, 1986   300 minutes   Color
CREDITS: Andrew V. McLaglen (Director); Lynn Raynor (Producer); Edgar J. Scherick (Executive Producer); Sam H.

Rolfe (Script); Bob Steadman (Photography); Michael Baugh (Production Designer); Javier Rodriquez (Art Director); Jorge La Borbolla (Set Decorator); Peter Saldutti (Costumes); Esther Oropeza (Make-up); Laurencio Cordero (Special Effects); Manuel Topete (Sound); Lawrence Rosenthal (Music Score). Based on the book by Ken Follett.
CAST: Burt Lancaster (Col. "Bull" Simons); Richard Crenna (Ross Perot); Paul Le Mat (Jay Coburn); Jim Metzler (Bill Gaylord); Louis Giambalvo (Paul Chiapparone); Esai Morales (Rashid); Robert Wightman (Keane Taylor); James Sutorius (Joe Poche); Lawrence Pressman (Gayden); Alan Fudge (Stauffer); Karen Carlson (Ruth Chiapparone); Diane Salinger (Emily Gaylord); Cyril O'Reilly (Sculley); Constance Towers (Margot Perot); Kabir Bedi (Mohammad); Richard Crenna Jr. (Ross Jr.); Bob Delegall (Davis); Patrick Collins (Howell); Martin Doyle (Shweback).

SYNOPSIS: In 1979 Iran, two Americans are jailed after the takeover of the country by the regime under Ayatollah Khomeini. The prisoners, Bill Gaylord and Paul Chiapparone, are executives representing the Texas-based Electronic Data Systems (EDS) headed by billionaire H. Ross Perot.

Vacationing, Perot learns of the imprisonment of his employees; he returns to Texas, but fails to free them through official channels. He then hires retired army colonel Arthur "Bull" Simons to help rescue the men.

A daring plan is devised for Simons to lead a group of Perot's executives as a commando team. They are referred to as eagles by the billionaire. Among their number are Jay Coburn, head of EDS personnel in Iran, and Rashid, an Iranian trainee with the company.

Under Simons's supervision, Rashid breaks Gaylord and Chiapparone out of jail. The contingent led by Simons is then forced to flee in land vehicles through mountainous terrain.

Numerous obstacles confront the eagles, including internment at an Iranian army compound. When Simons uses grenades to make the ruse of a full-scale enemy attack, they are able to escape. At the Turkish border, Perot waits for them.

The families of the commandoes greet them back in America. An official helps Rashid enter. Simons walks away, his job completed. Shortly after, he dies from a heart condition.

COMMENTARY: A true story, *On Wings of Eagles* was based on Ken Follett's 1983 best-seller from a script by Sam H. Rolfe. Lynn Raynor produced and Andrew V. McLaglen directed the miniseries, shown over two nights by NBC in the spring of 1986. The initial segment of three hours revealed the characters and the organization of the escape plan. The final two-hour segment detailed the trek out of Iran and its conflicts.

Exclusive promotional material for the miniseries was featured in *TV Guide* the week of May 17 to May 23 (including cover artwork by

On Wings of Eagles, with Richard Crenna, Burt Lancaster, and Paul Le Mat.

Richard Hess of Burt Lancaster in character as Arthur "Bull" Simons). The ratings were good but mixed; the first night's broadcast followed CBS's programs with a 17-point rating, and the second night's action led both CBS and ABC with a 21.2 rating.

Also nominated for an Emmy Award as Outstanding Miniseries, *On Wings of Eagles* was considered a realistic if sometimes plodding dramatization of the actual events that took place (locations in Mexico, including Mexico City, substituted for Iran). Its strong characterizations were especially notable.

It was great seeing Burt in a heroic action role again (this one and his ex-convict in the later *Tough Guys* were his last in that mode). The real "Bull" Simons would have been proud of the actor's blend of toughness and compassion in his portrayal.

Richard Crenna turned in his customary sincere performance, this time as Ross Perot (although looking nothing like him). Lancaster and Crenna worked together nicely, yet Esai Morales, as the energetic young Rashid, often locked horns with Lancaster. To Morales's credit, his youthful brashness toward Lancaster reflected quite well on the tense interchanges needed between their respective characters.

REVIEWS: *TV Guide:* "A rich production that captures the terrors of a country in turmoil, the film, rife with suspense, gives equal time to the human factor, delineating character and background with clarity and perception."

USA Today: "Burt Lancaster, a he-man's hero for the ages. Surly and stocky, a growlly bulldog of a guy, the seventy two year old star has the forceful command to make this a credible ... tale of glory."

Tough Guys

A Touchstone Pictures Presentation/In Association with Silver Screen Partners II   Distributed by Buena Vista   Released October 3, 1986   102 minutes   DeLuxe Color   Panavision   Rated PG

CREDITS: Jeff Kanew (Director); Joe Wizan (Producer); Ed Milkovich and Christopher Griffin (Assistant Directors); Richard Hashimoto and Jana Sue Memel (Co-producers); James Orr and Jim Cruickshank (Screenplay); King Baggot (Photography); Kaja Fehr (Editor); Todd Hallowell (Production Designer); Jeff Haley (Set Decorator); Erica Phillips (Costumes); Robert Schiffer and Michael F. Blake (Make-up); Chuck Gaspar, Joe D. Day, and Stan Parks (Special Effects); C. Darin Knight (Sound); James Newton Howard (Music Score).

CAST: Burt Lancaster (Harry Doyle); Kirk Douglas (Archie Long); Charles Durning (Deke Yablonski); Alexis Smith (Belle); Dana Carvey (Richie Evans); Darlanne Fluegel (Skye Foster); Eli Wallach (Leon B. Little); Monty Ash (Vince); Billy Barty (Philly); Simmy Bow (Schultz); Darlene Conley (Gladys Ripps); Nathan Davis (Jimmy Ellis); Matthew Faison (Man in Gay Bar); Corkey Ford (Gang Leader); Darryl Shelly, Kenny Ransom, Joe Seely (Gang Members); Rick Garcia (Federale Captain); Graham Jarvis (Richie's Boss); Doyle L. McCormack (Train Engineer); Bob Maxwell (Syms); Steven Memel (Derek); Jeanne Mori (Female Officer); Scott Nemes (Yogurt Boy); Ernie Sabella (Hotel Clerk); Hilary Shepard (Sandy); Jake Steinfeld (Howard); Charles Sweigart (Jarvis); Eleanor Zee (Restaurant Hostess); Ron Ryan (Prison Guard); Ruth De Sosa and John Mariano (Tellers); Larry Mintz and Dick Hancock (Bank Robbers); John Demy (Policeman in Park); Grant Aleksander (Bartender at Mickey's); Michael F. Kelly and Jeffrey Lynn Johnson (Ambulance Attendants); Hugo Stanger (Old Man); Jimmy Lennon (Jimmy Lennon); Philip Culotta (Slam Dancer); Donald Thompson (Boy Scout); Lisa Pescia, Jeff Levine, and Seth Kaufman

(Customers); Michele Marsh (Newscaster); Todd Hallowell (Todd Hallowell); Steven Greenstein (Bartender at Virginia's Bar); Thomas F. Maguire (Armored Truck Guard).

SYNOPSIS: After spending the last 30 years together in prison (for robbing a train), Harry Doyle and Archie Long are released into contemporary Los Angeles. When leaving the prison, they are ambushed by a near-sighted gunman out to kill them. But the pair get away from the mysterious assailant.

Meeting their parole officer, young Richie Evans (who idolizes them for having been the last train robbers in America), Harry and Archie are told they cannot see each other for three years. The 72-year-old Harry has to enter a nursing home, and the 69-year-old Archie has to go to work.

Archie and Harry are often together despite the rules of their probation. One time they stop a bank robbery and then steal the robbers' guns; another time they rough up a street gang.

At the nursing home, Harry is sullen and appalled by the conditions; the one bright spot is finding his old sweetheart, Belle, living there. Meanwhile, Archie enjoys a fling with a young aerobics instructor, Skye Foster, who is attracted to his virility and sense of humor. But Archie faces the humiliation of one menial job after another.

Deke Yablonski, the lawman who originally nabbed them, feels that Archie and Harry will go back to their old ways, and he follows them around. The tough guys do try to round up their old gang, but everyone is just too old; nonetheless, Harry and Archie rob an armored truck and then have a falling out.

Through all this, Richie remains understanding. The tough guys reunite to hijack the Gold Coast Flyer, the very train they once robbed, on its final run in California. They also meet the mystery gunman, who is named Leon B. Little and was hired to kill them years earlier. His help is now recruited in the hijacking.

Even Richie wants to help Harry and Archie in their scheme; however, he is talked out of a life of crime. With Deke hot on their trail, the tough guys drive the train to the end of the tracks and plow right into Mexico. When the Federales try to get them, Archie and Harry kick the captain in the groin.

Burt Lancaster and Kirk Douglas in a publicity pose for *Tough Guys*.

COMMENTARY: Burt Lancaster and Kirk Douglas were brought to Hollywood around the same time in the 1940s by producer Hal Wallis. Over the years they starred in five films together (*I Walk Alone, Gunfight at the O.K. Corral, The Devil's Disciple, Seven Days in May,* and *Tough Guys*), and they were involved in two more (Burt and Kirk guest starred in *The List of Adrian Messenger,* but shared no scenes in *Victory at Entebbe*). The duo were teamed for their last film together with *Tough Guys* in 1986.

Screenwriters James Orr and Jim Cruickshank saw the two actors together at the 1985 Academy Awards show and decided to write a script with them in mind. But it was not really believed that Kirk and Burt would actually be interested. They were, of course, with the screenplay focused on not just a long relationship but one edged with tempermental outbursts (as their actual professional relationship was as well).

Produced by Joe Wizan and directed by Jeff Kanew, under the Disney Company's Touchstone and Buena Vista aegis, *Tough Guys* proved to be rather lightweight material. While nice messages were reflected about friendship and the mistreatment of the elderly in nursing homes, a sense of flustered but jovial camaraderie dominated.

The climactic chase sequence was exciting fun with both stars doing their own stuntwork running atop the moving train. Lancaster was modest when he said, "It wasn't really a stunt. The train was only going twenty-five miles an hour." Nonetheless, for their efforts, Douglas and Lancaster were honored with a plaque by the Stuntman's Association of America.

A Southern Pacific locomotive built in 1940 was used for filming the chase sequence on the Eagle Mountain Line near Palm Springs, California. Most of the picture was filmed in areas of downtown Los Angeles.

Seemingly having a good time with their roles, Lancaster gave the more reserved performance to Douglas's spirited one (as was the case in all their work together). Despite the vigorous publicity campaign to fuel their reunion, *Tough Guys* was not a box office success; the initial domestic earnings of $9 million were less than it cost to make the picture. Any real success was in seeing the old pros together again.

Perhaps Burt summed it all up best when he said, "The characters of Harry and Archie have a certain respect for the old-world manners. In one sense, the movie was a return to our heroic personas of the past and has a built-in nostalgia."

REVIEWS: *Variety:* "*Tough Guys* is unalloyed hokum that proves a sad waste of talent on the parts of co-stars Burt Lancaster and Kirk Douglas."

Commonweal: "To watch Lancaster walk with his awkward ramrod dignity, or resolutely threaten Douglas with 'another hole in his chin' when they argue over the new caper, provides genuine small treats. But small treats are all that *Tough Guys* delivers."

Barnum

A Robert Halmi, Inc. Production Broadcast on CBS Television on November 30, 1986   120 minutes   TVC Laboratory   Color   Panavision

CREDITS: Lee Philips (Director); David J. Patterson (Producer); David Hood and Tommy Groszman (Assistant Directors); Robert Halmi (Executive Producer); Michael Norell (Script); Reginald Morris

(Photography); George Jay Nicholson (Editor); William Beeton (Production Designer); Claude Pare (Art Director); Jean Kazermirchuk (Head Set Decorator); Ann Marie Newson (Costumes); Jocelyne Bellemare (Head Make-up Artist); Don Cohen (Sound); Charles Gross (Music Score). Based on a story by Michael Norell and Andy Siegel.

CAST: Burt Lancaster (Phineas Taylor Barnum); Hanna Schygulla (Jenny Lind); John Roney (Young Barnum); Sandor Raski (Younger Tom Thumb); Patty Maloney (Older Tom Thumb); Laura Press (Charity); Kirsten Bishop (Nancy); Michael Higgins (Phineas Taylor); Lorena Gale (Joyce Heth); Deborah Hancock (Caroline); Andrew Bednarski (Little Phineas); Joe Cazalet (James Gordon Bennett); Rob Roy (Horace Greeley); Bronwen Mantel (Queen Victoria); Sean Hewitt (Coley Draper); Shawn Lawrence (R.W. Lindsay); Philip Spensely (Deacon Cox); Chris Wiggins (Olmstead); John McCorkell (Heckler Roberts); Harry Hill (Mr. Fish); Richard Dumont (Hummel); Rummy Bishop (Bank Doorman); Tony Robinow (Matthew Scott); Michael Sinelnikoff (Lord in Waiting); Joan Heney (Mrs. Stratton); Sam Lemarquand (Chauncey Jerome); Thick Wilson (Museum Passerby); John Stanzel (Tap Dancer); and the Royal Hanneford Circus.

SYNOPSIS: With a circus in the background, the spirit of showman P.T. Barnum tells the story of his own extraordinary life. He debunks the myths about himself, including never having said, "A sucker's born every minute." Having won and lost several fortunes, his dream was always to be more than a hustler of freak shows.

His promotion of a woman, Joyce Heth, claiming to be older than 150 years and the nursemaid of George Washington, turns sour. After she dies, Barnum discovers that she was only in her eighties. A museum is opened by Barnum, featuring such attractions as "The Strong Man" and "The Fattest Man."

A meeting between Barnum and Charles Stratton, a five-year-old who is but twenty-five inches tall, turns into a great success. Touring America together, the dwarf becomes known as General Tom Thumb. Eventually they travel to England for an audience with Queen Victoria.

Barnum goes to Germany to entice the singing star Jenny Lind to perform in America. Billed as "The Swedish Nightingale," her gentle exterior belies a shrewd business sense that was more than a match for him. She becomes another success for the showman.

When Barnum returns to his American Museum, a new selection of attractions are featured. Among the entries are the Siamese Twins Chang and Eng Bunker.

In his sixties and widowed (his late wife, Charity, never appreciated his imagination), Barnum marries again. His 20-year-old bride, Nancy, encourages him to enter the world of the circus. He creates his "Greatest Show on Earth" and merges to become Barnum and Bailey. Purchased in England, Jumbo the elephant is part of the successful American circus.

COMMENTARY: Phineas Taylor Barnum's spirit in *Barnum* (as grandly personified by Burt Lancaster in an insightful bit of casting) concluded his story with a beaming reflection. "What I saw that nobody else did was that out there in this rough-hewn country were millions of people waiting to be formed into an audience," he said. "That's what P.T. Barnum invented. I invented the audience."

Produced by David J. Patterson in Montreal, *Barnum* was a colorful presentation on the pioneer showman (who died in 1891). Director Lee Philips,

Barnum: Burt Lancaster as P.T. Barnum.

however, certainly had his hands full keeping the proceedings from seeming too episodic. The results from Michael Norell's script (from a story he put together with Andy Siegel) delved more on the pictorial rather than any in-depth dramatization. Yet there were some fine character interchanges, especially between Hanna Schygulla's Jenny Lind and Lancaster's Barnum.

Though the film did not perform especially well in the ratings for CBS Television (a 14.1 with its broadcast in 1986), Burt's lively performance cannot be slighted. His own circus background and films like *The Rainmaker*, *Trapeze*, and *Elmer Gantry* made him a natural for this role. Despite its flamboyance, the actor kept his tongue well in check. Lancaster elaborated, "You have to be careful not to go too far playing this type of character. You start out playing it fully, make yourself naked, give it everything and then take it back and shape it."

REVIEWS: *TV Guide:* "*Barnum*, a delightfully entertaining 'autobiography' of Phineas T. Barnum, that master showman of the 19th Century who is brought to zestful and charming life by Burt Lancaster, that master actor of the 20th Century."

Variety: "Lancaster, as narrator and protagonist, invests Barnum with something of the flair and personality one would expect of someone with his vaunted predilections."

Control

An Alliance Entertainment Corporation Presentation/In Association with Les Films Ariane   A Cristaldifilms Production Shown on HBO Cable Television on February 14, 1987   90 minutes   Color

CREDITS: Giuliano Montaldo (Director); Franco Cristaldi (Producer); Alexandre Mnouchkine (Co-producer); Denis Heroux (Executive Producer); Piero Angela, Giuliano Montaldo, Brian Moore, and Jeremy Hole (Script); Armando Nannuzzi (Photography); Ruggero Mastroianni and Frank Irvine (Editors); Luciano Ricceri (Production Designer); Nana Ceochi (Costumes); Ennio Morricone (Music Score). Based on a story by Piero Angela.

CAST: Ben Gazzara (Mike Zella); Kate Nelligan (Sarah Howell); Kate Reid (Camille Dupont); Burt Lancaster (Dr. Herbert Monroe); Ingrid Thulin (Mme. Havemeyer); Erland Josephson (Hans Swanson); Zeudi Araya (Sheba); Flavio Bucci (Herman Pundt); Andrea Occhipinti (Matteo); Andrea Ferreol (Rosy Bloch); Jean Benguigui (Max Bloch); Cyrielle Claire (Laura Swanson); William Berger (Peterson); Alfredo Pea (Dr. Paul Benoit); Amy Werba (Greta Hellstrom); Lavinia Segurini (Eva Bloch); Dean Magri (Jamie Howell); Achille Brunini (TV Announcer).

SYNOPSIS: In Frankfurt, West Germany, a press conference is held by Madame Havemeyer. Her Havemeyer Foundation has hired retired nuclear scientist Dr. Herbert Monroe to conduct an experiment using fifteen volunteers inside a fallout shelter. Each volunteer will get $10,000, plus a bonus of $5,000 if no one leaves the shelter during the twenty day experiment.

The volunteers have come from various countries. They are reporter Mike Zella; Dr. Paul Benoit; Mr. and Mrs. Bloch and daughter Eva; Sarah Howell and her son, Jamie; Camille Dupont; Hans Swanson and his wife, Laura; Sheba; Herman Pundt; Matteo; Greta Hellstrom; and shelter manager Peterson.

The experiment is going well when Matteo and Laura have an affair. After eleven days, the compressor malfunctions, causing a temporary breathing problem. Two days before the experiment is to end there is a nuclear threat—a missile has accidentally been launched from a submarine in the Atlantic Ocean.

Herman leaves the shelter to be with his family. People from outside try to get into the shelter for protection, only to be stopped by a few of the volunteers (although the majority had agreed with Mike to let them in).

The missile threat turns out to be a simulated test from Dr. Monroe. Havemeyer is upset, having known nothing about the test. Monroe defends himself by explaining it was done to show how people react to stress in such a situation and that the real problem is to stop building the weapons. Fearing an actual threat, Sheba tried to kill herself.

COMMENTARY: Threat of nuclear devastation and the fallout shelter as a danger of its own interested Burt Lancaster to participate in *Control* (albeit in another of those small, special billed roles). His performance as the deceptive scientist was earnest as usual, and the manipulative, reserved characteristics reflective of earlier roles with that trace of villainy as well.

To view Lancaster and Ingrid Thulin seated together at the start of the film, with the welfare of people hanging in the balance, was reminiscent of the pair side by side in *The Cassandra Crossing*. Ben Gazzara, Kate Nelligan, Erland Josephson, and Kate Reid were among the other international players who contributed reliable performances.

Although set in West Germany, the film was made in Rome (at the Cinecitta Studio). Originally called *Il Giorno Prima* (*The Day Before*), by the time this production—a joint Italian and Canadian offering, produced by

Franco Cristaldi—reached American shores, via cable television (HBO) in 1987, it was called *Control*.

Director Giuliano Montaldo, production designer Luciano Ricceri and composer Ennio Morricone all worked together on *Marco Polo*; their work on *Control* was less satisfactory due (among other reasons) to the overall routine conception. Piero Angela's original story was the basis for the script on which he, Montaldo, Jeremy Hole, and Brian Moore involved themselves.

REVIEWS: *Los Angeles Herald Examiner:* "Burt Lancaster, with a severe crew cut, is an eminent nuclear scientist hauled out of retirement to conduct the experiment—and to lead viewers quickly through the premise, which he does efficiently in about four minutes."

Long Island Newsday: "But, despite the best intentions of the scriptwriters to take a humanistic stand against war, the manhandling of emotions among *Control*'s characters is all too pat and black-and-white."

Sins of the Fathers

A Bavaria Atelier Production   In Association with Taurus Film/FR3/ORF/RAI-1   A Bernhard Sinkel Film   Shown on Showtime Cable Television on July 10 and 11, 1988   240 minutes   Color
CREDITS: Bernhard Sinkel (Director and Script); Jorn Schroeder and Helmut Krapp (Producers); Gunter Rohrbach and Bodo Scriba (Executive Producers); Dietrich Lohmann (Photography); Jean-Claude Piroue (Editor); Gotz Weidner (Set Designer); Barbara Baum and Munika Jakobs (Costumes); Ranier Wiehr and Werner Rohm (Sound); Peer Raben (Music Score).
CAST: Burt Lancaster (Carl Julius Deutz); Julie Christie (Charlotte Deutz);

Bruno Ganz (Heinrich Beck); Dieter Laser (Frederich Deutz); Tina Engel (Luise Beck); Rudiger Vogler (Ulrich Deutz); Martin Benrath (Victor Bernheim); Herberg Gronemeyer (George Deutz); Alexander Radszun (Dr. Sokolowski); Katherina Thalbach (Elli Deutz); Hannes Jaenicke (Max Bernheim); Christian Doermer (Dr. Korner); Cyrielle Claire (Anni); Martin Falk (Edmund Deutz); Burkhard Heyl (Carl Beck).

SYNOPSIS: In Salzburg, Austria, 1911, Carl Julius Deutz celebrates with his family the 25th anniversary of their chemical and dye company. A widower, he is fiercely determined to keep the family business independent from any cartel. Son Frederich has just returned from the United States and has ambitions to form a cartel with prominent American businesses; he had been banished for having an affair with Charlotte, the troubled wife of older brother Ulrich. Carl's daughter, Luise, is a scientist who marries a noted colleague, Heinrich Beck.

Involved in the family's ammonia plant, Heinrich has developed a process to be used for fertilizer to improve the growth of Germany's crops. He persuades Carl to cooperate with the Germans during World War I for the sake of nationalism. Heinrich's discovery is used by the German military as a deadly gas on the battlefield. Ulrich, Carl's heir, is killed in the war.

George Deutz, Charlotte's son, is now Carl's choice to take over the company. Disinterested, George instead becomes a filmmaker, ultimately making propaganda films for Hitler's Germany. Charlotte is having a romance with George's friend Max Bernheim. Her daughter, Elli, and Max are also involved romantically. To save Max's life, because he is Jewish, Elli agrees to marry Nazi sympathizer Dr. Sokolowski.

After Carl's death from a heart attack, Frederich and Heinrich compromise the chemical company so badly that it becomes a force for Nazism. An insecticide is used to exterminate Jews in concentration camps. Slave labor from the camp at Auschwitz is used to staff a plant. Following World War II, Heinrich and Frederich are among the war criminals on trial by the Allies at Nuremberg.

COMMENTARY: A $6 million multinational production, *Sins of the Fathers* was filmed in English in 1985 using several European sites (including Germany's Faber-Castell castle not far from Nuremberg and the Bavaria Film Studio in Munich). In 1986 and 1987, it was shown as an eight-hour miniseries on television in Europe—in Germany it was called *Vaeter und Soehne*, and in Italy it was *Padri e Figli* (with both titles translated as *Fathers and Sons*).

Producers Jorn Schroeder and Helmut Krapp, and especially director/writer Bernhard Sinkel must be commended for a rich and daring re-creation of a Germany in turmoil spanning two world wars. Sinkel's 600 page script utilized fictitious characters, but the story of the Deutz empire was based on the actual I.G. Farben chemical dynasty. Formed in 1916, Farben became involved with using Jewish slave labor from the Auschwitz camp for working a factory during World War II.

When the miniseries was aired on American television, via Showtime's cable network in 1988, it was with the title of *Sins of the Fathers*. Trimmed harshly to four hours, it lacked the clarity and the interest that specifically the Italian showing had enjoyed; a

Burt Lancaster in *Sins of the Fathers.*

heavyhandedness and pessimism that prevailed did not find favor with domestic viewers.

An international cast was headed by Burt Lancaster and Julie Christie, although the more pivotal roles went to Dieter Laser and Bruno Ganz. Burt displayed the appropriate authoritarian sturdiness and stateliness as the patriarch (a figure not unlike the ones he played in *The Leopard* and *1900*), who dies at the end of the second hour. Christie did a splendid job as his adulterous (and drug-addicted) daughter-in-law. As the son-in-law and younger son, respectively, Ganz and Laser conveyed

very well the not so evil but rather all-too-conflicting emotions, as they allow themselves to be swept away in the throes of the Nazi regime.

REVIEWS: *New York Daily News:* "A lavish and illuminating but sometimes plodding miniseries, clearly illustrates how one family, the force behind one of the largest prewar chemical companies, could succumb to Nazism."

Variety: "Acting is exemplary. Lancaster as pater familias stands assured, while Christie's complex Charlotte is a standout—the entire four hours could have been profitably used to explore the woman's complexities."

Rocket Gibraltar

A Ulick Mayo Weiss Production   A Columbia Picture   Released September 2, 1988   100 minutes   Duart Color   Rated PG

CREDITS: Daniel Petrie (Director); Jeff Weiss (Producer); Matthew Carlisle (Assistant Director); Michael Ulick, Geoffrey Mayo, and Robert Fisher (Executive Producers); Amos Poe (Screenplay); Jost Vacano (Photography); Melody London (Editor); Bill Groom (Production Designer); Betsy Klompus (Set Decorator); Nord Haggerty (Costumes); Steve Kirshoff (Special Effects); Bill Daly (Sound); Andrew Powell (Music Score).

CAST: Burt Lancaster (Levi Rockwell); Suzy Amis (Aggie Rockwell); Patricia Clarkson (Rose Black); Frances Conroy (Ruby Hanson); Sinead Cusack (Amanda "Billi" Rockwell); John Glover (Rolo Rockwell); Bill Pullman (Crow Black); Kevin Spacey (Dwayne Hanson); John Bell (Orson Rockwell); Nicky Bronson (Max Hanson); Dan Corkill (Kane Rockwell); Macaulay Culkin (Cy Blue Black); Angela Goethals (Dawn Black); Sara Goethals (Flora Rockwell); Emily Poe (Emily Rockwell); Sara Rue (Jessica Hanson); George Martin (Dr. Bonacker); Matt Norklun (Mo Plumm); Robert Compono (Tony Joe Basta); James McDaniel (Policeman); David Hyde Pierce (Monsieur Henri); Renee Coleman (Waitress).

SYNOPSIS: At his oceanfront home on Long Island, Levi Rockwell greets his family as they arrive to celebrate his 77th birthday. Levi is a widower and was once a blacklisted writer. His son Rolo is a film producer with a wife, "Billi," and four children, Orson, Kane, Flora, and Emily. Rose, Levi's oldest daughter, is married to baseball pitcher Crow Black, and they have two children, Dawn and Blue. Daughter Ruby is married to stand-up comic Dwayne Hanson, and they also have two children, Max and Jessica. Youngest daughter Aggie is single.

The varied personalities and problems of the entire family are explored. Kindly Levi is joined by all his grandchildren for a walk along the beach—he captivates them with a story of how the Vikings believed in immortality by placing a dead Viking warrior aboard a ship, then setting it aflame as it drifted out to sea and to Valhalla.

When the grandchildren overhear Doctor Bonacker talking to Levi of his fragile heart condition (a secret he keeps from his own children), they repair an old boat of his, the *Rocket Gibraltar*, as a Viking craft to be a gift for him.

After Levi quietly passes away in bed, the grandchildren, unbeknownst to their parents, wrap his body up and actually take him down to the beach and put him in the *Rocket Gibraltar*. The adults in the family catch wind of the matter, but they are too late to stop their children.

The *Rocket Gibraltar* is already afloat and in flames. The whole family sits on the beach to silently watch the burning craft drift out to sea and into the twilight.

COMMENTARY: Written by filmmaker Amos Poe, the screenplay for *Rocket Gibraltar* was sold to producer Jeff Weiss. Actual filming, during 1987, took place on Long Island in New York. Poe also initiated the directing, but was replaced after a few weeks by Daniel Petrie; apparently the production fell behind schedule and needed a more experienced hand as director.

Despite one rough encounter while filming where Burt Lancaster lost his temper at Petrie (but later apologized), the working relationship between the two went very well. For this, his last theatrical film in a starring role, Burt was paid $750,000. It was assuredly a handsome fee for an undeniably rich, but somewhat unappreciated, performance.

Rocket Gibraltar, sadly, was only given a minor release from Columbia Pictures in 1988. However, the final moments of the film were quite lovely, even though the concept of a Viking funeral nowadays might easily be construed as improbable if not outright illegal. While the family unity in the picture seemed to be its strength, the sequence where the kids carry their grandfather's body away was handled perhaps a bit too comically for its own good.

An especially enjoyable rapport was shared by six-year-old Macaulay Culkin and Lancaster, whose respective grandson and grandfather shared the same kindred spirit. Burt's beautifully warm acting glowed like Henry Fonda's did in 1981's *On Golden Pond*. The last scene, where his dying wish is fulfilled, fondly echoed Kirk Douglas's memorable demise in 1958's *The Vikings*.

REVIEWS: *People Weekly:* "Burt Lancaster is a great actor, but he can't work the miracle of saving this picture from jacked-up sentimentality."

New York Times: "Despite the glaring problems of the screenplay (by Amos Poe), Levi is a lovely character, and Burt Lancaster gives a wonderful performance in the role."

Burt Lancaster with Macaulay Culkin, who plays his grandson in *Rocket Gibraltar*.

Field of Dreams

A Gordon Company Production   A Phil Alden Robinson Film   A Universal Release   Released April 21, 1989   106 minutes   DeLuxe Color   Panavision   Rated PG

CREDITS: Phil Alden Robinson (Director and Screenplay); Lawrence Gordon and Charles Gordon (Producers); William M. Elvin (Assistant Director); Brian Frankish (Executive Producer); John Lindley (Photography); Ian Crafford (Editor); Dennis Gassner (Production Designer); Leslie McDonald (Art Director); Nancy Haigh (Set Decorator); Linda Bass (Costumes); Richard Arrington (Make-up); Russell Williams II (Sound); Industrial Light & Magic (Special Visual Effects); James Horner (Music Score). Based on the book *Shoeless Joe* by W.P. Kinsella.

CAST: Kevin Costner (Ray Kinsella); Amy Madigan (Annie Kinsella); James Earl Jones (Terence Mann); Timothy Busfield (Mark); Dwier Brown (John Kinsella); Frank Whaley (Archie Graham); Ray Liotta (Shoeless Joe); Burt Lancaster (Doc Graham); Gaby Hoffman (Karin Kinsella); James Andelin (Feed Store Farmer); Mary Anne Kean (Feed Store Lady); Fern Persons (Annie's Mother); Kelly Coffield (Dee, Mark's Wife); Michael Milhoan (Buck Weaver, 3B); Steve Eastin (Eddie Cicotte, P); Charles Hoyes (Swede Risberg, C); Art LaFleur (Chick Gandil, 1B); Lee Garlington (Beulah, Angry PTA Mother); Mike Nussbaum (Principal); Larry Brandenburg, Mary McDonald Gershon, and Robert Kurcz (PTA Hecklers); Don John Ross (Boston Butcher); Bea Fredman (Boston Yenta); Geoffrey Nauffts (Boston Pump Jockey); Anne Seymour (Chisholm Newspaper Publisher); C. George Baisi, Howard Sherf, and Joseph Ryan (Men in Bar); Joe Glasberg (Customer); Brian Frankish (Clean-Shaven Umpire); Jeffrey Neal Silverman (Clean-Shaven Center Fielder).

SYNOPSIS: In the cornfield of his Iowa farm, Ray Kinsella hears a mysterious voice. He is bewildered because his wife, Annie, and their daughter, Karin, do not hear it. Images of a baseball field and of Shoeless Joe Jackson are seen by Ray.

With Annie's support and their savings, Ray builds a baseball field in part of the cornfield for Shoeless Joe. Now deceased, he was one of eight Chicago White Sox players accused of throwing the 1919 World Series.

Appearing on the ball field one evening, Shoeless Joe meets the Kinsellas. Glad to be close again to the game he loves, however, he cannot cross over the foul line. He does vanish into the cornfield.

When Annie's family visits, her brother, Mark, urges Ray to sell the failing farm. Only the Kinsellas can see Shoeless Joe and the teammates he has brought back to play baseball in their field.

Ray learns that his late father's name, John Kinsella, was used as a character in one of writer Terence Mann's stories. Having heard the mysterious voice again, Ray interprets it and a dream shared with Annie as reasons to go find Mann in Boston.

Terence is somewhat disenchanted with his life, and Ray feigns a kidnapping to take him to a baseball game at Fenway Park. Both men hear the mysterious voice and also see a message on the scoreboard about Archibald "Moonlight" Graham from Minnesota, who played in one major league game in 1922 but never batted.

In Minnesota, Ray and Terence learn that "Moonlight" gave up his baseball career and became a small-town doctor. Although Doc Graham died in 1972, Ray is able to go back to that year and meet him. Doc wishes that he could have batted just one time in the majors.

Returning to Iowa with Terence, Ray picks up a hitchhiker, a young

Archie Graham, who wants to play base-ball. Ray confides to Terence about his father, a White Sox fan, who had played minor-league ball. In his teens, Ray had refused to play catch with his father and also told him that he had no respect for him because he liked Shoeless Joe.

Back home, the field is full of old-time ballplayers. Shoeless Joe puts Archie into the game, and the rookie gets a chance to bat.

Mark confronts Ray about selling the farm, but Karin tells her father that people will come and pay to see his field. Terence explains the people will want to relive the memories of the past and revel in the baseball.

When Karin is acciden-tally hurt, Archie steps over the foul line. He then turns into Doc, who saves the child from choking. But Doc cannot return to the game; after saying his goodbyes, he vanishes into the cornfield. Mark can now see the ballplayers, as the Kinsellas and Terence do, and implores Ray not to sell the farm.

Invited into the cornfield, Terence promises to bring back a description for an envious Ray. Shoeless Joe then points to the catcher and Ray under-stands that everything has led up to this moment. For the catcher is Ray's father, John, who is a young man again. As father and son play catch to-gether, miles upon miles of cars approach the farm.

COMMENTARY: Every Christmas season, the 1946 Frank Capra fantasy drama *It's a Wonderful Life*, starring James

Stewart, is shown on television. Inspired by a 1982 novel by W.P. Kinsella, direc-tor/writer Phil Alden Robinson made an old-fashioned movie, *Field of Dreams*, that was compared to the Capra classic because of the special ingredients of fable, family, and faith.

Though overly indulgent in its sen-timentality, on the nostalgia of baseball and on getting another chance at a dream, the 1989 Universal release (pro-duced by Lawrence and Charles Gor-don) was equally heartwarming and

A delightful pose from 1989's *Field of Dreams* con-veying Burt Lancaster's sincerity and charm.

enchanting. Kevin Costner conveyed the aura of a Jimmy Stewart, a decent, honest guy who tries to follow his heart.

The entire cast did a wonderful job with Costner. The gentle mystique surrounding this picture is unforgettable, made particularly so by the sweet nature of its ghosts played by Ray Liotta, Frank Whaley, Dwier Brown, and Burt Lancaster.

Burt had only two sequences in this, his very last theatrical feature, and they were overwhelming in their magical charm. The first encounter between Costner's Ray Kinsella and Lancaster's Doc Graham was filmed in the small town of Galena, Illinois (substituting for the film's Chisholm, Minnesota). Their second encounter was filmed on the actual baseball field used. It was constructed on two adjacent farms near Dyersville, Iowa (it later became a tourist attraction).

With its initial release, *Field of Dreams* made a very profitable $30 million at the box office. The film was also nominated for three Academy Awards: Best Picture, Screenplay Based on Material from Another Medium (Phil Alden Robinson), and Original Score (James Horner).

REVIEWS: *Detroit News:* "Patter about the magic of movies remains a staple of Hollywood press agentry, but only once in a great while does a movie make good on the promise behind the patter. *Field of Dreams* delivers, and then some. It's pure magic."

New York Post: "Burt Lancaster is a good choice for the old doctor who missed out on his big chance to play in the majors. His face and voice alone evoke the kind of longing for olden days (and better movies?) that fills everyone's heart in this film."

The Jeweller's Shop

A PAC/RAI-1/Alliance Entertainment/International Movies Production Previewed at the Vatican in 1989   90 minutes   Color

CREDITS: Michael Anderson (Director); Raimondo Castelli and Stephane Reichel (Producers); Pietro Bergni and Mario Bergni (Executive Producers); Jeff Andrus (Screenplay); Franco DiGiacomo (Photography); Ron Wisman (Editor); Luciano Calosso and Earl Preston (Set Designers); Nadia Vitali (Costumes); Janusz St. Pasierb (Literary Consultant); Michel Legrand (Music Score). Based on the play by Karol Wojtyla and First Italian Screenplay by Mario diNardo.

CAST: Burt Lancaster (The Jeweller); Ben Cross (Stephen); Olivia Hussey (Theresa); Daniel Olbrychski (Father Adam); Jo Champa (Anna); Andrea Occhipinti (Andrej); Melora Hardin (Monica); Jonathan Crombie (Chris).

SYNOPSIS: In 1939 Poland, a mysterious old jeweller watches some students talking with a priest, Father Adam. The jeweller seems interested in two particular couples—Stephen and Anna, and Andrej and Theresa.

In love, Theresa and Andrej buy their wedding rings from the jeweller, who speaks of the rings as symbols of eternal unity. The couple is wed by Father Adam. Also marrying, Anna and Stephen immigrate to Canada just before World War II begins.

Andrej becomes a soldier, is wounded, and dies with Father Adam at his side. Afterward, Theresa gives birth to Andrej's son and names him Chris.

Both Theresa and Chris are able to immigrate to Canada in 1947 with Stephen's help. Stephen and Anna have a daughter named Monica. Theresa is a concert pianist, and Stephen is a doctor.

In 1962, Chris and Monica, now grown, are in love. Anna and Stephen share an unhappy marriage, and this stress puts a strain on the younger couple as well.

Anna is so frustrated by her marriage that she tries to sell her wedding ring to a jeweller, who seems to resemble the old jeweller from Poland. He cannot buy it because his scales do not weigh metal, only people's relationships.

With both Father Adam and Theresa helping, Stephen and Anna renew their love. This also helps restore the love Monica and Chris have for each other and they decide to marry.

Theresa is playing at a concert in Poland, and

The Jeweller's Shop: **Burt Lancaster as The Jeweller.**

the young couple are wed there by Father Adam, after buying their wedding rings from the old jeweller. The jeweller looks back at all these people's lives and quietly savors the wonder of love.

COMMENTARY: A combined Italian-French-Canadian production, *The Jeweller's Shop* was filmed for $9 million in 1987. Raimondo Castelli and Stephane Reichel were the producers. Directed by Michael Anderson, the screenplay was first done in Italian by Mario diNardo, then by Jeff Andrus in English.

The story was based on a play written in 1960 by Pope John Paul II. At that time he was Monsignor Karol Wojtyla, auxiliary bishop of Krakow, Poland (he used the writing pseudonym of Andrzej Jawien). A poetic mediation on the institution of marriage, the play was printed in 22 languages and sold over 50 million copies; it was the first written work by a pope to be made into a film.

Pope John Paul II had given the script his blessing, and the Vatican in Rome had final approval of the film and of the cast, including Olivia Hussey, Ben Cross, and Burt Lancaster. "I'm very impressed by what the pope wrote," commented Burt at a news conference in 1987. "This is a new kind of story about what love means and the power of love."

A representative of the pope, Janusz St. Pasierb, was assigned to the film's locations in Poland (Krakow) and Canada (Montreal) as literary consultant to safeguard the theme of eternal love. He told the *Los Angeles Daily News*, "One of the problems we're trying to deal with in the movie is to make the jeweller appear more godlike." Lancaster was supposed to symbolize the deity with his role.

The Jeweller's Shop also had the problem of translating some of the pope's prose to a more natural speaking dialogue. It was alleged that six percent of the film's profits would go to the Vatican, where it was initially previewed. The pope was complimentary after the screening. Although it was reputed to have been shown as well on Italian television in 1989, the film was actually held up for a domestic release for the next few years.

Finally, by early 1992, New Line Television—an affiliate of New Line Cinema and a division of RHI Entertainment—picked up some domestic distribution privileges and the film began being shown on syndicated television stations. Out of a possible four stars, *TV Guide* gave it two for fair.

The acting by the principals was fine, although low-keyed as the rule. Burt Lancaster was particularly dignified in a small but vastly important role (which was filmed in a week in Krakow). The montage of scenes at the end, as the jeweller reflects on all that has come to pass, was very touching. Yet this rather simplistic drama (perhaps too much so) failed to ignite much interest with American viewers at least.

The Betrothed

A RAI Channel 1 Presentation   A RAI Uno, Hermes Film Munich, Bayerischer Rundfunk Gevest Holding B.V. Rotterdam, RTV Ljubljana Co-production   Broadcast on Italian television on November 12, 19, 26, and December 3 and 10, 1989   300 minutes   Color

CREDITS: Salvatore Nocita (Director); Alessandro Calosci and Anna Maria Denza (Executive Producers); Enrico Medioli, Roberta Mazzoni, Salvatore Nocita, and Pier Emilio Gennarini (Script); Zivko Zalar (Photography); Enrico Tovaglieri (Sets); Maurizio Monteverde and Franco Tirelli (Costumes); Ennio Morricone (Music Score). Based on Alessandro Manzoni's novel *I Promessi Sposi*.

CAST: Helmut Berger (Egidio); Gary Cady (Rodrigo); Mathieu Carriere (Attilio); Valentina Cortese (Donna Prassede); Delphine Forest (Lucia); Danny Quinn (Renzo); Fernando Rey (The Count Uncle); Jenny Seagrove (Gertrude); Gisela Stein (Agnese); Franco Nero (Fra Cristoforo); Alberto Sordi (Don Abbondio); F. Murray Abraham (L'Innominato); Burt Lancaster (Federigo).

SYNOPSIS: In 17th-century Lombardy, a landowner is killed in a dispute by a man called Ludovico. The landowner, however, slays Ludovico's servant Cristoforo in the process. Ludovico then becomes a Franciscan friar, calling himself Fra Cristoforo after his servant.

Years later, nobleman Don Rodrigo lusts after a woman who works at the silk mill. Her name is Lucia Mondella and she is betrothed to mill worker Renzo Tramaglino. Don Abbondio, the parish priest, is to marry Lucia and Renzo, but is afraid to because of Rodrigo's interference. Urged by the couple and Lucia's mother, Agnese, Fra Cristoforo tries without success to persuade Rodrigo to leave matters alone. When the friar has the mother, daughter, and promised bridegroom sent to safety, Rodrigo has his cousin, Attilio, arrange to have Cristoforo transferred.

With Renzo sent to Milan, Agnese and Lucia stay at the convent in Monza presided over by a nun named Gertrude. Aware of the nun's influence, Rodrigo turns to the services of the evil L'Innominato.

Egidio, Gertrude's secret lover, is a friend of this L'Innominato. Having killed a nun for discovering their affair, Gertrude is persuaded by Egidio to help L'Innominato kidnap Lucia in order to remove the dead body. Meanwhile, Renzo has become a fugitive from the bread riots.

Inside L'Innominato's stronghold, Lucia's grief causes the man to feel a great remorse—he visits Cardinal Federigo to make amends and begs Lucia for forgiveness. The cardinal sends Lucia to safety at the villa of Don Ferrante and Donna Prassede, and he scolds Don Abbondio for not marrying Renzo and Lucia. The cardinal orders all charges against Renzo being a fugitive dropped. Yet Lucia apparently cannot marry him, for she made a sacred vow not to while held by L'Innominato.

War has caused soldiers of fortune to pillage the countryside, and with their havoc a plague is spread. Don Ferrante and Attilio are among the victims.

Renzo seeks revenge against Rodrigo, but Fra Cristoforo moves him to forgive his enemy. The friar also releases Lucia from her vow, and she is free to marry Renzo. Rodrigo dies from the plague. Rain then falls, purifying everything and ending the pestilence.

COMMENTARY: "In Europe, the name obviously means something. I'm bankable. I give status to the release," said Burt Lancaster in 1988. And he undoubtedly proved this once again with an illustrious role as Cardinal Fed-

The Betrothed: **Burt Lancaster as Federigo.**

erigo in the multinational television miniseries *The Betrothed*.

The international cast joining Lancaster included Helmut Berger, Jenny Seagrove, Franco Nero, and Alberto Sordi. Delphine Forest and Danny Quinn portrayed the title's lovers. Somehow their romance was not found as powerful as it should have been. But powerful indeed was the sequence that highlighted the meeting between Burt's good and generous cardinal and F. Murray Abraham's L'Innominato [the unnamed], who seeks conversion from his vile past.

Lancaster's small role (he was billed as "special guest star") was filmed in seven days in 1988 at sites in Milan and Yugoslavia—the entire shooting schedule for the miniseries ran 32 weeks. Salvatore Nocita's tremendous direction utilized 284 actors and 10,000 extras.

The Betrothed was scripted by Enrico Medioli and Roberta Mazzoni, with the help of Nocita and Pier Emilio Gennarini. It was based on the classic Italian story written in 1827 by Alessandro Manzoni, entitled *I Promessi Sposi*. Long required reading in Italian government schools, the book's overwhelming tale of love and faith was derived from a historical background (the Thirty Years' War). Cardinal Federigo Borromeo was a real person.

Televised in Italy in late 1989, the five-part miniseries was reputed to be at that time the highest rated Italian programming in the history of RAI television. Although filmed in English and with lavish production values, *The Betrothed* failed to find any domestic distribution. It was apparently too long and slow-moving to attract attention outside of its native country.

The 1990s

The Phantom of the Opera

From Saban/Scherick Productions Broadcast on NBC Television on March 18 and 19, 1990   240 minutes   Color
  CREDITS: Tony Richardson (Director); Ross Milloy (Producer); Haim Saban and Edgar J. Scherick (Executive Producers); Arthur Kopit (Script); Steve Yaconelli (Photography); Bob Lambert (Editor); Jacques Bufnoir (Production Designer); Timian Alsaker (Visual Consultant); Philippe Turlure (Set Decorator); Jacqueline Moreau (Costumes); Sophie Landry (Makeup); Cedric Chami (Hair Stylist); Marc Marmier (Special Effects); John Addison (Music Score). Based on Arthur Kopit's play and Gaston Leroux's novel.
  CAST: Burt Lancaster (Gerard Carriere); Charles Dance (Erik, The Phantom); Teri Polo (Christine Daee); Adam Storke (Count Philippe de Chagny); Ian Richardson (Cholet); Andrea Ferreol (Carlotta); Jean Rougerie (Jean-Claude); Jean-Pierre Cassel (Inspector Ledoux); Andre Chaumeau (Joseph Buquet); Francois Lalande (Member of the Company); Marie-Christine Robert (Flora); Marie Lenoir (Florence); Anne Roumanoff (Fleure); Catherine Erhardy (Chorus Girl); Michel Feder (Music Director); Marie-Therese Orain (Madame Giry); Philippe de Brugada (Alfredo); Bernard Spiegel (Member of Audience); Luc Gentil and Jean-Claude Bouillon (Policemen).

SYNOPSIS: In 19th-century Paris, a man named Erik lives secretly beneath the opera house in the sewer tunnels. He has been there since childhood because his face is horribly disfigured. Gerard Carriere, the house manager, takes care of Erik. With a talent for music, Erik helps Gerard choose the best operas.

Gerard is replaced as manager by comic opera villain Cholet, who has bought the opera house so his wife, Carlotta, can sing there as the new diva. Known as The Phantom, Erik plays nasty tricks to make them leave.

Christine Daee has been brought to Paris by her suitor, Count Philippe, for singing lessons, but she works as Carlotta's wardrobe mistress. When Erik overhears Christine singing, her lovely voice reminds him of his deceased mother's.

The Phantom of the Opera, with Teri Polo, Burt Lancaster, and Charles Dance.

Erik then abducts Christine to his underground home to teach her to sing even better, and they become friends. But when she sees his face under the mask he wears, she is frightened and runs away. Both upset, Gerard tells Erik that he cares for him because Erik is his son.

During a performance of *Faust*, in which Christine is playing the heroine, Erik joins her in song from a box seat. Inspector Ledoux, who is hunting The Phantom, chases after Erik.

Forced to flee, Erik seems trapped on the roof of the opera house. To prevent Erik from being captured and turned into a freak show, Gerard shoots him. Christine kisses Erik's deformed face as he dies in his father's arms.

COMMENTARY: *The Phantom of the Opera* was originally written in 1911 by Gaston Leroux; the first film version was the 1925 silent theatrical classic starring Lon Chaney. Since then five additional *Phantom* films have been made (three theatrically and two for television). For the NBC television miniseries in 1990, Arthur Kopit's script (adapted from his 1982 play) replaced the horror in the famous story with romantic tragedy.

If not quite as thrilling as the earlier versions, it was a lavish treatment directed in Paris by Tony Richardson and produced by Ross Milloy. The singing was regarded as a high point, but the dubbing of the actual singing voices was faulted to a degree—Gerard Garino sang as Erik (played by Charles Dance); Michele LeGrange sang as Christine (played by Teri Polo); and Helia T'hezan sang as Carlotta (played by Andrea Ferreol).

Dance, in the title role, gave a noble performance. Burt Lancaster gave a quiet, sensitive one as the understanding father; he was nominated with a Golden Globe Award for Best Actor. In make-up similar to his role in *The Leopard*, Lancaster looked splendid. Being a true opera buff, he was very pleased to be part of the 11-week shooting schedule, which indeed filmed at the famed Paris opera house (and also at the Odéon Theater).

A pair of Emmy awards went to *The Phantom of the Opera* in the category of Miniseries or Special: Outstanding Art Direction (Timian Alsaker, Jacques Bufnoir) and Outstanding Achievement in Hair Styling (Cedric Chami). It also received three other nominations: Outstanding Costume Design (Jacqueline Moreau), Outstanding Achievement in Make-up (Sophie Landry), and Outstanding Music Composition (John Addison). Unfortunately, the production did not do well in the ratings—it averaged only a 12.3 for the two nights it was initially televised.

REVIEWS: *Variety:* "Plumping up Gaston Leroux's novel into an overwrought, explanatory meller, playwright Arthur Kopit has lost the tingle and the charm of other filmed versions."

TV Guide: "Richardson has given the four hour film an impressive look and he gets fine performances from his excellent supporting cast: newcomer Teri Polo (a find as Christine), Burt Lancaster, Ian Richardson, Adam Storke and French star Andrea Ferreol."

Voyage of Terror: The Achille Lauro Affair

Produced by Tribune Entertainment Company, Beta Taurus Group, RAIDUE, Filmalpha Productions, and TF1   Broadcast

on the Tribune Premiere Network (over Syndicated Television) on May 1 and 2, 1990
240 minutes   Color
CREDITS: Alberto Negrin (Director); David Lawrence (Line Producer); Mario Gallo and Fabrizio Castellani (Executive Producers); Alberto Negrin and Sergio Donati (Script); Giuseppe Ruzzolini (Photography); Richard Rabjohn (Editor); Mariolina Bono (Costumes); Ennio Morricone (Music Score).
CAST: Burt Lancaster (Leon Klinghoffer); Eva Marie Saint (Marilyn Klinghoffer); Robert Culp (General Walter Davies); Renzo Montagnani (Captain de Rosa); Dominique Sanda (Margot); Adriana Innocenti (Nonna); Said Amadis (Abul Abbas/Khaled); Brian Bloom (Antonio); Jochen Horst (Helmut); Joseph Nasser (Molqi); and Rebecca Schaeffer (Cheryl).

SYNOPSIS: In October 1985, the Italian cruise ship *Achille Lauro* sets sail for various ports in the Mediterranean. There are over 755 passengers and crew aboard; Gerardo de Rosa is the ship's captain.

Among the passengers are a group of American senior citizens, including husband and wife Leon and Marilyn Klinghoffer. Leon is confined to a wheelchair, having had a stroke, and Marilyn is suffering with cancer.

The Klinghoffers stay aboard when 666 passengers leave the ship for a sightseeing trip in Cairo. A few hours later, four terrorists, brandishing Soviet-made guns, take over the ship. Revealing themselves as part of the Palestine Liberation Front, the hijackers want 50 prisoners released from Israeli imprisonment.

Tired of waiting when their demands are not met, the terrorists take Leon away, shoot him, and throw his body into the sea. They threaten to kill a hostage every hour.

The leader of the PLF, Abul Abbas, commands the terrorists to abort their mission and instructs them to depart in an Egyptian airplane. American general Walter Davies attempts to intervene with commandos, but Italian troops advise him that the incident took place on one of their ships. But when the terrorists are airborne, Davies has U.S. naval aircraft force their plane down. The terrorists are then apprehended.

COMMENTARY: *Voyage of Terror: The Achille Lauro Affair* was based on a true story; a syndicated television miniseries, it marked the first production for the newly formed Tribune Premiere Network. Ten million dollars was invested into the film by the international interests involved. David Lawrence was the line producer, representing the American-based Tribune Entertainment.

Though overlong and not too surprising, the horror of the 52 hours of terrorism nonetheless remained quite harrowing. Portraying the tragic couple Marilyn and Leon Klinghoffer, Eva Marie Saint and Burt Lancaster did so most thoughtfully. Director Alberto Negrin (who also co-wrote the script with Sergio Donati) followed directors in Burt's later years who were understanding of his embarrassment at having trouble memorizing his lines on occasion.

The singer, Cheryl, involved with two male passengers in the film's romantic subplot, was portrayed by Rebecca Schaeffer. She was killed by a stalker before the program was aired in 1990. It was dedicated to her memory.

In February 1989, NBC televised an initial version of the hijacking, called appropriately *The Hijacking of the Achille Lauro*, with Karl Malden and Lee Grant

Voyage of Terror: Burt Lancaster and Eva Marie Saint with cast members.

as the Klinghoffers. Neither film was especially memorable, although *Voyage of Terror* was given more credence. Being the longer of the two, it gave a more detailed description of the events from 1985. It was also filmed aboard the actual 23,629-ton *Achille Lauro*, with the ship's captain acting as technical consultant.

REVIEWS: *Variety:* "The centerpiece is the seg in which Klinghoffer is gruesomely executed and Marilyn, tracked by Giuseppe Ruzzolini's camera, searches anxiously for him in the ship's salon; it's a moving, effective seg."

Dallas Times Herald: "Lancaster is always fun to watch, though it's unlikely that *Voyage of Terror* will be remembered as his finest moment, if it's remembered at all."

Separate But Equal

A New Liberty Production   In Association with Republic Pictures Television   Broadcast on ABC Television on April 7 and 8, 1991   240 minutes   Color

CREDITS: George Stevens Jr. (Director and Script); George Stevens Jr. and Stan Margulies (Co-executive Producers); Joel B. Segal and Ted Swanson (Associate Producers); Nic Knowland (Photography); John W. Wheeler (Editor); Veronica Hadfield (Production Designer); Francine Jamison-Tanchuck (Costumes); Gigi Coker (Make-up); Alixe Gordin (Casting); John Hope Franklin and E. Barrett Prettyman (Historical Consultants); Jim Zagami (Supreme Court Consultant); Ed Novick (Sound); Carl Davis (Music Score).

CAST: Sidney Poitier (Thurgood Marshall); Burt Lancaster (John W. Davis); Richard Kiley (Chief Justice Earl Warren); Cleavon Little (Robert Carter); Gloria Foster ("Buster" Marshall); John McMartin (Governor James F. Byrnes); Graham Beckel (Josiah B. Tulley); Ed Hall (Reverend J.A. DeLaine); Lynne Thigpen (Alice Stovall); Macon McCalman (W.B. Springer); Cheryl Lynn Bruce (Gladys Hampton); Henderson Forsythe (Justice Robert H. Jackson); Randle Mell (Charles Black); Tommy Hollis (Harry Briggs Sr.); John Rothman (Jack Greenberg); Damien Leake (Dr. Kenneth Clark); Albert Hall (Oliver Hill); Mike Nussbaum (Justice Felix Frankfurter); Hallie Foote (Julia Davis); William Cain (Judge Waties Waring); E. Katharine Kerr (Mrs. Elizabeth Avery Waring); Tom Aldregge (Justice Hugo Black); Leonard Jackson (Harold Boulware); Ed Seamon (E.R. Crow); Beeson Carroll (Judge John J. Parker); Samuel E. Wright (Artis Patterson); John Ottovino (Mark Baldwin); Jon de Vries (David Krech); Mark Hammer (Justice Stanley Reed); Charles Dumas (Bob Ming); Jeffrey Wright (William Coleman); Pearce Venning (Harry Briggs Jr.).

SYNOPSIS: In 1950 South Carolina, Harry Briggs Jr., a black boy, has to walk five miles to and from school. Reverend DeLaine, the school's principal, tries without success to get a bus for the black children. He is told to drop the matter by his own superintendent, W.B. Springer.

DeLaine, however, sends for Thurgood Marshall, the chief counsel for the NAACP (National Association for the Advancement of Colored People). To keep the NAACP from becoming involved, Governor James F. Byrnes is now prepared to spend equal funding for the black schoolchildren. But DeLaine is replaced as principal, and later he loses his home to arson.

The NAACP tries to challenge the segregation law in the state. In 1951, a three-judge court states that this law, separating the black and white children, must be upheld. Attorney John W. Davis is asked by the governor to defend the state law should the matter be taken to the Supreme Court.

Marshall decides that the time for desegregation has come. The NAACP takes several petitions from different areas of the country to the Supreme Court. Marshall's wife, "Buster," although suffering from cancer, supports his cause.

Davis is urged by his daughter, Julia, not to take the case because it will look like he is against black people. However, he believes in defending the law as written.

At the Supreme Court proceeding in 1952, a nine-judge court listens to Marshall and Davis on their opposing views. Both lawyers are quite persuasive, and the judges decide to allow them to reargue the case.

A new chief justice, Earl Warren, is appointed after his predecessor dies from a heart attack. Davis and Marshall then reargue their case in 1953, again in Washington, D.C., at the Supreme Court.

Realizing that segregation is wrong, Warren, with difficulty, manages to get the eight other judges to vote unanimously for desegregation the following year. Marshall and his colleagues rush back to the Supreme Court to hear the decision. Davis is told by Julia and he reflects that is the best thing for the country.

COMMENTARY: The miniseries *Separate But Equal* carried the following disclaimer preceding its television broadcast on ABC in 1991: "Tonight's

A landmark story, *Separate But Equal*, was Burt Lancaster's last film, here with Sidney Poitier and players.

film is a dramatization based on interviews and accounts of the time, and contains created scenes and dialogue."

Sidney Poitier, in his first dramatic televison role since 1956, played Thurgood Marshall; Burt Lancaster portrayed John W. Davis, "the lawyer's lawyer"; and Richard Kiley portrayed President Eisenhower's choice for chief justice, Earl Warren. Their performances were indeed excellent, as were those of the splendid supporting cast, including Gloria Foster as "Buster" Marshall and Ed Hall as Reverend DeLaine. Radiating from each of these five performers was a simple dignity.

Lancaster was particularly soft-spoken and gracious, and he reflected, "It's a great drama." He worked for three-weeks on the ten week shooting schedule, first in Charleston, South Carolina; then Washington, D.C.; and finally in Orlando, Florida. Concerned that his memorization skills would cause a problem with the extensive courtroom material, Burt once more found a director, George Stevens Jr., who helped him.

In Florida (on a Walt Disney World soundstage), teleprompters were placed for all the courtroom interiors filmed. They proved so helpful for Burt that both Kiley and Poitier used them, too. That he found a comfort in all this was reflected by Burt's good humor shared between scenes with the extras in the courtroom.

Separate But Equal: **Burt Lancaster as John W. Davis.**

Not only did Stevens direct but he also wrote the script and served as a co-executive producer (along with Stan Margulies). That the miniseries was quality television of the highest order was undeniable—it was dignified, intelligent, and with a powerful sense of justice. But the civil rights theme was deemed too slow-moving and predictable to excite viewers; this assessment apparently held true with the ratings—a low 11.9 was averaged.

Separate But Equal, however, did receive a number of major Emmy Award nominations in the category Miniseries or Special, including Lead Actor (Sidney Poitier), Supporting Actor (Richard Kiley), and Writing (George Stevens Jr.). It won two of the nominations: to Alixe Gordin for Casting, and as the Drama/Comedy Special and Miniseries of the year.

REVIEWS: *Washington Post:* "The film is beautiful to look at, and both Poitier and Lancaster are equipped with voices that are joys to hear. It's just a pity Stevens didn't move the story along a bit more zestfully."

Variety: "While it has its clumsy moments, *Separate But Equal* is an absorbing, persuasive telefilm that pays heed to the courage and vigor of the people championed by chief counsel Marshall.... Lancaster delivers a lovely perf filled with depth and awareness."

Bibliography

Alexander, Shana. "Will the Real Burt Please Stand Up?" *Life*, September 6, 1963.

Balio, Tino. *United Artists: The Company That Changed the Film Industry*. Madison: University of Wisconsin Press, 1987.

Beale, Lewis. "Burt Lancaster Dies." *New York Daily News*, October 22, 1994.

"Burt Lancaster." *Cincinnati Enquirer*, June 26, 1977.

Case, Christopher. *The Ultimate Movie Thesaurus*. New York: Henry Holt, 1996.

Champlin, Charles. "Burt Lancaster's Undimmed Magic." *Los Angeles Times*, September 10, 1988.

Clinch, Minty. *Burt Lancaster*. New York: Stein and Day, 1984.

Current Biography Yearbook. New York: Wilson, 1953 and 1986.

Demaris, Ovid. "He'd Rather Take a Chance." *Parade*, November 6, 1988.

Douglas, Kirk. *The Ragman's Son*. New York: Simon and Schuster, 1988.

Fishgall, Gary. *Against Type: The Biography of Burt Lancaster*. New York: Scribner's, 1995.

Gebert, Michael. *The Encyclopedia of Movie Awards*. New York: St. Martin's, 1996.

Graham, Sheilah. *Confessions of a Hollywood Columnist*. New York: William Morrow, 1969.

Hardy, Phil. *The Encyclopedia of Western Movies*. Woodbury, 1984.

Hunter, Allan. "A Perfectly Mysterious Man." *Films and Filming*, October 1983.

Huston, John. *An Open Book*. New York: Knopf, 1980.

International Dictionary of Films and Filmmakers. Vol. 2: *Directors*. Detroit: St. James/Gale, 1984. Vol. 3: *Actors and Actresses*. Detroit: St. James/Gale, 1986. Vol. 4: *Writers and Production Artists*. Detroit: St. James/Gale, 1987.

Itria, Helen. "Story of a Hard Man." *Look*, October 20, 1953.

Jarrell, Frank P. "Burt Lancaster." (Charleston) *News and Courier*, September 20, 1990.

Lantos, Jeffrey. "The Last Waltz." *American Film*, October 1986.

McDonald, Archie P. (ed.). *Shooting Stars: Heroes and Heroines of Western Film*. Bloomington: Indiana University Press, 1987.

Martin, Pete. "Hollywood Hard Guy." *Saturday Evening Post*, September 11, 1948.

_____. "I Drop In on Burt Lancaster." *Saturday Evening Post*, June 24, 1961.

Michael, Paul. *The Academy Awards: A Pictorial History*. 5th ed. New York: Crown, 1982.

Robbins, Fred. "Comeback of the Year: Burt Lancaster." *50 PLUS*, April 1982.

Scanlon, Christopher P. (ed.). *The Video Source Book*. Detroit: Gale Research, 1977.

Schuster, Mel. "Burt Lancaster." *Films in Review*, August/September 1969.

Shipman, David. *The Great Movie Stars: The International Years*. New York: St. Martin's, 1972.

Thirer, Irene. *New York Post*, October 10, 1948.

Thomas, Tony. *Burt Lancaster*. New York: Pyramid, 1975.

_____. *The Films of Kirk Douglas*. Secaucus, NJ: Citadel, 1972.

Vermilye, Jerry. *Burt Lancaster*. New York: Falcon/Crescent, 1971.

Wallis, Hal, and Charles Higham. *Starmaker: The Autobiography of Hal Wallis*. New York: Macmillan, 1980.

Wiley, Mason, and Damien Bona. *Inside Oscar: The Unofficial History of the Academy Awards*. 4th ed. New York: Ballantine Books, 1993.

Windeler, Robert. *Burt Lancaster*. London: W.H. Allen, 1984.

Index

Abbott, Bud 66
Abbott, Philip 12
Abraham, F. Murray 231
Addison, John 234
Adelson, Merv 182
Adler, Buddy 70
Adler, Luther 34
The Adventures of Don Juan (movie) 48
The Adventures of Robin Hood (movie) 48
Airport (book) 152
Airport (movie) 15, 17, 23, 70, 150–153, 155, 180
Aldrich, Robert 75, 78, 80, 160, 182
Alexander, Fay 88
Ali, Muhammad 16
All My Sons (movie) 8, 22, 34, 35–37, 39, 40, 85
All My Sons (play) 37
Allen, Lewis 32
Alsaker, Timian 234
Altman, Robert 17, 176
Alwyn, William 61
An American Christmas: Words and Music (TV program) 21
Ames, E. Preston 152
Anastasia (movie) 91
Anderson, John 136
Anderson, Maxwell 16
Anderson, Michael 229
Andrews, Dana 21
Andrews, Edward 115
Andrus, Jeff 229
Angela, Piero 221
Anthony, David 167
Anthony, Joseph 91
Apache (movie) 10, 22, 73–75, 77, 78
The Apartment (movie) 113
Arcalli, Franco 187
Armstrong, Tex 159
Asquith, Anthony 105
Astor, Mary 32, 33
At This Very Moment (TV program) 21

Atlantic City (movie) 1, 18, 19, 23, 195–198, 199

Bacall, Lauren 37
Bach, Catherine 168
The Bachelor Party (movie) 11, 12, 96
Bad for Each Other (movie) 10
Bailey, Charles W., II 131
Baldwin, Earl 66
Balsam, Martin 132
Bancroft, Anne 202
Barnum (TV movie) 19, 23, 217–220
Barnum, Phineas Taylor 218, 220
Bartok, Eva 61
Basehart, Richard 186
Baxter, Anne 13
Beach, Edward L. 99, 100
Begley, Ed 37
Belafonte, Harry 16
Bellah, James Warner 58
Bellamy, Ralph 105
Ben-Hur (movie) 13
Benton, Thomas Hart 82
Bercovici, Leonardo 40
Berger, Helmut 174, 231
Bergman, Ingrid 45, 91
Bernstein, Elmer 137, 141
Bernstein, Walter 40, 134
Bertolucci, Bernardo 17, 187, 188, 189
Bertolucci, Giovanni 173
Bertolucci, Giuseppe 187
The Betrothed (TV miniseries) 19, 20, 23, 230–232
Bettger, Lyle 95
Bickford, Charles 31, 55, 109
The Big Event (TV series) 17
Birdman of Alcatraz (movie) 1, 13, 14, 23, 116, 120–124, 132, 135, 141
Birdwell, Russell J. 55
Birnbaum, Roger 209
Biroc, Joseph 160
Bischoff, Sam 66
Bishop, Joey 21

Bisset, Jacqueline 152
Black, Jennifer 206
The Black Pirate (movie) 61
Blackmer, Sidney 63
Blair, Betsy 11
Blair, Linda 178
Blaustein, Julian 51
Blum, Edwin 66
Blyden, Larry 12
Blyth, Ann 31
Bodoh, Allan F. 191
Boenisch, Carl 147
Bogart, Humphrey 37, 45, 46
Bone, Jackie 15
Bonicelli, Vittorio 170
Booth, Shirley 62, 63, 64
Borgnine, Ernest 11, 12, 13, 14, 78, 86
Borromeo, Federigo 232
Boyle, Edward G. 132
The Boys in Autumn (play) 19
Brand, Neville 123
Brando, Marlon 85, 155, 156, 186
Bredell, Woody 27
Brent, Curley 4
Brice, Monte 33
Bricken, Jules 134
Bridges, Lloyd 90, 91
Bright Path (story, tribal name for Jim Thorpe) 55
Broken Arrow (movie) 75
Broncho Apache (book) 75
Bronson (Buchinsky), Charles 75, 78, 158
Brooks, Richard 15, 31, 111, 112, 113, 139, 140
Brown, Anthony 7
Brown, Dwier 228
Brown, Harry 7
Brown, Phil 8
Brute Force (movie) 8, 22, 27, 28–31, 32, 33, 35, 37, 46, 111
Buffalo Bill and the Indians (movie) 17, 20, 23, 174–176, 178, 200
Bufnoir, Jacques 234
Buntline, Ned 176, 200
Burgess, Anthony 170

Burgoyne, "Gentleman Johnny" 105
Burman, Tom 186
Butler, David 202
Butler, Gerald 40
Butler, Hugo 11
The Butter and Egg Man (play) 66

Cahn, Sammy 67
Calley, John 146
Calvet, Corinne 46
Cannold, Mitchell 191
Capaldi, Peter 205, 206
Capra, Frank 227
Captain Horatio Hornblower (movie) 60
Cardinale, Claudia 130, 138, 140, 174, 201
Carpenter, Carleton 53
Carradine, John 82
Casablanca (movie) 45
Cass, David 185
The Cassandra Crossing (movie) 17, 20, 23, 179–181, 182, 183, 184, 208, 221
Cassavetes, John 124, 125
Castellani, Renato 18, 19
Castelli, Raimondo 229
Castle Keep (movie) 15, 23, 144–147, 149
Cattle Annie and Little Britches (movie) 18, 23, 198–200
Catto, Max 88
Cavani, Liliana 201
Cavett, Dick 21
Cetshwayo 193
Chaikin, Judy 20
Chambers, John 186
Chami, Cedric 234
Chandler, John Davis 116
Chaney, Lon 234
Chaplin, Geraldine 176
Chase, Borden 72, 78
Chayefsky, Paddy 11, 12
Cheever, John 143, 144
Chelmsford, Lord 193
A Child Is Waiting (movie) 14, 23, 124–126
A Child Is Waiting (TV program) 124, 125
Chomsky, Marvin J. 178
Christians, Mady 36
Christie, Julie 223
Christine, Virginia 27
Clanton, Ike 95
Clanton, Phineas 95
Clark, Mark 201
Clark, Petula 21
Clark, Susan 158, 167, 168
Clift, Montgomery 68, 70, 105, 119
Cobb, Lee J. 158

Cody, William "Buffalo Bill" 176
Coen, Franklin 134
Cohen, Ronald M. 182
Cohn, Harry 69
Colby, Anita 31
The Colgate Comedy Hour (TV series) 10, 20
Collette, Chea 212
Colquhoun, Archibald 129
Come Back, Little Sheba (movie) 10, 22, 61–64, 86, 161
Come Back, Little Sheba (play) 63
Comer, Sam 86
Coming Home (movie) 191
Connors, Chuck 65, 66
Conrad, William 28
Control (TV movie) 19, 23, 220–221
Conversation Piece (movie) 17, 23, 172–174, 188
Cooper, Ben 85
Cooper, Gary 33, 53, 76, 77, 78, 99, 105
Cooper, Gladys 102
Cooper, James Fenimore 161
Coppola, Francis Ford 189
Corcoran, Kevin 12
Corey, Wendell 32, 33, 34, 91
Corkery, Paul 209
Cosmatos, George Pan 181
Costello, Lou 66
Costner, Kevin 161, 228
Cravat, Nick 3, 4, 6, 9, 48, 58, 59, 60, 61, 100, 142, 159, 168, 186
Crenna, Richard 214, 215
Crichton, Charles 123
The Crimson Pirate (movie) 10, 22, 58–61, 66, 72, 73
Criss Cross (movie) 8, 22, 42–44, 60
Cristal, Linda 12
Cristaldi, Franco 221
Cronyn, Hume 31
Crosby, Bing 33
Crosland, Alan, Jr. 78
Cross, Ben 229
Cruickshank, Jim 217
Cry Tough (movie) 11, 12, 108, 109
Culkin, Macaulay 225
Cummings, Bob 11
Curtis, Tony 87, 88, 89, 97, 98, 127
Curtiz, Michael 55
Cypher, Jon 155

D'Amico, Suso Cecchi 172
Dance, Charles 233, 234
Dances with Wolves (movie) 161
Dannenbaum, Jed 20

Danson, Ted 212, 213
Darcel, Denise 78
Dare, Daniel 33
The Daring Young Man (composition) 88
Dark City (movie) 51
Dassin, Jules 30, 31
Davenport, Nigel 194
Davis, Frank 58, 134
Davis, John W. 238
Davis, Ossie 141, 142
Davis, Peter S. 208
Davison, Bruce 159, 160, 161
Dawn's Early Light: Ralph McGill and the Segregated South (TV program) 20
Death in Venice (movie) 174
De Bosio, Gianfranco 170
Decae, Henri 146
DeCarlo, Yvonne 31, 43, 44
Dee, Ruby 12
De Haven, Carter 160
Dekker, Albert 28
Delon, Alain 22, 128, 130, 163
Del Ruth, Roy 67
DeMille, Cecil B. 20, 195
De Niro, Robert 189
Depardieu, Gerard 189
Desert Fury (movie) 8, 9, 22, 31–33, 34, 35, 66
The Devil's Disciple (movie) 12, 22, 104–106, 108, 217
The Devil's Disciple (play) 104, 105
The Devil's Disciple (TV program) 105
Dexter, Brad 100
Dieterle, William 45
Dietrich, Marlene 119
Dighton, John 13, 105
di Lampedusa, Giuseppe 129
diNardo, Mario 229
Disraeli, Benjamin 193
Donahue, Phil 21
Donati, Sergio 235
Doniger, Walter 45, 46
Douglas, Kirk 19, 21, 22, 34, 93, 94, 95, 105, 106, 127, 131, 132, 178, 216, 217, 225
Douglas, Melvyn 183
Douglas, Robert 48
Dowdy, Kathleen 20
Dragnet (TV series) 27
Dreyfuss, Richard 178
Drought, James 149
Dru, Joanne 53
Duff, Howard 31
Duggan, Pat 116
Duning, George 70
Durnford, Anthony 193
Durning, Charles 183, 184
Dutton, George 95
Duvall, Robert 157, 158

Earp, James 95
Earp, Wyatt 93, 95, 158
Eastlake, William 146
Eastwood, Clint 158
Eisenhower, Dwight 238
Elliott, Denholm 202
Elmer Gantry (book) 111, 114
Elmer Gantry (movie) 1, 13, 14, 15, 23, 110–114, 139, 220
Endfield, Cy 193
The Entertainer (movie) 113
Epstein, Julius J. 12
Ernst, Ora 6
Erskine, Chester 37
Evans, Maurice 105
Executive Action (movie) 17, 18, 23, 163–166
Exodus (movie) 113
Eyre, David 200

Fairbanks, Douglas, Sr. 3, 48, 61
Falk, Peter 147
Farnon, Robert 72
Farnsworth, Richard 159
Farrell, Bernard 134
Ferreol, Andrea 234
Field of Dreams (movie) 19, 20, 23, 226–228
Fierro, Paul 38
Fight of the Champions (boxing event) 16
The Fighters (short film) 16
Finch, Peter 178
First Love (proposed film) 13
The First Time (movie) 11
Fisher, Kate 95
Flaherty, Vincent X. 55
The Flame and the Arrow (movie) 9, 19, 22, 46–50, 57, 58, 60, 61, 72
Fleming, Rhonda 95
Fletcher, Lucille 39
Flight from Ashiya (movie) 14
Follett, Ken 214
Fonda, Henry 198, 225
Fontaine, Joan 41, 42
Ford, Daniel 190
Ford, John 108
Forest, Delphine 231
Forsyth, Bill 205, 206
Foster, Dianne 81, 82
Foster, Gloria 238
Foster, Norman 42
Fracci, Carla 19
Frankenheimer, John 14, 116, 123, 132, 134, 135, 149
Frazier, Joe 16
Freed, Donald 165
Freeman, Al, Jr. 145
Freeman, Devery 66
Frings, Ketti 64
From Here to Eternity (book) 69, 70, 88

From Here to Eternity (movie) 1, 10, 11, 22, 67–70, 86, 100, 149, 196
Le Front de l'art (book) 134
Frost, David 21
Fuchs, Daniel 43, 88

Gable, Clark 99, 100
The Gabriel Horn (book) 82
Gaddis, Tom 123
Ganz, Bruno 223
Gardner, Arthur 141
Gardner, Ava 27, 28, 132, 181
Garino, Gerard 234
Garland, Judy 37, 119, 124, 125, 126
Garrison, Jules 49
Garson, Greer 114
Il Gattopardo (book) 129
Il Gattopardo (movie) 127
Gausman, Russell A. 42
Gay, John 99, 102, 103, 136
Gazzara, Ben 221
Gebert, Gordon 47
Geer, Will 165
Gennarini, Pier Emilio 232
Gibbs, Alan 163
Gierasch, Stefan 178
Gigi (movie) 103
Gillette, Anita 16
Gilmore, Stuart 152
Il Giorno Prima (TV movie) 221
Gish, Lillian 109, 119
Go Tell the Spartans (movie) 18, 23, 189–191
The Godfather II (movie) 189
Gold, Ernest 113
Goldbeck, Willis 58
Goldsmith, Jerry 127, 183
Goldsmith, Jonathan 190
Golitzen, Alexander 152
Gordin, Alixe 239
Gordon, Charles 227
Gordon, Lawrence 227
Goulding, Edmund 51, 52
Grade, Lew 170
Graham, Sheilah 30
Grant, Cary 77
Grant, Lee 235
Green, Gerald 72
Griffin, Merv 21
Grimaldi, Alberto 188
Gruppo di Famiglia in un Interno (movie) 172, 173
Guare, John 196, 198
Guenette, Robert 178
Guffey, Burnett 70, 123
Gulick, Bill 136
Gunfight at the O.K. Corral (movie) 10, 19, 22, 91, 92–95, 158, 217
Guthrie, A.B., Jr. 82

Gwenn, Edmund 51, 52
The Gypsy Moths (movie) 14, 15, 23, 147–149, 158

Hackman, Gene 149
Hailey, Arthur 152
Hale, Barbara 11, 152
Hall, Conrad 139
Hall, Ed 238
Hallelujah Trail (book) 136
The Hallelujah Trail (movie) 14, 15, 23, 135–137, 139, 142
Hallmark Hall of Fame (TV presentation) 105
Hamilton, Guy 105
Hanley, William 149
Happy Birthday Hollywood (TV program) 21
Happy Days (TV series) 209
The Happy Thieves (movie) 14
Harlan, Russell 100
Harris, Richard 181
Harrison, Susan 97
Hartmann, Edmund 33
Haskin, Byron 8, 34, 72
Hatcher, Mary 33
Hathaway, Henry 152
Hauer, Rutger 208
The Hawk and the Arrow (screenplay) 48
Hawks, Howard 157, 158
Haworth, Edward S. 11
Hayden, Sterling 189
Hayes, Helen 152, 179
Hayward, Susan 103
Hayworth, Rita 103
Head, Edith 63, 86, 152
The Heart of Show Business (short film) 20
Hecht, Harold 1, 7–14, 40, 42, 48, 57, 58, 60, 66, 71, 75, 77, 80, 86, 88, 96, 97, 99, 100, 102, 103, 105, 108, 109, 116, 123, 141
Heeren, Astrid 146
Heflin, Van 152, 153
Heller, Otto 61, 73
Hellinger, Mark 8, 27, 30, 31, 43
Hemingway, Ernest 27
Henreid, Paul 45, 46
Hepburn, Audrey 13, 70, 108, 109, 110
Hepburn, Katharine 90, 91, 92
Heroux, Denis 196
Herrmann, Bernard 82
Herzbrun, Bernard 42
Hess, Richard 215
Heston, Charlton 13, 16, 51
Heyman, Barton 155
Hickox, Douglas 193
High Noon (movie) 75, 95
The Hijacking of the Achille Lauro (TV movie) 235, 237

Hill, James 1, 11, 12, 13, 14, 72, 78, 88, 89, 96, 99, 102, 103, 105, 108, 109, 116, 141
Hill, Steven 126
Hiller, Wendy 103
Hilton, Arthur 27
His Majesty O'Keefe (book) 72, 73
His Majesty O'Keefe (movie) 10, 11, 22, 66, 70–73, 78
Hitzig, Rupert 199
Hodiak, John 32
Holden, William 70, 91
Hole, Jeremy 221
Holliday, David 16
Holliday, John "Doc" 93, 95
Holliman, Earl 90, 91
Holt, Felix 82
Hope, Bob 33
Hopkins, Anthony 178
Horn, Robert 144
Horner, James 228
Horton, Louise 36, 37
Horvath, Charles 72
Howard, Dennis 190
Howard, Trevor 113
Howe, James Wong 86, 98
Hudson, John 94
Huebsch, Edward 182
Hunter, Evan 116
Hunter, Ross 152
Hurt, John 208
Hurt, William 21
Hussey, Olivia 229
Huston, John 27, 109, 110, 127
Hutton, Jim 137
Hutton, Lauren 209

I Love Liberty (TV program) 21
I Walk Alone (movie) 8, 9, 19, 22, 33–35, 46, 93, 217
I Want to Live! (movie) 103
I Who Am, Who Am I? (short film) 144
Incident at Muc Wa (book) 190
Infell, Howard 134
Inge, William 63
Inherit the Wind (movie) 113
Ireland, John 53, 95
The Island of Dr. Moreau (movie) 17, 23, 184–186, 194
The Island of Lost Souls (movie) 186
It's a Wonderful Life (movie) 227

Jacobs, Irving 7
Jaeckel, Richard 159, 161, 183
Jaffe, Herb 212
Jaffe, Sam 46
Jarre, Maurice 139
Jawien, Andrzej 229
The Jeweller's Shop (movie) 19,

20, 23, 228–230
Jim Thorpe—All American (movie) 10, 22, 53–56
John Paul II 229, 230
Johnny Belinda (movie) 39
Johnson, Lamont 200, 201
Jones, Carolyn 12
Jones, James 69, 88
Jones, Shirley 113
Jordan, Glenn 16
Jordan, Richard 158
Josephson, Erland 221
Joy, Robert 198
Judgment at Nuremberg (movie) 14, 21, 23, 117–120, 123, 124, 125, 130
Judgment at Nuremberg (TV program) 118, 119
Julius Caesar (movie) 70

Kanew, Jeff 217
Kanter, Hal 85
Kaquitts, Frank 176
Karmen, Roland 18
Katz, Robert 181, 201
Kaufman, George S. 66
Kazan, Elia 37
Keith, Brian 137
Kellerman, Sally 21
Kelley, DeForest 94
Kelly, Gene 37
Kelly, Paul 34
Kennedy, Arthur 37
Kennedy, George 152
Kennedy, John F. 132, 165, 166
Kennedy, Robert 122
The Kentuckian (movie) 1, 12, 22, 78–82, 161
Kerr, Deborah 69, 70, 102, 103, 149
Kibbee, Roland 17, 58, 60, 66, 67, 78, 105, 156, 167
Kidder, Margot 212, 213
Kiley, Richard 238, 239
"The Killer" (article) 93
The Killers (movie) 1, 8, 22, 25–28, 30, 31, 33, 35, 37, 39, 43, 44, 46, 60
The Killing Frost (book) 88
King, Alan 199
King, Martin Luther, Jr. 16
King: A Filmed Record ... Montgomery to Memphis (documentary film) 16
Kinoy, Ernest 177, 179
Kinsella, W.P. 227
Kiss of the Spider Woman (movie) 21
Kiss the Blood Off My Hands (book) 40
Kiss the Blood Off My Hands (movie) 8, 22, 39–42, 43, 46
Kleiner, Harry 12

Klingman, Lawrence 72
Knebel, Fletcher 131
Knickerbocker Holiday (play) 16
Knight, Ray 7
Knudtson, Frederic 119
Kohn, Nate 193
Kopit, Arthur 176, 234
Kraike, Michel 43
Kramer, Stanley 118, 119, 124, 125
Krams, Arthur 86
Krapp, Helmut 222
Krasker, Robert 88
Kristien, Stanley 166

Labella, Vincenzo 170, 202
Ladd, Alan 33
Laine, Frankie 95
Lambert, Jack 28
Lamour, Dorothy 33
Lancaster, Elizabeth (née Roberts) 3, 4
Lancaster, Florence 3
Lancaster, James (brother) 3, 4, 14
Lancaster, James (father) 3, 4, 14
Lancaster, James (grandfather) 3
Lancaster, James Steven (son) 8
Lancaster, Jane 3
Lancaster, Joanna Mari 10, 15, 19, 22, 212
Lancaster, June (née Ernst) 6
Lancaster, Norma (née Anderson) 7, 8, 9, 10, 15, 40
Lancaster, Sighle-Ann 10, 15
Lancaster, Susan (née Scherer) 21, 22
Lancaster, Susan Elizabeth 9, 15
Lancaster, Susanna (née Murray) 3
Lancaster, William (brother) 3, 4, 8
Lancaster, William Henry 8, 168, 170
Landau, Eli 16
Landers, Hal 149
Landry, Sophie 234
Lane, Diane 200
Lane, Mark 165
Lang, Andrew 3
Lang, Charles, Jr. 45, 95, 103
Lansbury, Angela 13
Larsen, Tambi 86
Laser, Dieter 223
LaShelle, Joseph 11
The Last of the Mohicans (book) 161
Last Tango in Paris (movie) 189
Laszlo, Ernest 75, 78, 80, 119, 152
Laughton, Charles 186

Laven, Arnold 141
Law, John Philip 149, 180
Lawler, Ray 13
Lawman (movie) 17, 23, 156–158, 161
Lawrence, David 235
Lawrence, Jody 58
Lawson, Denis 205, 206
Leacock, Philip 12
Legacy of the Hollywood Blacklist (TV program) 20
The Legend of the Lone Ranger (movie) 199
LeGrange, Michele 234
Lehman, Ernest 97
Leigh, Vivien 102
Leighton, Margaret 101, 102
Le Mat, Paul 214
LeMay, Alan 108
Lemmon, Jack 113
Leonard, Elmore 156
Leonard, Jack E 67
The Leopard (book) 129
The Leopard (movie) 14, 18, 22, 23, 127–130, 172, 188, 223, 234
Leotard 88
Leroux, Gaston 234
Leslie, Bethel 12
Leve, Samuel 7
Levene, Sam 7, 28, 31, 67
Levy, Jules 141
Levy, Louis 72
Lewis, Edward 127, 132, 149, 165
Lewis, Jerry 10, 20
Lewis, Roger 144
Lewis, Sinclair 111, 112, 114
The Life of Verdi (TV miniseries) 18, 19
Liotta, Ray 228
The List of Adrian Messenger (movie) 14, 23, 126–127, 217
Litel, John 82
Little Treasure (movie) 19, 20, 23, 212–213
Litvak, Anatole 38, 39
Livadary, John P. 70
Local Hero (movie) 18, 20, 23, 204–206, 208
Loden, Barbara 144
Lollobrigida, Gina 88, 89
Lombardo, Goffredo 130
Lord, John 18
Loren, Sophia 21, 181
Lorre, Peter 45, 46
Louis, Jean 70, 120
Low, Warren 64, 86, 95
Lubin, Arthur 66
Ludlum, Robert 207
Lugosi, Bela 186
Lukas, Paul 119
Luke, Jorge 159, 161

Lumet, Sidney 16
Lussier, Dane 11
Lynn, Diana 82
Lyon, William 70

McCarthy, Jack 6
MacDonald, Donald 81, 82
MacDonald, Philip 127
McGavin, Darren 91
McGill, Ralph 20
McGraw, Charles 28
McGregor, Rob Roy 100
McGuire, Dorothy 51, 52
McIntire, John 75, 82
MacKay, Fulton 205, 206
McKelway, St. Clair 51
MacKendrick, Alexander 96, 105
McKenzie, James 19
McKuen, Rod 18
McLaglen, Andrew V. 214
McLaren, Hollis 198
MacRae, Gordon 67
Maddow, Ben 40, 109
Magnani, Anna 84, 85, 86
Magurie, Hal 159
Mahlor, Jack 7
Malaparte, Curzio 201
Malden, Karl 123, 235
Malle, Louis 196, 198, 201
Mangano, Silvana 174
Mankiewicz, Joseph L. 16
Mankiewicz, Tom 81
Mann, Abby 118, 119, 120, 124
Mann, Daniel 64, 86
Mann, Delbert 11, 12, 102, 103, 108
Mantell, Joe 11
Manzoni, Alessandro 232
March, Fredric 131, 132
Marchand, Nancy 11
Marco Polo 202
Marco Polo (TV miniseries) 19, 20, 123, 201–204, 221
Margulies, Stan 239
Mark of Zorro (movie) 3
Markland, Ted 159
Marre, Albert 16
Marshall, E.G. 12
Marshall, George 33
Marshall, Ken 202
Martin, Dean 10, 20, 152, 153
Marty (movie) 1, 11, 12, 14, 86, 102
Marty (TV program) 11
Marvin, Lee 138, 139
Marx, Harpo 61
Masters, Ian 208
Mastroianni, Marcello 201
A Matter of Conviction (book) 116
Matthau, Walter 82
Mayes, Wendell 190
Mayo, Virginia 48, 65, 66

Mazurki, Mike 34, 35
Mazzoni, Roberta 232
Medioli, Enrico 172, 232
Megna, John 190
Merkel, Una 82
Merrill, Dina 116
Metty, Russell 42
Michaels, Mickey S. 152
The Midnight Man (movie) 17, 23, 166–168
Miles, Vera 183
Millar, Stuart 123
Miller, Arthur 37
Miller, David 165
Miller, Iva 55
Miller, J.P. 12, 108, 116
Miller, Kristine 32
Milloy, Ross 234
Mills, John 13, 192, 194
Milner, Martin 97
Milo, George 120
Minciotti, Esther 11
Miracle on 34th Street (movie) 51, 52
Mirisch, Walter 163
Mister 800 (movie) 10, 22, 50–52, 53, 86
Mitchell, Cameron 168
Mitchum, Robert 127, 196
Mondellini, Rino 146
Montalban, Ricardo 21
Montaldo, Giuliano 202, 221
Montiel, Sarita 78
Moore, Brian 221
Moore, Jack D. 152
Moore, Kieron 57, 58
Moore, Terry 64
Moore, Tom 19
Moorehead, Agnes 38, 39
Morales, Esai 215
Moreau, Jacqueline 234
Moreau, Jeanne 134
Moriarty, David 152
Morricone, Ennio 221
Morris, Wayne 27
Morrow, Douglas 55
Moses, the Lawgiver (TV miniseries) 17, 23, 168–172, 202
Mueller, Edward 51
A Mule for the Marquesa (book) 139
Murphy, Audie 109, 110
Murray, Don 12

The Naked City (movie) 27
Nash, Johnny 12
Nash, N. Richard 91
Nayfack, Nicholas 53
Negrin, Alberto 235
Nelligan, Kate 221
Nelson, Barry 152
Nelson, Craig T. 208
Nelson, Gene 67

Nephew, Neil 116
Nero, Franco 231
Nesbitt, Cathleen 102
Neuman, Alan 17
Newman, Alfred 152
Newman, Paul 16, 175, 176
Newton, Robert 42
Nimoy, Leonard 202
1900 (movie) 17, 20, 23, 186–189, 223
Niven, David 103
Nocita, Salvatore 231, 232
Nolan, Lloyd 152
Norell, Michael 220
Norman, Leslie 13
North, Alex 86, 92
North, Sheree 149, 158
Norton, William 141
Novecento (movie) 186, 188
Nugent, Frank 72

Oakley, Annie 176
Ober, Philip 68
O'Brian, Hugh 53
O'Brien, Edmond 28, 123, 132
O'Brien, Liam 88
Odell, Gary 132
Odets, Clifford 97, 98
Old Eight-Eighty (story) 51
Old Gringo (movie) 21
Olivier, Laurence 102, 105, 113, 119, 130
On Golden Pond (movie) 198, 225
On Wings of Eagles (TV miniseries) 19, 23, 213–215
O'Neal, Patrick 147
An Open Book (book) 109
Operation: Thunderbolt (movie) 178
O'Rourke, Frank 139
Orr, James 217
The Osterman Weekend (movie) 18, 20, 23, 207–208
Oswald, Lee Harvey 165
O'Toole, Peter 192, 194

Padri e Figli (TV miniseries) 222
Page, Geraldine 91, 102
Palance, Jack 139, 140
Panzer, William N. 208
Papas, Irene 170
Parrish, Robert 58
Pascal, Gabriel 105
Pascal, John 159
Patterson, David J. 218
Patterson, Robert 31
Pavan, Marisa 85, 86
Paynter, Robert 163
La Peau (movie) 201
Peck, Gregory 21, 122
Peckinpah, Sam 207, 208
La Pelle (movie) 19, 23, 200–201, 202

Penn, Arthur 134
Pereira, Hal 86
Peres, Shimon 178
Perot, Ross 215
Perry, Eleanor 143, 144
Perry, Frank 143, 144
Peters, Jean 75
Peterson, Louis, S. 12
Petrie, Daniel 224
The Phantom of the Opera (book) 234
The Phantom of the Opera (TV miniseries) 19, 23, 232–234
Philco TV Playhouse (TV series) 11, 91
Philips, Lee 218
Pickup, Ronald 19
Pierce, Ronald 152
Playhouse 90 (TV series) 113, 118
Pleasence, Donald 137
Plummer, Amanda 200
Poe, Amos 224, 225
Poitier, Sidney 16, 238, 239
Pollack, Sydney 116, 141, 144, 146, 155, 156
Polo, Teri 233, 234
Ponti, Carlo 181
Portman, Eric 101
Post, Ted 191
Potter, Joan 91
Powell, Jane 67
Pretty Baby (movie) 196
Previn, Andre 113
Price, Dennis 105
Priestley, Robert 11
Pro Football: Big Game America (TV program) 16, 17
The Professionals (movie) 15, 23, 137–140, 141, 160
I Promessi Sposi (book) 232
Prud'homme, Cameron 90, 92
Psychic Phenomena: Exploring the Unknown (TV program) 17
Puttnam, David 205

Quayle, Anthony 170
Quinn, Danny 231

The Rabbit Trap (movie) 11, 12, 108
Rabin, Yitzhak 177, 178
Race to Oblivion (short film) 20
Raid on Entebbe (TV movie) 178, 178
Raines, Ella 31
The Rainmaker (movie) 10, 22, 89, 92, 220
The Rainmaker (play) 91, 92
The Rainmaker (TV program) 91, 92
Rains, Claude 45, 46
Raksin, David 103

Ramrus, Al 186
Rankin, William M. 66
Ransohoff, Martin 146
Rattigan, Terence 101, 102, 103
Ravetch, Irving 53
Rayfiel, David 146, 156
Raynor, Lynn 214
Red River (movie) 53
Reed, Carol 88
Reed, Donna 70
Reed, Pamela 209, 210, 211
Reeves, Theodore 34
Reichel, Stephane 229
Reid, Kate 198, 221
Reis, Irving 37
Remick, Lee 137
Ricceri, Luciano 221
Rice, Joan 72
Rich, David Lowell 209
Richardson, Don 7
Richardson, Ian 234
Richardson, Tony 234
Rickles, Don 100
Riegert, Peter 205, 206
Ringo, Johnny 95
Rintels, David W. 163
Rio Lobo (movie) 158
Riskin, Robert 51
Ritchey, Bruce 125
Ritter, Thelma 122
The Robe (movie) 70
Roberts, Bobby 149
Roberts, James 3
Roberts, Jennie (née Smith) 3
Robertson, Cliff 21
Robinson, Edward G. 20, 36, 37
Robinson, Phil Alden 227, 228
Rocket Gibraltar (movie) 19, 20, 23, 224–225
Rodman, Howard 209
Roland, Gilbert 57, 58
Rolfe, Sam H. 214
Roman Holiday (movie) 70
Rope of Sand (movie) 8, 22, 44–46, 48, 64
The Rose Tattoo (movie) 10, 22, 82–86, 92
The Rose Tattoo (play) 85, 86
Ross, Frank 48
Rossellini, Renzo 201
Rossen, Robert 32
Rotunno, Giuseppe 129
Rouveral, Jean 11
Rowlands, Gena 126
Rozsa, Miklos 27, 32, 42, 44
Rozycki, Christopher 206
Rudolph, Alan 176
Rule, Janice 144
Run Silent, Run Deep (book) 99
Run Silent, Run Deep (movie) 12, 22, 98–100
Ruocheng, Ying 202
Rush to Judgment (book) 165

Rustichello of Pisa 202
Ruzzolini, Giuseppe 237
Ryan, Robert 138, 139, 158, 164, 165, 166

Sabath, Bernard 19
Sabbatini, Enrico 204
Sabela, Simon 194
Sabol, Ed 16
Sabol, Steve 16
Saint, Eva Marie 235, 236
St. Pasierb, Janusz 229
Salisbury, Harrison 18
Salt, Waldo 48
Salute to Oscar Hammerstein II (TV program) 21
Sampson, Will 176
Sanda, Dominique 174, 189
Sandrelli, Stefania 189
San Juan, Olga 33
Sarandon, Susan 195, 198
Sasamoni, Shigeko 20
Savalas, Telly 115, 122, 142
Saxon, John 12, 109
The Scalphunters (movie) 14, 15, 23, 140–142, 144, 146, 155, 161
Scandal Sheet (TV movie) 19, 23, 209–211, 212
Schaeffer, Rebecca 235
Schell, Maximilian 21, 118, 119, 120
Schiffer, Robert 122
Schnee, Charles 34
Schroeder, Jorn 222
Schygulla, Hanna 220
Scofield, Paul 134, 162, 163
Scorpio (movie) 17, 18, 23, 161–163, 208
Scott, George C. 127
Scott, Lizabeth 32, 33, 35, 51
Scrooge (movie) 21
Scullin, George 93
Seagrove, Jenny 205, 231
The Searchers (book) 108
Season of Passion (movie) 11, 12, 13, 14
Seaton, George 152
Seberg, Jean 152
Second Annual Super Comedy Bowl! Gridiron Follies (TV program) 21
Separate But Equal (TV miniseries) 1, 19, 20, 21, 23, 237–239
Separate Tables (movie) 12, 22, 101–103, 105, 108
Separate Tables (play) 101, 102
Serling, Rod 132
Seven Days in May (book) 131, 132
Seven Days in May (movie) 14, 23, 130–132, 134, 181, 208, 217

Shakespeare, William 3
Shane (movie) 70, 75
Shaner, John Herman 186
Shapiro, Stanley 66
Sharp, Alan 160, 208, 212, 213
Shaw, George Bernard 104, 105
Sheen, Martin 181
Sheldon, Ernie 137
Sherin, Edwin 155, 156
Shore, Dinah 21
Short, Luke 53
Shulman, Irving 12
Siegel, Andy 220
Simmons, Jean 112, 113
Simon, Michel 134
Simonds, Walter 11
Simonides 191
Simons, Arthur "Bull" 215
Sinatra, Frank 16, 70, 127
Singer, Marc 190, 191
Sinkel, Bernhard 222
Sins of the Fathers (TV miniseries) 19, 20, 23, 221–223
Siodmak, Robert 27, 44, 60
Sitting Bull 176
The Skin (movie) 200, 201
Smith, Bernard 112, 113
Smith, Robert 34
Sons and Lovers (movie) 113
Sordi, Alberto 231
Sorry, Wrong Number (movie) 8, 9, 22, 34, 37–39, 46, 64
Sorry, Wrong Number (radio play) 38, 39
A Sound of Hunting (play) 7, 40
South Sea Woman (movie) 10, 22, 64–67
Spiegel, Sam 144
Stalag 17 (movie) 70
Stallings, Laurence 72
Stanley, Paul 12
Stanwyck, Barbara 33, 39
Stapleton, Maureen 85, 152
Star Wars (movie) 185
Stars and Gripes (war revue) 7
Steiger, Rod 11, 199, 200
Steiner, Ira 155
Steiner, Max 48
Steloff, Skip 186
Sternad, Rudolph 120
Stevens, George, Jr. 19, 239
Stewart, James 20, 227, 228
Stewart, Ramona 32
Stoloff, Morris 70
Storaro, Vittorio 189
Storey, Anthony 193
Storke, Adam 234
A Streetcar Named Desire (play) 85
Striepeke, Dan 186
Strode, Woody 138, 139
Stroud, Robert 122, 123
Studio One (TV series) 125

Sturges, John 95, 137
Summer of the 17th Doll (movie) 13
Sutherland, Donald 189
Sweet Smell of Success (movie) 12, 22, 95–98, 99, 211
The Swimmer (movie) 15, 23, 142–144, 146
The Swimmer (story) 143, 144

Take a Giant Step (movie) 11, 12, 108
Taradash, Daniel 69, 70, 146
Taras Bulba (movie) 14
Tarkington, Booth 4
Tashlin, Frank 11, 33
Taylor, Don 186
Taylor, Elizabeth 113, 178, 179
Temple-Smith, John 186
Ten Tall Men (movie) 10, 11, 22, 56–58, 60
10th Annual Circus of the Stars (TV program) 21
Terzieff, Laurent 170
Thatcher, Torin 61
Thaxter, Phyllis 55
T'hezan, Helia 234
Thom, Burton 3
Thorpe, Jim 16, 55, 56
Thorpe, Richard 53
Three Pills in a Bottle (play) 4
Three Sailors and a Girl (movie) 10, 22, 66–67
Thulin, Ingrid 170, 180, 221
Tiomkin, Dimitri 72, 95, 110
To Kill a Mockingbird (movie) 122
Tosi, Piero 130
Tough Guys (movie) 19, 23, 215–217
Tourneur, Jacques 48
Tournier, Jean 134
Tracy, Don 43
Tracy, Spencer 102, 113, 119, 120
The Train (movie) 14, 23, 132–135, 141, 146
Trapeze (movie) 12, 22, 86–89, 92, 108, 220
Trosper, Guy 123
Trumbo, Dalton 165
Turner, Don 49
Twain, Mark 19
Twilight's Last Gleaming (movie) 17, 23, 181–184

Ulzana's Raid (movie) 17, 18, 23, 158–161
The Unforgiven (movie) 12, 23, 107–110, 141, 161
Unger, Joe 190
The Unknown War (TV miniseries) 18
Urich, Robert 209

Uris, Leon 93, 95
Ustinov, Peter 113

Vaeter und Soehne (TV miniseries) 222
Valdez Is Coming (movie) 17, 23, 154–156, 158, 161
Valland, Rose 134
Van Der Vlis, Diana 143
Van Druten, John 13
Van Fleet, Jo 95
Variety Girl (movie) 8, 22, 33
Veiller, Anthony 27, 127
Vengeance Valley (movie) 10, 22, 52–53, 86
Vera Cruz (movie) 10, 11, 22, 75–78, 80, 100
Verdi, Giuseppe 19
Vernon, Richard 40
Victoria (queen of England) 193
Victory at Entebbe (TV movie) 17, 20, 23, 176–179, 217
The Vikings (movie) 225
Violence et Passion (movie) 173
Viper Three (book) 182
Visconti, Luchino 17, 18, 129, 130, 172, 173, 174
Vogel, Tony 202
Voyage of Terror: The Achille Lauro Affair (TV miniseries) 19, 20, 23, 234–236

Wager, Walter 182
Walker, Robert 53
Wallace, Mike 21
Wallach, Eli 86
Wallis, Hal B. 7–10, 32–35, 37, 39, 45, 46, 51, 53, 64, 85, 8l6, 91, 93, 217
Ward, Eddie 88
Ward, Robert 200
Ward, Simon 192, 194
Warden, Jack 12, 100, 178
Warner, David 202
Warren, Earl 238
Washington, Ned 95
Wasson, Craig 190, 191
Waxman, Franz 64
Wayne, John 158, 161
Webb, James R. 75, 78, 88
Webster, Paul Francis 72
Weill, Kurt 16
Weiner, Fred 18
Weiss, Jeff 224
Welch, Robert 33
Wellman, Paul I. 75
Wells, H.G. 186
West Side Story (movie) 116
Westmore, Bud 127
Westmore, Wally 63
Whaley, Frank 228
What Price Glory? (movie) 66
Widmark, Richard 119, 183
Williams, Tennessee 85

Wilson, Gerald 158, 163
Wilson, Scott 149
Wilson, Whip 82
Winchell, Walter 97
Winfield, Paul 183
Winkler, Henry 209
Winner, Michael 157, 158, 163
Winters, Shelley 116, 142
Wise, Robert 100
Wiseman, Joseph 109
Wizan, Joe 217
Wojtyla, Karol 229
Wolper, David L. 178
Wolseley 193
Woodward, Joanne 16
Wottiz, Walter 134
Wyman, Jane 39
Wynter, Dana 152

York, Michael 186
Young, Burt 183
Young, Ned 134
The Young Savages (movie) 14, 23, 114–116, 125, 141
Yulin, Harris 168, 178

Zavitz, Lee 134, 146
Zinnemann, Fred 70, 196
Zulu (movie) 193
Zulu Dawn (movie) 18, 23, 191–195